ANGELS
and
HEROES

Robert D. Lesslie, M.D.

HARVEST HOUSE PUBLISHERS

EUGENE, OREGON

Cover by Left Coast Design, Portland, Oregon

Cover photos © Thinkstock Images / Comstock Images / Getty Images; James Steidl / Shutterstock Images; SVLuma / Shutterstock Images

Back-cover author photo © Penny Young

All the incidents described in this book are true. Where individuals may be identifiable, they have granted the author and the publisher the right to use their names, stories, and/or facts of their lives in all manners, including composite or altered representations. In all other cases, names, circumstances, descriptions, and details have been changed to render individuals unidentifiable.

ANGELS AND HEROES
Copyright © 2011 by Robert D. Lesslie, M.D.
Published by Harvest House Publishers
Eugene, Oregon 97402
www.harvesthousepublishers.com

Library of Congress Cataloging-in-Publication Data
  Lesslie, Robert D., 1951-
  Angels and heroes : true stories from the front line / Robert D. Lesslie.
    p. cm.
  Summary: "Angels and Heroes Dr. Robert Lesslie 978-0-7369-3775-7 Dr. Lesslie shares amazing experiences of the courageous men and women who exhibit the grace and strength of angels in the face of danger every day."
  Provided by publisher.
  ISBN 978-0-7369-3775-7 (pbk.)
  ISBN 978-0-7369-4131-0 (eBook)
  1. Hospitals—Emergency services—Popular works. 2. Emergency medical personnel—Popular works. I. Title.
  RA975.5.E5L469 2008
  616.02'5092—dc22
                                                                    2011007094

Printed in the United States of America

11 12 13 14 15 16 17 18 19 / LB-NI / 10 9 8 7 6 5 4 3 2 1

Readers respond to Dr. Lesslie's previous books, *Angels in the ER* and *Angels on Call*

"Thank you for the two *amazingly awesome* books you have written. As a Christian pursuing a career in medicine, I find them really inspiring. I had tears in my eyes many times, especially in *Angels on Call*. I love, love, love these books!"

Alina

"The book was an inspiration during a difficult time in our lives... Your humility and humanity jumped out at me. I truly believe God works through us and that there are angels among us."

Chuck

"I am a busy working mother but managed to read the entire book in less than three days. The way you described the people and the situations was brilliant...You see things in a very special way and have made me see...thank you."

Jamie

"I loved every bit of it. It touched me greatly and I have told my friends about it...It also gave me a much better understanding on what goes on in an ER. I sincerely believe it should be read in high schools, colleges, etc."

Mosheh

"I recently visited the USA from Finland...My husband and I have enjoyed these little stories...Great book and wish you would write more."

Inka

"The most inspiring and relatable book I have read throughout my college career in nursing school…I often feel that my small contributions of extra time with patients or a simple smile have no impact on anyone's life. I was inspired by your book and appreciated the Bible verses throughout."

Katie

"Just read your book *Angels in the ER* and loved it. Couldn't put it down. Very well written. Excited to see another one is on the way! God bless you."

Bill

"Having spent ten years as a coordinator for our emergency department, I was very intrigued to read your stories…You have a very eloquent way of relating things that most people will never experience, but probably should…Your kindness, care, and compassion shine through."

Alicia

"Your stories touched me deeply…I am a retired RN…7 years in infant ICU. We got the worst of the worst. It was a hard job, but so worth it… On a brighter note, your book made me feel that I still might have a purpose…I keep praying for God's will to be done in my life."

Jackie

"The Bible verses, along with the stories, had me searching my heart for peace and grace (something I haven't felt in some time). Thank you for your dedicated care to all of the people whose lives you have touched, and thank you for reminding me that God really is with us all of the time."

Terri

*To the men and women
who put their lives
on the line every day—
for each one of us.*

Acknowledgments

With special thanks...

To Les Stobbe, my agent (and Rita, his wife), who believed in my work and found it a home.

To Paul Gossard, my editor, who has refined my manuscripts, tried (sometimes with success) to teach me proper grammar and style, and taught me that the *delete* button is my friend.

To my wife, Barbara, who has always been a faithful encourager, and my worst and best critic.

To the dedicated people at Harvest House Publishers, who have always been professional, caring, and helpful, and who allowed the people in these pages to tell their stories.

And especially to those who shared their stories with me—Jerry Waldrop, Mike Blackmon, T.R. Jones, and Cathy "Crash" Adams.

Contents

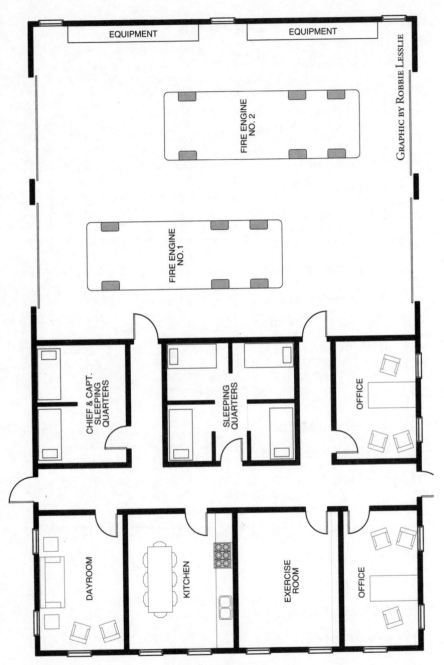

Fire Station No. 1

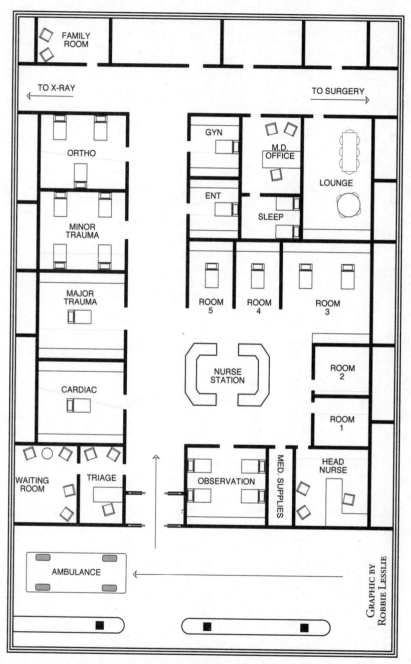

Layout of the ER

O reader!
Had you in your mind
Such stories as silent thought can bring,
O gentle reader!
You would find
A tale in every thing.

WILLIAM WORDSWORTH (1770–1850)

Angels on the Front Line

Would you lay down your life to save another? Maybe your child, or your spouse. But what about a total stranger?

It takes a special man or woman to be willing to put him or herself in harm's way in order to save another person. Most of us can't understand that kind of thinking, that kind of deliberate self-sacrifice.

The true stories in these pages are from people who have done just that. They are the firemen, policemen, and paramedics who stand between each of us and certain disaster. And they do it every day.

As I talked with these professionals, I was humbled by their willingness to share their most profound and sometimes troubling experiences. And I was inspired by their unshakable faith, which they demonstrate in their words and through their actions.

It is my hope that in these pages you will also find inspiration, and a new appreciation for the heroes among us.

1

Salt Lick Road

This is my Father's world.
O let me ne'er forget
That though the wrong seems oft so strong,
God is the ruler yet.

"This Is My Father's World"
Maltbie D. Babcock (1858–1901)

Friday, 2:15 p.m. Sharon and Mike Brothers were putting the final touches on EMS Unit 5. The Hickory Grove Christmas parade was scheduled to start in less than two hours, and they had waxed and polished the ambulance until it sparkled. They were to be the lead vehicle, and if the parade was anything like last year's, they would be followed by a vintage Plymouth, two fire trucks, and a tractor pulling Santa on a hay wagon. It wasn't going to be a very long parade, and they wanted to be sure their ambulance made the right impression.

Mike was standing behind the vehicle, trying to attach a large wreath to the back doors. So far, he wasn't having much success.

Sharon opened the front door and slid into the driver's seat. As she was hanging some brightly colored balls from the rearview mirror, the dash radio crackled to life.

"Good grief!" she exclaimed, dropping and breaking one of the ornaments.

Then she heard one of her friends from dispatch say, "We've got an accidental shooting on the west side of the county. No other report yet, but it doesn't sound too bad."

There was silence as Sharon began picking up the broken decoration. She was off duty, and she waited for someone to respond to the call.

"Sharon, are you there?" the dispatcher asked.

"Doggone it," Sharon muttered to herself.

She picked up the radio receiver and answered. "This is Sharon. I'm not workin', and I'm out at the house with Mike. We're getting ready for the Hickory Grove parade."

Sharon suspected what was coming next, and she was right.

"We've got every unit out on a call," the dispatcher informed her. "You guys are pretty close, maybe a mile and a half away. Is there any way…"

Sharon sighed and looked at her watch. If it was a simple call, they could probably get to the scene, pick up the patient, get to the hospital in Rock Hill and then back to Hickory Grove just in time to make the parade.

"Sure, we can do it," she answered. "But you know it's me and Mike," she added.

It was contrary to EMS policy for a husband and wife to work on the same unit. They both had different partners when they were working, but today they had scheduled themselves to be off for the parade.

"That's fine," the dispatcher responded. "The shift supervisor is aware and says it's okay. This should be a routine run."

Sharon wrote down the address of the call, tossed the radio receiver into the passenger seat, and jumped out of the ambulance.

"Mike, come on! We gotta go!" she called out to her husband.

"What's going on?" he asked. His wreath was dangling from one of the door handles, and when he stepped away to find Sharon, it fell to the ground. He mumbled something incoherent, shook his head, and then kicked the greenery over into the yard.

Sharon walked around to where he stood and quickly told him about the call.

"Let's get going!" he said to her, quickly moving to the driver's door and jumping in. She hurried around to the passenger side, shaking her head as she saw the disheveled wreath lying in the grass.

"Oh, well," she sighed.

As Mike turned the ambulance around in their driveway, she glanced at the notes she had made and told him where they were headed.

"Salt Lick Road."

"Isn't that a dirt road off Highway 5?" he asked her. "Some ol' loggin' trail?"

"I think you're right," Sharon answered, pulling a county map out of the glove compartment. "Let me be sure."

She knew just about every road and cow path on this side of the county, but she wasn't familiar with Salt Lick Road. She traced Highway 5 with her finger, searching for this obscure location.

"There it is," she exclaimed. "About a mile past Shiloh Church."

They were now on Highway 5, and Mike switched on the lights and siren.

"What did they say was the problem?" he asked Sharon.

"A shooting accident of some kind," she answered. "Didn't sound serious, but Cheryl was dispatchin', and she didn't have much information."

Mike slowed as they sped past Shiloh Church, and Sharon peered ahead on their left for the road sign.

"Look, there it is!" she called out to him, pointing to a neglected wooden sign haphazardly nailed to a pine tree. "Salt Lick Road," she read.

They turned onto the dirt track and had to slow to a crawl to battle the ruts and twists of the old lumber trail.

"You think anybody lives out here?" Mike asked her. "I mean, this place is the middle of nowhere."

Sharon glanced down at her note. "That's what Cheryl told me," she answered, shaking her head. "Salt Lick Road. There must be a house out here somewhere."

The road seemed to be getting narrower, and they had to drive across fallen branches and dodge an old truck tire. Mike was about to stop and turn around when just up ahead, they saw an old clapboard house standing in the middle of a small, grassless field. The yard around it was littered with trash. Sharon noticed a small child's bike, its front wheel bent and useless.

On the right side of the house was an old Chevy truck, its axles propped up on cinder blocks, wheels and tires missing.

There was no driveway or gravel, just the bare dirt. Mike got as close to the house as he could.

Odd. Nobody came to the door or peered out from any of the windows. Their siren was still on, and somebody should have heard them approaching.

For the first time she could remember, Sharon felt uneasy. There was something wrong about this place.

"Let's go," Mike said, jumping out of the ambulance and heading to the rear of the vehicle. He was opening the doors and taking down the collapsible stretcher as Sharon stepped down and turned toward the house. She scanned the door and windows again for any movement. Nothing.

Mike had turned off the engine and the siren. As Sharon stood in front of the house, she became aware of the eerie silence. Nothing seemed to be moving or alive. Suddenly she felt an uncomfortable chill. It was a mild December day, but something made her shiver.

The loud cackle of a crow startled her. She looked away from the house. There, behind the beat-up truck and near the edge of the clearing, stood a dying black walnut tree. Its once proud and strong limbs were now reduced to a few spindly, twisted branches, dark black and silhouetted against the winter sky. Two crows were perched on the topmost branch and peered down at these recent intruders. With another cackle directed at Sharon, they took off from their limb and disappeared over the tops of the surrounding pine trees.

Silence again.

Mike walked around from behind the ambulance, pushing the unit's stretcher before him.

"Did Cheryl say the county had been notified?" he asked, wanting to be sure that law enforcement was on the way.

"I thought she did," Sharon replied hesitantly, not completely sure of her answer.

Mike glanced up at the gloomy and depressing house. He wasn't satisfied with Sharon's response. "Let's hold on before we go in there. I'll call dispatch and make sure an officer is on his way."

He let go of the stretcher and turned back to the ambulance and its dashboard radio.

Sharon was only twenty feet from the front door and for the first time noticed it was cracked open, but only an inch or so. Its rusted and torn screen door was closed, but the door itself was ajar and obviously not latched. She stepped toward the house and onto the small concrete slab that served as the front stoop.

As she opened the screen door, the screeching of its rusted hinges caused her to shiver again, and she thought about waiting for Mike. But something was pulling her into the house. She reached out and tapped lightly on the wooden front door and then pushed it in a little ways.

"Anybody here?" she called out into the silence. "This is the EMS. Is anybody hurt?"

She strained to hear any response, but there was only the sound of the breeze in the pines behind her, stirring as the evening was coming on.

"Anybody here?" she called again, pushing the door wide open and stepping into the house.

Am I crazy? she thought. *What if…*

And then the smell overwhelmed her. It was a combination of decomposing garbage, urine, and some musty odor she couldn't recognize. But it was awful. Although she had been in a lot of places, including a lot of rundown and neglected houses and apartments, this was the worst.

As her eyes grew accustomed to the darkness, she was shocked by what she saw. The room she was standing in was large and square, with a few dirty windows on two sides covered with old and yellowed sheets. The wooden floor was littered with debris and scattered pieces of what seemed to be clothing. A door to her left led to the kitchen, where most of the foul odor seemed to be coming from. She could see stacks of dirty dishes on the small table, all containing unrecognizable remnants of food. On one of the two kitchen chairs, there was a pizza box. It was open, and Sharon could see a few moldy pieces of discarded crust in the bottom of it. A milk carton was overturned on the worn green linoleum floor, with a small puddle spreading out in front of it. It was starting to dry, and must have been there for a while.

This must be a mistake, Sharon thought. She wondered if she had written down the wrong address, or if someone had phoned in a bogus call. No one had been living in this place for a while.

"Hello! Is anybody here?" she called out once more.

She glanced around the room again, listening for any sign that someone else was in the house. It was completely quiet.

She looked over to her right, to a doorway that probably led to the bedrooms. Against the wall beside that door was a sleeper sofa. Its mattress was pulled out, and Sharon could see that it was filthy and partially covered with an old army blanket.

She wondered if hoboes had been living in this house, or druggies, or…maybe worse. Then she felt that chill again. She turned to the front door, ready to get Mike and get out of this place.

Sharon took two steps and heard the floor creak beneath her. It startled her, and she chuckled nervously at her own silliness. Then she heard the clatter of stretcher wheels as Mike approached the front door. His presence brought a welcome sense of relief.

She was reaching for the front doorknob when she heard it. She froze where she stood and then spun around, searching for the source of the noise.

It was coming from the direction of the doorway to the bedrooms, but somehow it had seemed closer. And then she heard it again. It was a whimper. The kind made by a small child.

Mike stepped through the door. "What ya got, Sharon? Cheryl said a county deputy should be here in—"

"Shh!" she quieted him, pointing to the right side of the room. Her finger jabbed the air, and she whispered, "Listen!"

"Wha—" he started to say.

"Shh!" Sharon repeated, pointing now to the sofa.

And then they both heard it. It *was* the whimper of a small child. Then it was joined by another.

Mike and Sharon bolted toward the sofa, each grabbing one side to move it. It didn't weigh much and was threatening to fall apart, so they had no trouble pulling it out from the wall.

Sharon gasped, unable to speak.

"Good Lord!" Mike sighed heavily.

Sitting on the floor with their backs to the wall were three little blond-headed girls. The oldest couldn't have been more than four. They were filthy—each wore only soiled and tattered panties. They looked up at Mike and Sharon with wide, sad eyes, not moving at all. The youngest started to whimper again, and then they all began to. The lower lip of the oldest girl began to tremble, and large tears streaked down her dirt-covered face.

Sharon sprang into action, quickly getting to the girls while taking off her jacket.

"Come here, sweethearts," she whispered to them soothingly, drawing them to her and covering them with her jacket. They didn't resist, and they pressed themselves against the warmth of her body.

Sharon looked up at Mike, a mother hen protecting her brood. He just shook his head and began to glance around the room.

"I think the bedrooms are that way," Sharon told him, motioning with her head to the nearby doorway.

They both heard the siren of the county patrol car as it approached through the woods.

"Good," Mike said with relief. "I'm going to see if anyone else is in the house. It looks like somebody abandoned these kids—just left them here."

"But what about the gunshot?" Sharon asked him. "Somebody called in an accidental shooting. Maybe they got tired of waiting and just took off without the children."

"Could be," he replied, moving toward the doorway. That didn't make much sense, though. Something else was going on here.

"Be careful," Sharon said to him, clutching the little girls even tighter. They were quieter now, and had stopped their whimpering.

Mike disappeared toward the bedroom as the county car came to a stop in the front yard. Sharon heard a door slam as the deputy got out and approached the house.

"Oh no!"

It was Mike. Sharon could hear the shock and disbelief in his voice. John Pendergrass, the county deputy, was coming through the front door just as Mike uttered this exclamation. He heard it too, and immediately drew his revolver.

She motioned to the door but didn't say a word.

"Sharon!" Mike called out. There was a tone of desperation in his voice she had never heard before.

"It's John Pendergrass," the deputy called out, heading quickly to the doorway. "Where are you, Mike?" he asked. Then he disappeared as well.

Mike was easy to find. He was standing on the far side of the only bedroom in the house. It was small, and just as filthy as the living room and kitchen.

"Mike…" John called out. Mike's back was to the deputy, and he was standing in the bathroom doorway, steadying himself with one hand tightly gripping the door jamb. He didn't turn around when John spoke his name, but just kept staring into the small room.

"Mike," John repeated, stepping over to where he stood and standing behind him. He looked over the medic's shoulder into the bathroom and gasped as if all the air had been knocked out of him.

Against the far wall was the bathtub. And in the bathtub was the body of a young woman. She was fully clothed. There was no water in the tub—it looked as if she had just climbed in to relax for a while. She was leaning comfortably back against the end of the tub, with her head resting on the edge. Most of her brains and the back of her head were missing, splattered against the tiled wall. Her mouth was partially open, where she had inserted the business end of a handgun.

Her left arm was draped over the side of the tub, and on the floor, just out of reach of her lifeless fingers, was a cordless phone.

Mike and John were silent for a moment, staring in horror and disbelief. Then John spoke. "We ran down this address and the names of the people who live here. The husband works over in York, and we got in touch with him. He should be here any minute."

Mike just nodded his head without saying a word.

Another deputy sheriff pulled into the yard, and after the two officers had talked, they made a sweep of the rest of the house and the surrounding yard and woods. Nothing else turned up, just the bleak realization of the desolate and distorted world of these little girls.

Sharon had bundled them up as best she could and was sitting with them in the back of one of the deputies' cars. They would be taken to Rock Hill General to be examined. And then there would be the decision of finding a safe place for them to stay.

"Billy and Samantha Myers," the second deputy had told John and Mike. "That's Samantha in there," he added, motioning toward the house. "Billy should be here any minute. But I don't think the kids need to be here. We need to move them on to the hospital."

Mike agreed and said he would follow the deputy to the ER in his ambulance. He had completely forgotten about the Hickory Grove parade. It would be starting in about five minutes without them.

"I'm not sure I want to be here either," he added, his initial shock now giving way to anger. "What kind of a father would allow his children to live like this? How could *he* live like this?"

"You guys go on," John replied. "I'll wait here on Billy Myers. I have a couple of questions for him myself."

Sharon shepherded the three girls through the back entrance of the ER and led them into the empty ortho room. They needed some privacy—and to be out from under the curious eyes of strangers. Word was starting to filter through the community about the tragedy somewhere off Highway 5. The girls hadn't said a word during the thirty-minute trip to the hospital, and when Sharon tried to lift them up onto one of the stretchers, they clung desperately to her legs. She grabbed a blanket from a nearby counter and sat down on the floor, wrapping it around herself and the girls, and cradling them once more.

Later that evening Sharon and Mike learned that Billy Myers was in jail, with multiple charges pending. The three girls had been examined by the ER doctor and were okay. They were undernourished, but there was no evidence of physical abuse. Their emotional health was a different matter. They were now in the emergency custody of an aunt who lived on the northern side of Rock Hill. The girls had recognized their Aunt Ruth but had only hesitantly left the protective embrace of Sharon when their aunt and uncle had arrived in the ER. Sharon had been reluctant to let them go, but the agent from the Department of Social Services had assured her they would be safe.

Samantha Myers had shot herself shortly after Billy had left the house for work. She had been struggling for several years with depression and, according to another sheriff's deputy, because of the physical and emotional abuse of her husband. Something had snapped this morning. She had found Billy's handgun, gone into the bathroom, and left her three daughters forever motherless.

As they drove home in the winter darkness, Sharon and Mike were silent, each uneasy from their own troubled thoughts.

As a mother, Sharon couldn't begin to understand what had happened in that lonely house today. She couldn't understand how that family had so utterly disintegrated into the waste and depravity they had witnessed. And what was to become of those girls? Their father obviously wasn't capable of or interested in taking care of them. And how long would their aunt and uncle be willing to provide for them?

They were turning into their driveway when she realized what she needed to do.

"Mike, I've got a thought, and I need to make sure it's okay with you," she began. "If it's not—well, that's fine."

Mike pulled the ambulance to a stop and cut off the motor. Then he took the key out of the ignition, sat back in his seat, and turned to his wife.

"What's on your mind?" he asked her.

She hesitated for a moment, still wrestling with her decision. But only for a moment.

"I know how much you've been wanting that new Beretta over-and-under 20-gauge shotgun," she began. "And I've been puttin' some money back each month and next paycheck should just about give me enough. I was goin' to surprise you with it at Christmas, but I...I think we need to spend that money on those little girls. They need some clothes, and I didn't see a single toy in that house, and I..."

Mike started laughing, and Sharon stopped mid-sentence.

"What's so funny?" she asked him. "What are you laughin' at?"

He shook his head and just smiled at her.

"Let me tell you what *I've* been thinkin'," he told her.

He proceeded to tell her of his plans to surprise her with a Caribbean cruise in January. They had never been on one, and Sharon had wistfully expressed her hopes that someday they would be able to do just that. They both knew how expensive it would be, yet Mike had somehow been able to put the money aside without his wife's knowing about it.

"I was really excited about surprising you with that at Christmas," he told her. "But on the way home, I was thinkin' about those little girls and how we should best use that money. If it's okay with you, let's put our money together and see what we can come up with."

"A cruise!" Sharon exclaimed. "Why you ol'...How did you keep your mouth shut about that? A shotgun...I mean, that's just a...well, a shotgun. But a cruise!"

She leaned over and hugged him around his neck. Then she kissed him on his cheek and mussed his hair.

"A cruise!" she cried out again. "Why, of course we'll give that money to the girls."

After a few days of shopping, they loaded up their SUV and headed to the home of Ruth and Fred Biggers, the girls' aunt and uncle.

Sharon had called and talked at length with Ruth about how they were doing and what they needed most. They pulled into the driveway, parked, and walked up the steps to the front door. They were empty-handed, having decided to bring the gifts in later. They just wanted to see the girls. This would be the first time since that terrible afternoon less than a week ago.

Sharon looked over at Mike. He nodded at her, smiled, and rang the doorbell.

From within, they could hear the scamper of little feet, and a deep voice calling out, "Not so fast, girls! Take your time."

The door opened, and there stood Karlie, Sue Ellen, and Jasmine. Jasmine was the youngest, and she bolted through the door and grabbed Sharon around her knees, burying her face in her cotton slacks. The other two were jumping up and down and calling out Sharon's name. Then Karlie, the oldest girl, reached out and took Mike's hand in hers, looking up at him with those same large, brown eyes. This time, unlike their first meeting, she was smiling.

❧

Fifteen years had gone by. Sharon and Mike were driving down Highway 5 on their way to the mountains for a weekend getaway. They had just left the Biggers's house, having dropped off Christmas gifts for the three girls, something they had been doing for a decade and a half.

Karlie had been away at Clemson, where she was in nursing school. She was doing well with her class work, and during her clinical rotations she demonstrated a rare gift of empathy, something she attributed to "Aunt Sharon." She planned on becoming a nurse practitioner and wanted to specialize in pediatrics.

Sue Ellen was a senior in high school, and was struggling. She found books "boring," and Ruth and Fred were having problems with her behavior. The last time Mike and Sharon had visited, he had made it a point to have a talk with her. They had discussed a lot of things, and she had opened up with Mike, telling him what was troubling her. On the way home that night, he had told Sharon, "Sue Ellen is going to be okay. It may take a while, but she's going to be okay."

And Jasmine. She was a junior in high school and was wide open. She played volleyball, sang in the chorus, was president of her class, and was a favorite of her teachers. She didn't remember anything of Salt Lick Road, and none of them ever talked about it. They did know about their father, Billy, and that he had spent time in prison. When he got out, he had disappeared. The last anyone had heard of him, he was somewhere in Tennessee.

"The girls seem to be doing fine," Mike said as they drove down the highway.

"Yeah—they do, don't they?" Sharon agreed.

As they slowed to negotiate one of the many sharp turns, they both glanced over to their left, toward the entrance to a well-worn logging road. The rutted dirt track disappeared forlornly into a large stretch of pine forest. Still nailed to one of the first trees was a wooden sign, now barely hanging on by one remaining nail and pointing to the ground. Most of the letters were now faded, but you could still just make out "Salt Lick Road."

Sharon glanced up at Mike as they passed, and she saw the smile forming on his face. She gently patted his leg, and turned again to the road ahead.

2

A Line in the Sand

The brave man is the one who faces and who fears
the right thing for the right purpose
in the right manner
at the right moment.

ARISTOTLE

Everything was going wrong.

Michael Greenfield had stuck to his routine this morning, just like he always did. He had been up and showered and out the door at 6:30. Now he was sitting in his patrol car, checking out his equipment, just like always. He had unloaded his firearm and placed the clip on the seat behind him, inspecting the barrel, making sure it was clean. Just like always. And then he realized he hadn't packed his lunch. For a moment he thought about going back inside and quickly making a sandwich. But he glanced at his watch and realized he didn't have enough time. This was his first day riding solo, and though he knew he was ready, he was still more than a little nervous. And he didn't want to be late.

After all, Michael was a rookie, and the fact that he had finished number one at the police academy would mean there would be a lot of eyes on him. He would just have to pick up lunch somewhere.

He was satisfied with the condition of his duty weapon and was reaching toward the seat beside him when his radio suddenly demanded his attention. He tossed the handgun down and picked up the receiver. The loaded clip of bullets bounced to the back of the seat and underneath several loose pages of yesterday's reports.

"Any units in the vicinity of Mt. Gallant and Celanese, report to the scene of a 10-50. No PI's" (personal injuries), the dispatcher reported. Michael was all the way across town and not officially on duty yet. Besides, this sounded like a routine fender-bender, with no one really hurt. He listened as two units near the accident responded. They were en route. That should handle it. He put the receiver back into its holder on the dash. Then he put his gun back into its holster and backed out of his driveway.

His assignment today was patrolling a quiet area of town. Shouldn't be too demanding. Yet it was his first time riding alone, and there was still that uneasy, nervous feeling in the pit of his stomach. Excitement, he supposed. And that was okay. His chief had told him that if you weren't at least a little nervous, you were in danger of becoming overconfident. And when you were overconfident you made mistakes. He wasn't going to tell his chief that he forgot to pack his lunch on his first day solo.

Michael chuckled, laughing at himself. He reached for his left breast pocket and for the pen he kept there.

"Doggone it!" he exclaimed, feeling his face flush. As he brushed his hand against his chest, he quickly realized he hadn't put on his Kevlar vest. It wasn't mandatory, at least not yet with the police department. His wife—well, that was a different matter. She had insisted from the very beginning that he wear the protective vest anytime he was on duty.

"If you don't worry about yourself," she had said, "You should worry about me and about Jenny. We want you to come home at night, you know."

Jenny was only a year old and wasn't yet aware of what her father was wearing, or even that he was a policeman. But Michael had promised his wife he would wear the vest, and so far, he had done that.

But today he had left it hanging over the back of the chair in their bedroom. He thought about turning around and heading back home, but decided against it. It was now a quarter of seven, and he was officially on duty. And anyway, his assignment was pretty cushy. Busting a few jaywalkers would probably be the extent of his excitement. No, he would head over to his patrol area and wait until he got home this afternoon to apologize to Becca.

Then he thought about his lunch again and decided to stop at Sam's Market and pick up something there. It was on the way to his patrol area, and it would only take a minute.

Michael picked up his radio and reported his location.

"10-4," the dispatcher responded. "Keep your radio open."

Everything was going wrong.

Roddy Anderson stood in the middle of the convenience store and wondered how things had suddenly gotten so complicated.

It was a simple plan, and foolproof. Or so he had thought. Roddy had been released from the "big house" in Columbia a week ago and had met with his parole officer yesterday. Clean as a whistle, he had convinced the officer that he was about to get a job and get his life in order.

"Just stay out of trouble, Roddy," the man had told him, even patting him on the back. "And I'll see you in a week."

The problem was that Roddy didn't have a job yet and he needed some money. Not a lot, just enough to get him by for a few days. Something would come along for him, it always did. But he was a multiple offender, and one more conviction would put him away for life. He had to be careful.

That's why this job had seemed perfect. It was going to be simple, with no fuss and no trouble. Just walk into the store, show his gun to the attendant, grab the money, and be gone. At this hour of the morning, there shouldn't be many, if any, customers in the place, and it all should take a minute or two at the most. He would wear a mask and gloves, and be gone without a trace.

But it had all turned south in a hurry.

When he got to the store, he had seen the old man behind the counter reading his newspaper. Roddy quickly put on his gloves and slipped the ski mask over his head, adjusting the eyeholes as best he could. They weren't quite big enough, and he had trouble seeing very much peripherally. But it would have to do.

He had stepped into the store and toward the checkout counter. The old man had looked up at him and then over to his right somewhere. Roddy had followed his glance and had seen the middle-aged couple standing in front of the milk and juice refrigerator. They were studying the label of a container of orange juice and hadn't looked in his direction.

Roddy pulled out his .38 and silently pointed it at the man behind the counter. He held his other hand palm up, nervously gesturing for the old man, now pale and shaking, to get whatever money he had out of the cash drawer.

That's when things went haywire. He heard the woman behind him scream loudly, and then something dropped on the floor. It was the container of orange juice. It burst and went everywhere. Roddy looked back at the couple just as they ducked out of view behind the refrigerator. Something made him step back from the counter, and it was a good thing. The baseball bat missed his head by only an inch or two, and he could feel and hear the whoosh as it swept by him. He turned and faced the old man, now wide-eyed and ready to swing at him again. Roddy thought about shooting him but was worried about the noise it would make. He swung the revolver, backhanding the man, striking the right side of his face and splitting the top of his ear.

The blow stunned the old man, and he slumped to the countertop, dropping the bat and grabbing the side of his bleeding face.

During all of this, the ski mask had shifted on Roddy's head, and he could only see out of one eyehole. Without thinking, he pulled it off and stuffed it into his pants. The old man raised his head and stared at Roddy, noting every detail of his face, recording it forever in his mind. Roddy knew what he was doing, and he swore.

He held the gun on the man and said, "Listen, it's nothin' for me to shoot you, you hear me? I don't care if I do or don't. It's up to you."

The man nodded silently, his blood dripping onto the newspaper.

Roddy had called out to the two in the back of the store, threatening to shoot the man in front of him if they didn't come up to the front. It had worked, and now here they were. Roddy was holding his gun on the old man. The couple was sitting on the floor a few feet away where Roddy could keep an eye on them, and he was.

The woman was sobbing, and tightly holding on to her husband. She looked up at the bleeding man behind the counter and sobbed, "Sam…"

A new understanding spread across Roddy's face and he said, "So, you the owner of this place?"

Sam didn't say anything, but just kept holding his wounded ear.

"Well, that makes things a little easier," Roddy went on. "Just hand me the money in that drawer, and make it quick."

He motioned toward the cash register with his gun, and then glanced down at the couple sitting on the floor. The man was starting to have a cramp in his leg and was trying to straighten it out.

"Sit still!" Roddy yelled at him. "I don't want either of you moving."

The man grabbed the back of his thigh and winced, rocking a little back and forth in obvious pain.

"What's the matter with you?" his wife blurted. "Can't you see he's hurting!"

Roddy looked at the man and said, "You need to keep her quiet. And if you can't, I will."

"Here's the money," Sam said from behind him, trying to draw his attention from the couple.

Roddy spun around and looked down at the counter. He could see three twenty-dollar bills, a five, and some loose change.

He swore again and then stepped closer to Sam. "Are you sure that's all you have?" he asked him, the barrel of his gun now pressed between Sam's eyes.

Sam didn't blink, but just looked calmly at him and said, "This is a small store, son, and this is all I have."

"I'm not your son!" Roddy snapped. "And I can't believe this is all I get for my trouble." He reached down, grabbed the loose bills and change, and stuffed it all in his pants pocket.

"Now, old man, I'm sure you have a storage room somewhere in the back here," he said, glancing to the rear of the small store. "I think it's time we all take a little walk."

Sam could see Roddy's mind working, and he didn't like the look on his face.

"Listen, mister," he spoke quietly to him. "Just let these two people go, and you can do whatever you want with me. They haven't done anything to you, and I'm sure—"

"Shut up!" Roddy yelled at him. "We're way past that. I'm not about to go back to Columbia for a pitiful sixty-five dollars! Come on, you two, get up on your feet."

"But—" Sam began to plead.

"I said shut up!" Roddy yelled, drawing his gun back as if to strike him again. "Come on out from behind that counter."

Once again Sam's eyes betrayed him. It had been a fleeting glance, but Roddy had noticed it, and he turned in the direction of the front door.

He swore once more, this time barely under his breath. A police car had pulled up in front of the store and an officer was getting out. Roddy stepped back, out of sight of the front door, and pointed his gun again at Sam's forehead.

"Don't make a sound," he told him menacingly.

Michael Greenfield's father had been good friends with Sam Keeches, and Michael had grown up coming to this small store for candy and occasionally lunch. He wished he had some time to talk with Sam this morning, but that would have to wait. He was in a hurry.

Reflexively, he patted the butt of his handgun and slipped his radio into its holder on his belt. Then he got out of the patrol car and walked toward the store.

Through the glass of the front door, he could see Sam standing behind the counter on the right side of the store. He was staring straight in front of him, probably talking with an early morning customer. Michael pushed the door open, and the faint tinkle of a bell announced his arrival.

"Hey, Sam—it's Michael!" he called out, stepping quickly over toward the counter.

Sam was slow to turn to his young friend, and when he did, Michael could see the blood dripping down the right side of his face. He stopped dead in his tracks and reached down for his weapon.

"I wouldn't do that," Roddy said quietly, stepping out from behind a rack of chips and crackers, his .38 now pointed directly at the policeman's head. "Just stop where you are and don't move."

He glanced over Michael's shoulder and asked, "Anybody with you? You got a partner?"

"No, just me," Michael answered, wishing this wasn't his first day solo.

"Good," Roddy said. "We've already got a crowd here."

For the first time, Michael noticed the couple cowering on the floor. He quickly put things together and said, "Listen, whatever your name is. Just let these people leave the store and you and I can work things out. I know you don't want anyone getting hurt."

"Well, buddy," Roddy said with a smirk, "I'd say it's a little too late for that." He glanced over at Sam's bleeding face.

"It can stop here," Michael persisted gently. "We can all walk away from this without anyone else getting hurt."

"And where am I going to walk to?" the ex-con asked. "Like I said, it's a little late for that."

He glanced around the store, quickly formulating a plan.

"Take your gun out and drop it on the floor," he told Michael. "And do it real slow. I've shot a man before, and a police officer might be sort of fun."

Sam looked at his young friend and slowly nodded his head, confirming his fears about this desperate man.

Michael reached down and unsnapped the strap of his holster, then slowly began to remove the gun with his thumb and index finger.

"Real slow," Roddy reminded him.

Sam shuffled the newspaper on the countertop, causing Roddy to glance over at him. It was only a split second, but it was enough time for Michael to draw his handgun and level it at Roddy's head.

"Don't do anything crazy," Michael said to the startled man in front of him. Roddy's eyes had widened when he saw the barrel pointed at him, but then a snarl spread across his face.

"Looks like we got ourselves a real Mexican standoff," he quipped. "Let's just see who blinks first."

The butt of Michael's firearm was resting in his left palm, and some-thing just didn't feel right. Then with a sinking feeling, he knew. There was no clip in the gun. It was empty. The clip was lying uselessly some-where in the front seat of his patrol car. And he knew there was no bul-let in the chamber.

Michael stared at Roddy Anderson and watched as beads of sweat began to appear on the man's forehead. Anderson's gun trembled for a moment, but he noticed it and struggled to hold it steady.

"Do you want me to call 9-1-1?" Sam asked Michael.

"You do, and I'll kill him!" Roddy called to the store owner with no hesitation, not looking away.

"Just hold steady, Sam," Michael told him. "I'm sure we're going to come to some understanding here."

He stared at a small freckle between Roddy's eyes and was surprised to realize how calm he was. He should have been scared to death, try-ing to face down a criminal with an empty pistol in his hand. Yet some-how he remained cool and was able to think clearly. At one point, his mind began to drift to thoughts of his wife and little girl, and what they would be doing right now. But he quickly put that aside and stared harder at that freckle.

Michael Greenfield knew the situation here, and he knew what he had to do. If he put the gun down, this man would kill him and every-one else in the store. He was that desperate. Sam knew it, and now so did Michael. Somehow he had to get the man to give himself up and lay down his weapon. It was the only chance these people had of stay-ing alive, even if it meant giving up his own life.

That's when it struck him that he had to be willing to die so the other people in the store could live. Two were complete strangers and one was a friend, an old man. Then, with a calm certainty, he realized he could do that, and that he *would* do it. And with that certainty came an unexpected but overwhelming peace.

He continued to stare at the freckle. Then out of nowhere, he chuck-led aloud. This whole thing was really absurd. Didn't a Mexican stand-off require that both participants have loaded guns?

"What are you laughin' at?" Roddy demanded, blowing the sweat from his upper lip.

"Nothing." Michael answered, quickly removing the grin from his face. He didn't need to provoke this man more than he already was.

The radio at his side suddenly crackled to life.

"Officer Greenfield, this is dispatch. What's your location?"

No one in the store moved.

"Officer Greenfield—what's your location?" the voice repeated itself, this time with an edge of impatience.

"Tell her you're somewhere downtown," Roddy told Michael. "And that you're headed toward Cherry Park."

Both locations were far from Sam's Market and would distract anyone searching for him for at least fifteen or twenty minutes.

"Go ahead, tell her!" Roddy insisted.

Michael reached with his left hand for the radio, careful not to let this man see the empty butt of his weapon. He took the radio out and held it to his face, pushing the send button.

"Dispatch, this is Officer Greenfield," he calmly spoke into the receiver. "I'm at Sam's Market and I need backup."

"You sorry—!" Roddy began, stepping toward the policeman.

Michael straightened his arm out, pressing the barrel of his gun firmly against the ex-con's forehead.

"Repeat, dispatch. I need backup right now."

He turned the radio off and dropped it on the floor, once again cradling the pistol in both hands.

Roddy Anderson was speechless with rage and a sudden helplessness. He had lost control of this situation, and he stood there staring at Michael, his eyes wide and his lips now trembling. He was struggling for an idea, some way of knowing what he should do next.

Michael knew that anything could happen and that this man was at his most dangerous. Yet he still remained calm and steady.

That bothered Roddy more than anything, and it made him mad. His finger began to twitch on the trigger, and for the first time Michael thought he might die in this store, on this morning, at any minute.

But he knew time was on his side. Backup was on its way, probably only a matter of minutes. And then…then, anything could still happen. He needed to try one more time.

"Listen, you can still end this, you know," he spoke quietly to the man standing right in front of him. "No one needs to die here. But that's up to you. This place will be crawling with police in about five minutes, and I see only a couple of choices. You and I can kill each other…I'm not going to miss from this distance. But should you somehow make it out of the store, you'll just die in the street. Or, and this is the best choice, you can put your gun down on the floor and walk out of here with me. No one else gets hurt. There's no more blood on your hands."

He paused and then added, "It's up to you now."

In the distance, they heard the wail of fast-approaching police sirens. Sam glanced at the door and then back at Michael. The couple on the floor slid even closer to each other.

Roddy was really sweating now, the perspiration dripping into his eyes. He desperately wanted to wipe them with his shirt sleeve.

He glanced at the door and then back to Michael. His trigger finger continued to twitch, as if it had a mind of its own and would be making this decision.

"It's the only choice," Michael repeated softly.

With that, Roddy let out a sigh and dropped the gun to the floor. Michael quickly kicked it away as the man slumped down on his knees, exhausted.

Four police officers burst into the store, weapons drawn, quickly spreading out in all directions. Two officers brusquely pulled Roddy's arms behind his back and cuffed him.

One of the officers walked up and said, "Well, well. If it isn't Roddy Anderson." He looked over at Michael and said, "I need to hear about this one, Greenfield. This is one bad dude you've arrested."

They were hustling Anderson out of the store as Sam Keeches came from behind the counter and put his arm around Michael.

"Thanks, son," he said to him. "You saved my life." Sam looked over to the couple, now standing by the counter, holding each other, and sobbing. "You saved all of us today. Your dad would be proud of you."

Sam didn't understand, and he never asked his young friend about it. But at that moment, he felt Michael Greenfield slump against him, and he had to brace himself to hold the two of them up. And then Michael stood up straight and took a deep breath.

"I'm just glad I happened along when I did," he said. "I'm glad I could help."

He didn't tell Sam about the empty handgun. He never told anyone, not even his wife.

"Now," he said with more animation. "What about one of your chicken salad sandwiches to go?"

3

If the **Shoe Fits...**

*The most wasted of all days
is one without laughter.*

E.E. CUMMINGS

A ndy Wilson was at his breaking point.
He had been a good sport through it all—the short-sheeting, the jalapeno-laced scrambled eggs, even having the legs of his brand-new uniform sewn together. But when was this "rookie orientation" going to end?

He had been assigned to Station 6, one of the busiest fire stations in the city, and had quickly meshed with the group of veterans working there. He liked the chief, Rick Stevens, and everyone on his crew. He even liked the "Big Swede," Eric Larson, even though Larson was clearly the ringleader when it came to practical jokes. But what were you going to do? Andy was just a rookie, three weeks out of training, and Eric Larson was...well, he was six-foot-five and weighed a trim 260 pounds. Andy was just going to have to wait him out. But it was getting old.

"Good job today, kid," Stevens said, slapping Andy on the back. "That attic was a little tricky, and you handled it well."

Their crew had responded to a house fire, a small wooden structure only a quarter of a mile from the station. They had had to go through the roof, and Andy had been assigned the lead. He had quickly cut a hole through the shingles and rafters, then made his way through the narrow attic, carrying the heavy hose by balancing precariously on the rickety rafters. They were able to save most of the house, and no one had been hurt.

"Thanks, Chief," Andy responded shyly. "Just trying to do my job, and learn from you guys."

Eric Larson walked by just then, carrying his jacket in one hand and his hat in the other. "Yeah," he muttered as he passed them. "Not too bad for a newbie."

Andy's eyes followed Larson as he walked through the engine bay and toward his locker. He shook his head, just a little, but Rick Stevens noticed it.

"Put your stuff up and then come to my office," he told Andy. Then he turned and walked away.

Andy wondered if he was in trouble. He quickly stowed his gear and headed to the chief's small office in the front of the station.

"Close that door, Andy," Stevens told him. Then motioning to the chair in front of his desk, he said, "Have a seat."

Nervously, Andy sat down. This had never happened before. Had he forgotten to do something? Missed some important protocol? Failed to properly use some equipment?

He leaned forward in the chair, his hands gripping the armrests.

"Listen, I know things haven't been exactly easy for you around here," the chief began, drumming his fingers on the top of his desk. "Especially with Swede."

Andy stiffened a little in the chair.

"Chief Stevens," he muttered in a confused response. "I—"

"How would you like to get even with Larson?" Stevens interrupted, looking directly at his rookie fireman and smiling mischievously.

"'Get even'? What do you mean?" Andy asked him, his mind racing.

"Look, we all know that Larson is the instigator of the practical jokes around here," the chief continued, leaning back comfortably in his chair and folding his hands behind his head. "He's the real mastermind. Has been for years. Just ask the guys. By the way, have those bald patches on your head started filling in?" He moved his own head from side to side, pretending to examine Andy's hair. "Who do you think put that super glue inside your helmet?"

Without thinking, Andy reached up and patted the irregular areas on the back of his scalp, remembering that embarrassing moment and the clipped clumps of glued hair left on the locker-room floor.

"I thought it might be him…" he mumbled.

"Of course it was him!" Stevens laughed. "He takes great pride in being the master joker around here. Now it's time to turn the tables."

He paused, watching the young rookie in front of him. Andy was obviously deep in thought, and the chief gave him a moment to chew on the idea.

The young fireman continued to study the back of his head with his fingers. Then he looked up at the chief and with determined resolve asked, "What do we do?"

Stevens leaned forward, slapped his hands on the desk, and said, "Attaboy! I knew you'd be up to this!"

He leaned even closer to Andy, glanced with mock caution at the office door, then motioned the rookie to come nearer.

"I've got an idea," he whispered. "And it can't fail."

Now becoming excited at the prospect of teaching the Big Swede a lesson and giving him a dose of his own medicine, Andy nodded expectantly and waited.

"Okay," the chief began, still whispering. "Here's what I'm thinking."

He proceeded to give Andy a brief history of Swede's favorite pranks. It would be hard to catch him in one of his own traps, so they would need to expose one of Larson's weaknesses and exploit it.

"And I know just what that is," Stevens proclaimed confidently.

Since his earliest days with the unit, Eric Larson had always been a creature of habit, to the point of obsessiveness. He had become entirely predictable in his daily routine. He got up at the same time each morning, he went to bed at the same time, he set his clothes out the same way every night. It was all like clockwork.

Stevens explained these quirks to Andy Wilson and then leaned back in his chair, quietly studying the rookie's response.

There was a confused look on Andy's face, and he finally said, "I don't understand, Chief. How are we supposed to use that? I mean, what are we going to do with the fact that he's so predictable?"

"You'll see, Andy," Stevens answered, smiling knowingly. "Tonight, you'll see."

At 10 p.m., right on cue, the Big Swede stood up in the dayroom and said, "All right, that's it for me. I'm heading to bed. You guys handle any emergency," he quipped, patting Andy on his shoulder as he walked by him and out of the room.

Chief Stevens glanced over at his fellow conspirator and silently nodded, smiling.

Forty-five minutes later, they could hear Larson's quiet snoring just down the hallway. Stevens stood up and motioned for Andy and the two other firemen in the room to follow him into the kitchen. He quietly closed the door behind them and with a finger to his lips, signaled them to be silent.

Whispering, he told the group his plan.

"Here's what we're going to do," he began, with a twinkle in his eye. "Anytime there's an alarm, Swede jumps out of bed, always to the left and just beside his boots. Then he pulls his pants on and steps into the boots while he's pulling the suspenders over his shoulders."

"You got it, Chief!" one of the firemen excitedly whispered. "I've watched him do it a hundred times. Sometimes even in his sleep, without waking up!"

Andy and the others chuckled at this, a little too loudly for Stevens.

"Shh!" he quieted them. "Don't wake him up."

"I don't think you *can* wake him very easily," one of them said. "He sleeps pretty hard, and sometimes the alarm doesn't even do it."

"I know," the chief agreed. "And that's going to help us. We're going to go into his room in a minute and a couple of us are going to pick up his bed and move it around, reversing it."

There was a puzzled look on Andy's face, and Stevens went on to explain.

"Swede always jumps out of bed on the *left* side, landing right beside his boots."

He waited for the men to show some sign of understanding. After a moment one of the firemen said, "I get it! This time, when he tries to get out of bed, the left side will be up against the wall. He won't be able to find the floor!"

"The only thing he'll find is that big Pittsburgh Steelers flag he hung up there a couple of years ago," one of the men threw in. "It's as big as a barn."

"One other thing…" the chief added, stepping over to the refrigerator and opening the cabinet above it. He retrieved a pair of old, beat-up boots and quietly put them down on the table.

Andy reached over and picked up one of the black lace-up boots.

"These things are tiny!" he whispered. "They can't be more than size 8."

"7," Stevens informed him. "And Swede wears a size 15. We're going to swap them."

This time there was no puzzled look on Andy's face. "And then we pull the alarm!" he said excitedly, imagining what was soon to transpire. "This is perfect, Chief!" he told him. "What a great idea!"

"Can't fail," Stevens agreed knowingly. "Let's get at it."

The group of grown-up kids quietly made their way down the hallway and toward Eric Larson's bedroom. When they reached the doorway, Stevens resorted to hand signals to direct his men. The room was dark, but there was enough light to easily see the huge outline of Swede under his blanket.

Two of the firemen grasped the foot of his bed while Stevens and Andy took hold of the head. Silently mouthing the words "one…two…three," Stevens signaled them to pick it up. They raised it off the floor smoothly and began to circle clockwise. This was the critical moment. If they could do this without waking him up, they were home free.

Swede was a bigger load than they had imagined. But they were able to swing the bed around without jostling him, and he snored the entire time.

They set the bed down carefully, and then Stevens swapped Swede's size 15 boots for the tiny pair they had brought with them.

He motioned to the neatly folded pants on the floor beside the boots, ready to be pulled on at a moment's notice. Then he raised his right index finger in the air, raised his eyebrows, and pulled a half-dozen huge safety pins out of his pocket. He leaned down and began to pass them through the lower part of each pants leg, securely pinning them together.

One of the firemen began to snicker, but a quick glance from the chief silenced him.

Stevens stood up, examined their handiwork, and then motioned everyone to move toward the doorway. Once again, he put his finger to his lips, commanding their silence. When he was satisfied that everything was ready, he reached down to a transmitter on his belt and pushed its button.

There were three deafening blasts from the overhead speakers, followed by the almost painfully loud wailing of a siren.

How could anyone sleep through this?

Larson sat straight up in his bed with his eyes still closed. He shook his head, trying to clear it.

"What the…!" he muttered, still not completely awake.

Bam!

There was a loud noise as something crashed into the wall.

Chief Stevens reached behind him and switched on the lights in the room.

Andy could barely contain himself. The scene playing out in front of the group of firemen was beyond anything they could have hoped for.

The comatose Swede had recognized the wail of the alarm and instinctively swung around to his left—and into the wall. It hadn't been there when he had gone to bed, but there it was now. He groped with both hands, trying to find the open space in his room. His eyes were still closed, and he floundered in the bed, both legs seeming to climb up the wall in front of him.

Then he grabbed the Steelers flag and yanked it down on top of himself.

"What the…!" he repeated, this time louder and more animated.

The flag landed on top of him, and his flailing arms quickly caused it to wrap around his head and torso. Now he was locked in mortal combat with this unyielding cloth that had attacked him, and the impenetrable object in front of him.

He was finally waking up a bit, and though he was unable to see because of the flag, his movements became more purposeful. He began to feel along the sides of the bed, and he quickly discovered the open area off to his right. He swung his legs around, planting them squarely on the floor just to the side of the waiting boots.

All the while the alarm continued to howl, causing his movements to become even more energetic.

Swede somehow found his pants and shoved his feet into them. He gripped his trousers with one hand and continued to battle the flag with the other.

But something was wrong. His feet quickly came to the obstruction in his pants legs caused by the safety pins, and would go no further down.

He started yelling angrily. None of the other men in the room could understand Swedish, but the meaning was very clear.

The big fireman let go of the flag and grabbed his pants with both hands. Then, with a herculean effort, he jammed his feet into the legs, determined to get the trousers on. There was a loud ripping sound, and his feet suddenly poked through the sides. The safety pins had held, but the inside seams of the legs had given way, splitting all the way down.

He leaned back on the bed and held his stockinged feet up in the air, feeling them and making sure they were now free. The tattered ends of his pants flapped helplessly.

By this time, his audience was red-faced. Each man was trying desperately to contain himself.

Swede then searched beside him for his boots, located them, and began to put them on. He had a peculiar way of doing this, as the chief had pointed out earlier. He would get one foot started into one boot, and then the other. Once this was done, he would stand up and stomp around a little bit, driving his feet into his boots. A quick lacing up and tying of knots and he was done.

Not tonight.

Chief Stevens reached over and tapped Andy on the shoulder.

"This is gonna be good!" he whispered in his ear, nodding at Swede and grinning.

Andy was grinning too. This was all going better than any of them had hoped.

Not for Swede, though. He was trying to jam his enormous feet into the size 7 boots, and it wasn't happening. He was up on his tiptoes, since that was about the only part of his feet he could get in, and for a moment, he almost looked like some overgrown and amazingly clumsy ballerina.

That's probably what did it. The sight of him perched awkwardly in the tops of those boots, his ripped pants flapping haphazardly, and the yellow-and-black Steelers flag still wrapped around his head and shoulders, was all that one of the firemen behind Andy could take. He lost control and burst out laughing, and the others joined in. The chief immediately tried to shush them.

It was too late. Swede had heard the laughter, and he froze where he stood, precariously perched on the tiny boots. His knees were bent, and he was groping around, trying to find where the laughing came from. He was beginning to understand.

"Wait'll I get my hands on you…" he growled, now violently trying to grab whoever it was standing in front of him.

"Who's there?" he bellowed. He reached out again, trying to grab the source of this laughter. The effort did him in. His arms began to flail wildly as he lost what little balance he had, and he fell straight down toward the floor. He was able to break the fall with his arms and hands, barely saving his face from an unwanted impact.

The big fireman was an even more absurd vision now, lying sprawled on the floor, and everyone in the room broke out in uncontrollable laughter. Everyone except the Swede. He was reaching out helplessly, trying to locate the people who had done this to him.

Somehow, his fall had partially disentangled the flag draped around his head and upper body, and he reached up to it, grabbing an edge and beginning to pull it down.

"Uh-oh," Stevens whispered with alarm, the laughter in the room suddenly coming to a stop.

Andy stood motionless, staring down at their handiwork. This was something Swede wouldn't forget for a long time. None of them would.

He turned to the door and took a step, then stopped abruptly. It was closed, and he was the only one in the room. He and Eric Larson.

He glanced back over his shoulder and was shocked to see that Swede had almost freed himself from the flag. His eyes were still covered, thankfully, and Andy just had time to—

The door was locked! He twisted the handle again just to be sure. But it wouldn't budge. On the other side of the door, he could hear muffled laughter.

Andy Wilson stood up straight, took a deep breath, and turned around.

Swede had just unwrapped the flag from around his head and was now struggling to get his eyes used to the light. He shook his head, trying to clear it. Andy remembered thinking it was what an angry bull might do.

And then his eyes locked on those of the younger fireman.

Wilson's knees almost buckled.

But after a few agonizing moments, Larson's scowl began to relax, and a slight smile began to tug at his face. There was even a tiny twinkle in his eye as Swede uttered a drawn-out, almost sympathetic, "Sooo…"

Humor is the shock absorber of life;
it helps us take the blows.

PEGGY NOONAN (1950–)

4

An Answered Prayer

The Spirit helps us in our weakness.
We do not know what we ought to pray for,
but the Spirit himself intercedes for us
with groans that words cannot express.

ROMANS 8:26

Andy Wilson was becoming a fireman. He was bright, aggressive, and eager to learn everything he could from everyone in the department. Even from Swede Larson.

In fact, he and Swede were becoming good friends, and they spent a lot of time together on duty at Fire Station 6.

In spite of his reputation of being the department's prankster, Larson had a lot to teach Andy. He had been doing this for a long time, and he had seen a lot and learned a lot. Some of it had been the hard way. He shared some of these experiences with Andy, hoping he wouldn't have to learn most things the way he had.

Late one weekday afternoon, Swede and Andy were sitting in the day-room, talking and absently watching TV.

"Swede," Andy said to the nearly snoozing Larson. "Why don't we have a firehouse dog here? Why don't we have our own dalmatian?"

The big fireman opened one eye and rolled it in his direction.

"Well, boy, we did," Swede told Andy. He sat up a bit and looked over toward the entrance. "You want to tell him about Lucky, Chief?"

Chief Rick Stevens had just walked through the door and over to one of the sofas. He plopped himself down.

"Yeah, we had our own dalmatian, named Lucky." He settled back and stretched his legs out in front of him. "One morning we got up and found this dalmatian pup sitting in a basket on the front walkway. Pitiful-lookin' pup, too. Remember, Swede?"

"Oh yeah, I remember," Larson agreed, slowly nodding his head. "Skinny, dirty, and with the floppiest ears you've ever seen."

"That's right," Stevens agreed. "Anyway, we took a vote and decided to keep him. After all, what's a firehouse without a firehouse dog? Well, we all pitched in and got him a bed, and food, and a couple of different collars. Had a tough time comin' up with a name for him, though. Then one of the guys remarked about how he was lucky to have come our way, and it just sort of stuck, I guess. Anyway, we named him Lucky."

"And boy did that dog grow!" Larson exclaimed. "He ate almost as much as I did, and before long, he must have weighed seventy or eighty pounds."

"Good-lookin' dog, too," Stevens added.

"But not very bright," Swede lamented, shaking his head. "I suppose it was centuries of inbreeding. I guess you breed in the spots and breed out the brains. Anyway, we had a hard time teaching him to do anything."

"Especially teaching him where his bathroom was," the chief added. "All of us worked with him, used the crate method, everything. But he somehow got it in his head that the engine bay was his special latrine. Never could get him broke of that."

"Nope." Swede grimaced. "That turned out to be a real chore, cleanin' up after that dog."

"And then he was always gettin' into things," Stevens continued. "You couldn't leave any of your stuff out or it would be gone. And I mean *anything*. Equipment, shoes, helmets, your wallet. Anything. But in a couple of days, it would turn up somewhere—sometimes in some pretty strange places."

"You remember the time Lucky got into the refrigerator, Chief?" Larson asked him.

"Do I!" Stevens rolled his eyes. "A couple of our wives had fixed a Sunday lunch for us, and we put the leftovers in the fridge for later on.

Fried chicken, potato salad, coleslaw, baked beans. And that dog some-how opened the refrigerator door and cleaned it out. All of it!"

"We were wonderin' why he was just lying around that afternoon," Swede remembered. "With his stomach making all kinds of strange noises. And then one of the boys went to the refrigerator and saw what Lucky had done."

"That might have been the final straw," the chief observed solemnly. "That, and cleaning up the engine bay the next morning."

"The final straw?" Andy asked him.

"Yep, that was it," Stevens explained. "We took another vote and decided it was time to get rid of Lucky. He was way too much trouble, and…well…it was time to do something about it."

"Who did you give him to?" Andy asked, curious about the where-abouts of the dalmatian.

"Nobody," Stevens answered grimly. "Nobody would take him."

The meaning of this statement was beginning to dawn on Andy, when the chief added, "Larson volunteered to take him to the pound, and that was that."

Andy's head snapped over in the direction of Swede.

The big fireman was staring down at his lap and rubbing his hands together. He didn't look up.

"Haven't seen that dog since," the chief said with finality. He stood up and walked to the doorway. Pausing there he turned and faced the two men. "Better get some rest, boys. I've got a funny feeling about this afternoon." Then he turned and walked down the hallway to his office.

Eric Larson got up from his chair and looked down at his younger partner.

"Better pay attention when the chief has a feelin'," he said. "He's usu-ally right. We ought to close our eyes for a while."

"Wait a minute," Andy said, not yet finished with the previous con-versation. "I want to know what happened to Lucky. You mean you just took him to the pound and they put him to sleep? Just like that?" There was accusation in his eyes, as well as surprise. He thought he was getting to know Larson pretty well, and this revelation came as a shock.

Swede glanced at Andy and over to the doorway. When he looked back to the young fireman, he winked.

"Lucky's at my house," he said, smiling.

Chief Stevens was right—again. An hour later, the station alarm went off and the crew was dispatched to a house fire. The address was on a small street about a half mile away.

As they jumped into their gear, Eric Larson said to Andy, "Make sure to get a couple of those waters. It's hot out there."

He was pointing to a cooler full of ice and bottled water. And he was right about it being hot. It was the middle of July, and the temperature was in the mid-90s. The humidity was not far behind.

Andy grabbed two of the water bottles and piled into the back of the engine. He was adjusting the straps on his jacket as the unit pulled out of the firehouse and onto the highway. Larson was at the wheel, and he gave two loud blasts from the air horn, making sure that any drivers on the road knew they were coming.

Chief Stevens was sitting on the bench next to Andy. He leaned over and cupped his hand to his mouth, trying to make himself heard over the roar of the motor and the occasional blast of the air horn.

"Structural fire," he yelled. "It's a residence, with possible entrapment."

He nodded knowingly at the younger man, raising his eyebrows for some acknowledgment.

Andy knew what this meant, and what his job was going to be. "Got it!" he shouted back.

It took them less than three minutes to get to the scene. During that time, Andy rechecked his equipment and went over in his mind the things he would be counted on to do. Since Eric Larson was the driver of this unit, he would be expected to lead a team through the front of the house, searching for any survivors. Andy Wilson was on that team and would be right behind Swede.

"Air pack ready?" the chief hollered at him, tapping the equipment in Andy's lap.

"Yeah!" he responded. "Ready!"

He glanced out the side window and could see black smoke billowing up into the summer sky somewhere just up ahead. And then the engine came to a sudden stop.

"Let's go!" the chief called out to Andy and the other men in the cab.

They jumped to the ground and ran to the side of the truck, quickly grabbing their equipment from the storage compartments. Swede opened his door and dropped down from the driver's seat. He snatched up his air pack and hat and then headed straight for the burning house.

Andy had a fleeting moment to take in his surroundings. The house was a two-story structure with white vinyl siding. He could see flames leaping behind the upstairs windows, and smoke escaping from two blackened holes in the shingled roof. And there was that roar—the awful sound that only an angry and all-consuming fire can make.

"Hurry! I think there's someone still inside!"

Andy glanced to his right and saw a middle-aged woman pointing desperately to the front door of the house.

"Quick!" she called out again. "There are two kids in there!"

He noticed the group of people gathering behind her, and more running toward them from somewhere down the street.

He turned back to the house just as Larson was disappearing through the front door. He hurried to catch up with him and found Swede standing in the middle of the living room. He was studying something, listening carefully, and looking from the kitchen door to the steps leading upstairs.

Wilson came up behind him and stopped, listening as well.

"What do you—" Andy began.

"Shh!" Larson interrupted. "Listen!"

Andy cocked his head again, wondering what Swede was hearing. All he could hear was the sound of the fire upstairs and the shouting of the other firemen as they worked their way through the back of the house. And then there was the sound of pouring water as the hoses began to unload on the roof.

Larson strained to hear, not moving a muscle. They would have precious little time, and it was critical that they make the right decision about where to search. Standing beside him, Andy suddenly realized how hot he was. He regretted not drinking some of that water on the way over. He reached down to his big side pocket, making sure he had stowed the bottles away.

Empty! Then he remembered leaving them on the seat of the cab as he made a final adjustment to his air pack.

"Let's go!" Larson said decisively, pointing to the stairs. "I heard a dog crying, and I bet he's upstairs with the kids. We'd better hurry."

He bounded up the steps, two at a time, reached the landing, and immediately turned to his right. Andy was slower, feeling every ounce of the equipment he was carrying, and sweating profusely beneath the protective layers of his uniform. He prided himself on being in good shape, but this was hard, and he noticed his own labored breathing when he reached the top of the stairs.

Larson had his hand on a closed bedroom door, checking for heat. Satisfied, he tried to open it, but the material of the door had expanded in the heat of the fire and it was jammed. He motioned with his head for his partner to come over with his ax.

Andy grabbed the pointed tool from behind him, and with a few blows, splintered the door. Larson put his shoulder to what remained of it, and burst into the small bedroom. Andy was right behind him.

Black smoke was starting to fill the room, but they could see well enough to quickly scan the area. A single bed was pushed up against the far wall, and on the bed was a white Maltese. She hadn't barked when the men exploded into the room, but had just stayed on the bed, whimpering. Occasionally she let out a faint, frightened cry.

How had Swede heard that? Andy thought.

As Larson stepped toward the bed the dog didn't move, or growl, or bark. She just sat there, refusing to leave the two little girls sitting behind her.

They were three or four years old, probably sisters, each with curly blond hair. And they didn't move either. They just looked up at the big fireman with their thumbs in their mouths. As Swede got closer, the younger girl reached up to him and started crying.

Andy stepped over to the bed and picked up the other girl and the little dog.

"Let's get them out of here!" Larson yelled, nervously looking up at the ceiling. It was starting to buckle and would be collapsing in a matter of minutes.

Andy heard a loud, cracking sound as they stepped out into the hallway. It came from somewhere in the attic, and it had caused Swede to flinch and tuck his neck protectively over the child in his arms.

They hurried down the stairs, through the living room, and out into the front yard.

Andy gently put the dog down in the soft grass. She sat at his feet, trembling and staring at the burning house. The middle-aged woman who had earlier hollered at him now came running over, scooping the little girls into her arms.

"Their parents are at work, and their older brother is still in there!" she said to them. "He's ten, and we can't find him!"

"Let's go!" Larson said, turning once again to the burning house. This time, Andy could see flames through the downstairs windows. Things were getting worse.

They made their way into the living room once more and met up with two other firemen.

"Everything's clear down here," one of them told Larson.

"We'll check upstairs again," Swede said, motioning for his partner to follow him.

When they reached the top of the stairs, Andy was exhausted. His breaths were coming in ragged gasps, and he was baking inside his uniform. He had never been this hot in his life, but for some reason, he had stopped sweating. And for the first time, he realized he was getting light-headed.

So this is what it feels like, he thought, surprised by the pleasant sensation of floating, of losing the heaviness in his arms and legs. And then everything began fade, to become hazy, and then somehow cloudy and dark…

Eric Larson had seen the first stumble, the first awkward sideways step of Andy's right foot. And then he had caught the barely notice-able tilting of his head to one side. He stepped over to him, knelt down, and effortlessly threw the young fireman over his shoulder. He carried him down the stairs and out of the house.

"Chief!" he called over to Stevens, who was standing by one of the engines, directing his team.

Four hours and three liters of IV saline later, Andy was sitting up on a stretcher in the ER, trying to remember what had happened in the house.

"Don't worry about any of that." Eric Larson was sitting nearby, grin-ning. "It happens to the best of us. Just ask the chief."

Rick Stevens was leaning against the wall in the small cubicle, and he blushed when Swede said this.

"That was a long time ago," he muttered. "Anyway, Wilson, you did a good job in there. Those girls are going to be fine."

"What about their brother?" Andy asked, remembering at least that much.

The chief raised an eyebrow. "He wasn't even in the house. He had been upstairs working on a model, and went down the street for a min-ute to get one of his friends. Problem is, he left his glue gun on, and it fell over and caught his bedspread on fire."

"Who was looking after them?" Andy asked, upset that the kids had been alone in the house. "I mean, the oldest was only ten!"

"That's a good question," Larson observed. "I think the parents are downtown answering that right now."

The young man sat back in his bed and shook his head.

❧

It didn't take Andy long to recover, just a day or two. And the rookie fireman had learned an important lesson.

Two weeks later, he and Larson were again sitting in the dayroom, relaxing. They hadn't talked much about that house fire, and Andy turned to the big fireman and said, "Swede, I want to thank you for helping me in that fire…I mean, I was passing out, and who knows what would have happened if you hadn't—"

"That's what we do," Larson interrupted. "We look out for each other."

"I know," Andy insisted. "But I just want to say that—"

"Don't worry about it," his partner interrupted again, waving his hand.

The overhead alarm blasted and the dispatcher broke into their conversation.

"All units, respond to 129 Caldwell Street. Warehouse fire."

"All units?" Andy asked, surprised.

"Must be a big one," Larson calmly replied, jumping up from his chair. "Better get going."

Carson's Warehouse and Storage was a huge, sprawling red-brick building, located in what used to be the industrial center of Rock Hill. Now it was falling into disrepair, suffering from more than 20 years of neglect. Areas of collapsed roofing had allowed rainwater to collect in several uneven and sunken places in its concrete floor. One of the town's previous mayors had described the building as "a death trap" and "the breeding place of Rock Hill's mosquitoes."

Andy Wilson had heard a lot of stories about the warehouse but had never been in it. That was going to change, he thought, as their engine pulled into the weed-infested parking lot and the crew jumped down to the ground.

Chief Stevens gathered his men around him and began giving them their assignments. Behind him, flames and an odd greenish smoke were billowing from second-floor windows and some of the holes in the roof.

"Why don't we just let this thing burn to ground?" one of the firemen asked, not completely in jest.

"Probably a good idea," Stevens chuckled. "But dispatch has been told there are chemical drums in there, and some other old stuff. Not sure what all we might find, but we need to get this fire under control as quickly as possible. So be sure your air packs are working properly and that you use them!"

Andy strapped his mask over his face, checking for a tight seal. Then he adjusted the heavy cylinder on his back, trying to find the most comfortable position for it. There was none. He patted his coat pocket, checking for water bottles. This time they were there. The men around him were doing the same thing, and then Eric Larson said, "Let's go, guys."

The quickest way into the building was through a small office that connected the parking area with the warehouse itself. The door was chained closed, but this proved no match for a single blow from Larson's ax. He and Andy led the men into the cluttered room and down a dark hallway. A door at the end of the short corridor read "Employees Only." It was unlocked, and they stepped through it and into a room that set a bewildering array of choices before them. It was twenty feet wide and maybe thirty feet long. Each of its concrete-block walls contained several doorways. Some of the doors were still in place, while others were barely hanging from rusted and worn hinges.

"What now?" Andy asked Swede. They would need to check out the entire structure, and these doorways provided a confusing and complex set of options. Which one should they search first?

Larson looked around the room, searching for a map of the place, some layout of the warehouse attached to one of the walls. That was too much to hope for, and the only thing he saw was a "No Trespassing" sign and the names of a couple of young lovers who had apparently visited here ahead of them.

"We'll just start over here," he said, pointing to the door nearest them on the right wall. "This one first."

He reached into one of the pockets of his heavy coat and took out a can of marking paint. It was bright orange, and he would use it to indicate the rooms and areas that had been cleared.

As they stepped over to the door, Andy heard the sound of water cascading onto the metal roof above them. The units outside had begun to spray the building, trying to quench the spreading fire.

The young fireman glanced around, and for the first time realized there was no smoke in this area—no water on the floor. Maybe the chief had been wrong about that mosquito business.

Swede pushed the door open in front of him and quickly scanned what appeared to be a utility room. Nothing stored in here, and no fire or smoke. He held up the can of paint and sprayed a bright orange "X" just to the right of the door.

As he and Andy turned toward the next door, the echoing sound of an explosion caused them to freeze where they stood. The loud boom had come from somewhere deep in the warehouse—and from straight ahead, through the door at the far end of the room.

Eric Larson struggled for a moment, trying to decide whether to continue the methodical clearing of this area or to hunt down the source of the explosion. Time might be running out on them.

"Follow me," he told Andy. Then he directed the men with them to keep checking the remaining doorways while he and his partner headed toward the other end of the room.

The door in the middle of that wall opened easily, and led the two men into a cavernous storage room. The light was better in this area, but it was still a pale gray, diffused by the windows of darkened glass just under the distant ceiling. And for the first time, Andy noticed the smoke. It was a greenish black. And seemed to be seeping into the area from a number of places. Most of it was coming from an arched opening in the wall on the left, about a hundred feet away.

And here was the water Chief Stevens had been talking about. *This room must be lower than the front area and office,* Andy thought, seeing the pools of standing water scattered across the floor. And then water began to pour through the dilapidated roof above them, the result of the efforts of the men on the hose trucks outside.

Larson pointed to the opening on the left, which seemed to be the major source of smoke. Without saying a word, he quickly headed in that direction.

Stepping through the arched passageway, they came into another small chamber, this one with only a doorway off to the right and one to the left—no other options. The doors were partially open, and they could see smoke coming from both of them. It was starting to get thicker.

The floor in this room was covered completely in water, and they found themselves standing in at least two inches of brown, murky liquid.

Another explosion boomed out, this one closer but not as loud as the first. Swede cocked his head, trying to determine its direction. The echoes in the warehouse made it confusing, and he decided they should split up.

"Check out that area," he instructed his rookie partner, pointing to the doorway off to their right. "I'll go over here," he added, jerking his head in the direction behind him. "But don't go too far. Just into the next couple of rooms."

Andy didn't like the idea of separating. They were supposed to stay together, to have each other's back. He reached down into his right-side coat pocket, trying to locate his radio. With a sinking feeling he realized he had left it charging in the dayroom back at the station.

Boom!

Another explosion, this one off to the left, startled him, and he realized that time was really running out. There was something in this building that didn't like the heat, and they needed to find it before things really got bad.

He nodded his understanding to Swede, and turned to his right and to the half-open doorway. As he sloshed across the floor, he glanced down and was dismayed to see the water halfway up his boots, a good six inches deep now.

Andy glanced over his shoulder and watched his partner disappear through the far doorway. He turned and grabbed the handle of the door in front of him and opened it wide. The room ahead was strangely bright, with sunshine streaming down from two large holes in the ceiling. The smoke in this area seemed to just be drifting in, with no obvious source of flames. In the far corner of the room was a large stack of wooden pallets, but nothing else. Another doorway led off somewhere to his left. *What a peculiar maze of a place this is!* he thought.

He was about to head in the direction of that other door when something made him stop. It was a feeling, nothing more—not something he heard or anything he saw. It was just a feeling.

The hair stood up on the back of his neck, and he shivered.

Suddenly turning around, Andy retraced his sloshing steps and walked quickly back into the room where he and Larson had parted.

Ahead of him was the passage Swede had taken, and the rookie fireman headed directly for it.

This room was the size of the one he had just left, but it was much darker. There were no holes in the ceiling, no sunlight penetrating the smoky, greenish haze. In the far wall was an open doorway through which smoke was pouring and quickly drifting upward to the ceiling. They were getting closer.

But where was the big fireman?

Andy stepped through the doorway, about to call out his partner's name, when something caught his eye. He looked down into the murky water at his feet and saw something orange. He reached down and picked up a cylindrical can of some sort…it was Larson's marking spray! What was it doing here? He must have dropped it, but that didn't—

Andy looked up quickly toward the far doorway and loudly called out, "Swede! Swede, do you hear me?"

There was no answer. He was about to take a step in that direction when something stopped him. It was that feeling again, that same odd shiver and then the hair on his neck stood up again.

Then he did something strange, something he would never be able to explain. He got down on his knees and began to feel the floor ahead of him. He couldn't see anything through the brown, filthy water—he was groping blindly, not sure of what he might find. He edged forward another foot or two when suddenly…the floor disappeared!

He froze, and felt along the concrete edge of a drop-off. It extended to his right and to his left, as far as he could reach in either direction.

In the middle of this room there seemed to be a sunken concrete pit, who knew how large and deep. Whatever it had stored in the past was probably gone now, and all it held was this dark, murky water.

And Eric Larson!

Suddenly Andy knew what had happened. Swede had stepped right into this pit and sunk straight to the bottom. His equipment and uniform would act like anchors, holding him under while he desperately struggled to free himself. His air pack would provide a few minutes of precious oxygen, but it wasn't designed for underwater work.

Larson was going to drown. That realization struck Andy like a lightning bolt, and a wave of nausea washed over him. What could he do? He didn't have anything to help him here, no rope or pole or hook. Nothing.

Then he noticed the small bubbles breaking the surface of the water just in front of him. They only confirmed his worst fears.

Powerless to do anything, Andy just began screaming. "Swede! Swede!"

It would do no good to call for help—there was no one to help him. The other men were scattered in distant areas throughout the warehouse and couldn't possibly hear him. He was alone.

He was kneeling on the edge of this unseen pit, helpless, not knowing what he should do. And he found himself praying.

"Lord, help me. I don't…please…"

No more words would come, and he was silent.

Finally, he whispered, "Save my friend."

Then in an instant he would never forget, an unexpected calmness flowed through him. He planted his left hand firmly on the edge of the pit, grabbing the rim tightly. And then he leaned out as far as he safely could, and put his hand into the dark, cold water.

He didn't thrash around aimlessly, but with a purpose not his own he reached down and held his hand open and still.

It had been only a few seconds when he felt something brush the back of his fingers.

Then a hand grabbed his, and being careful not to lose this one opportunity, Andy grasped it with all of his strength.

He leaned back on his heels, digging in as best he could. Then he felt another hand grabbing hold. Swede kicked up from the bottom of the pit, and together they were somehow able to raise the big fireman up enough to clear the surface of the water.

Andy held on with everything in him, and pulled his friend to the edge of the pit.

Swede released one hand and grabbed the concrete edge, using it as leverage for the two of them to get his water-soaked body and gear over the brink and onto the floor.

He was struggling for breath as he ripped off his mask. Somehow he managed to get onto his hands and knees.

Andy sat back, his hands on the floor behind him. He was exhausted.

Neither of them said a word as Larson continued to gasp loudly, trying desperately to catch his breath.

Finally he looked over at his partner, and their eyes met. They didn't say a word—just sat there. Then suddenly, two nearby explosions got their attention and they scrambled to their feet, with Andy helping his unsteady partner.

Larson looked over in the direction of the explosions and shook his head. Someone else would have to continue checking the warehouse.

The younger man put his arm around Swede's waist and led him through the building and out into the parking area. They walked over to one of the engines and sank down on the cracked and uneven pavement. Without saying a word, they stripped off their equipment and jackets, down to their soaked T-shirts.

After a few minutes, Swede looked over at Andy and asked, "How... how did you ever find me?"

Andy looked at his partner and thought about that moment on the edge of the pit.

"It wasn't me."

Though I walk in the midst of trouble,
you preserve my life...
with your right hand you save me.

PSALM 138:7

5

To Have and to Hold

Husbands, love your wives...

EPHESIANS 5:25

Tuesday, 6:35 p.m. Lori Davidson was working triage. The ER had been steady this spring afternoon, but not overwhelming.

It's a good thing we haven't been too busy, she thought as she led a thirty-five-year-old woman into the ER and over to room 4. She was a little concerned about one of the new ER doctors, Duff Sims, who had just started working in the department three weeks earlier. Sims had finished his residency the year before and had worked in a very low-volume emergency department before coming to Rock Hill General. Lori knew he was bright and well-trained, but he needed some experience under his belt. He would get that pretty quickly here, but then he would need to couple that experience with judgment—and that would take more than just time.

Duff Sims was working the overlap shift today, 11 a.m. until 11 p.m. He was standing at the nurses' station as Lori pulled the curtain of room 4 closed behind her and walked over beside him. She made a few more notes on the chart in her hand and then put it into the "To Be Seen" rack.

"What ya got?" Sims asked, looking up from his notes on the clipboard of room 3.

Lori glanced briefly back at room 4.

"A thirty-five-year-old woman with a bruised shoulder. She told me she fell in the shower last night and landed on it."

She paused and was about to add something when Sims interrupted her.

"Sounds straightforward to me. I could use something simple right now."

He finished making some notes on the chart in front of him and then slid it across the counter to Amy Connors, the unit secretary this evening.

"We need an X-ray on this three-year-old's wrist," he told her. "Right wrist."

Then he reached over to the "To Be Seen" rack and pulled out the clipboard of room 4.

"That's all?" he asked Lori, studying the chart. "A bruised shoulder?"

"That's all she complained of," she answered, deciding not to tell him about a nagging feeling she had about this patient. All the time in triage, the woman had never looked up at Lori, but had just stared at the floor. She was in no distress and looked like she had just come from a party in one of the upscale neighborhoods in town. Yet there was something there, this unwillingness to meet her eyes, that bothered Lori. *A red flag,* she had thought.

"Okay, I'll go see," Duff Sims said lightly, taking the clipboard and walking over to room 4.

Jenny Bristol was sitting on the stretcher as Sims pulled open the curtain of the room and walked in.

"Hello, Ms. Bristol," he said, glancing down quickly at the chart to find her name. "I'm Dr. Sims. What can we do for you today?"

Jenny Bristol barely looked up as the young doctor walked into the room, and then she quickly averted her eyes. This unusual reaction was lost on Duff, and he pulled the curtain closed behind him and plopped down on the single chair in the small cubicle.

"I…I slipped in the shower last night, and fell on my left shoulder," she quietly explained. "I don't think it's broken, but it hurts and I… just want to be sure."

She had put on the hospital gown Lori had given her and now pulled up its loose-fitting left sleeve, revealing an ugly, purplish bruise on her shoulder area.

"Wow," Sims remarked. "You must have really taken a tumble."

He stood up and stepped over to the edge of her stretcher.

"That's quite a bruise there," he added.

He made a few notes on her chart, then asked her, "Did you get hurt anywhere else? Any head trauma or neck pain? Did you hurt your hips or wrists or…anything else?"

Jenny Bristol shook her head. "No, just my shoulder. Nothing else."

Sims put the clipboard down on the stretcher beside Jenny and began to gently examine her injury.

The bruise covered most of the top and front of her shoulder, and it extended down over the upper part of her chest. Surprisingly, there was very little bruising on the side, over the deltoid area, where you would expect most of the blow to be absorbed.

Duff Sims was focused on the range-of-motion of the joint and on any possible neck tenderness. Satisfied with that, he listened to her lungs, making sure the breath sounds were equal and there was no obvious rib fracture.

"Okay, let's get a couple of X-rays, just to be sure," he told her, picking up the clipboard once again. "I don't think you've broken anything, but we can't take any chances."

She didn't respond or look up at him. There was only a silent nod of her head as she folded her arms around herself.

Sims walked over to the nurses' station and ordered an X-ray of Jenny Bristol's left shoulder. But before he gave the chart to Amy, he stared at her record and tapped it thoughtfully with his index finger.

Lori Davidson walked over from the medicine room and stood beside him.

"Well, what do you think about Mrs. Bristol?" she asked him.

He had been lost in thought, contemplating some potential what-ifs as Lori said this.

He looked over at her. "Something's just not right about that woman."

Lori looked up at him expectantly, curious as to his sense about Jenny.

"I don't think she has a fracture," he began to explain. "And that bruise is huge. Something doesn't match up here."

"I think you're right," Lori agreed. "She just—"

"I wonder if she has a bleeding problem," Sims interrupted without hearing her. "I wonder if she has a problem with her platelets, or maybe even something worse. I've seen a couple of people with early leukemia who presented like this—bad bruising and nothing else."

Lori looked up at him, not sure what to say.

Sims picked up Jenny's chart and headed back over to her room.

"I'm going to ask her a few more questions," he tossed over his shoulder. "We might need to get some blood work, so hold on before ordering anything, Amy."

He disappeared behind the curtain of room 4. Amy Connors looked up at the nurse and asked, "What's wrong, Lori? Somethin's botherin' you about that woman."

She and Lori had worked together for more than a dozen years, and Amy sensed that something was troubling her friend.

"I don't know," Lori answered, slowly shaking her head. "Probably nothing."

She had been looking at the closed curtain of Jenny Bristol's room, thinking. Now she turned back to Amy. "I'd better get back out to triage."

Duff questioned Jenny Bristol about any easy bruising or unexplained weight loss. He asked her about headaches and about any prescriptions, over-the-counter medications, or herbal remedies. He was very thorough as he pursued any possible clues as to why she might be bruising like this.

Then he asked her to lie down on her back, and he made sure she had no enlargement of her liver or spleen. Normal. And he didn't see any other bothersome bruises anywhere.

He missed the one behind her left ear. It was covered by her curly brown hair, and she didn't volunteer anything about it.

"Well," Sims said thoughtfully, cupping his chin in his hand, satisfied that he wasn't missing anything unusual or significant. "I think we can just focus on your shoulder today, and make sure that's okay."

He turned and walked back over to the nurses' station.

The X-rays of Jenny Bristol's shoulder were normal, with no obvious fracture or any bone problem. What he could see of the underlying ribs and lung was normal as well.

"Contusion of left shoulder" was the diagnosis he wrote on her chart. He gave her a prescription for something for pain, instructed her in the use of ice, and told her to come back to the ER if she had any problems.

"Thanks, Doctor," she said in a soft, flat voice. "I'll be fine."

Lori Davidson was bringing another patient back into the department as Jenny was leaving. She looked up at Lori as they passed in the hallway, and their eyes met. Jenny quickly looked away and hurried out of the ER, leaving the nurse with an uneasy feeling.

Wednesday, 11:30 a.m. It had been a little more than two weeks since Jenny Bristol had been in the ER. And here she was, once again sitting in triage, this time in front of Jeff Ryan.

Jeff had been in the emergency department for almost fifteen years, and was one of the most experienced and seasoned nurses there. He had an uncanny ability to cut to the chase and quickly determine who was sick and who wasn't. And just like Lori Davidson, he sensed that something wasn't adding up with Jenny.

"Mrs. Bristol," he said patiently to the woman sitting calmly in the triage chair. "Let's go over that one more time. What is the main problem that brings you to the ER today?"

Jenny studied the backs of her hands and quietly repeated what she had just told him.

"I've been having headaches lately, and some chills. I thought I had a fever when I got here, but you told me…Anyway, and I've been having some stomach cramps."

She placed her right hand over her mid-abdomen, indicating the site of her pain.

"Anything else?" Jeff asked, making notes on her clinical encounter form. Her temperature was normal, as were her pulse and blood pressure. She seemed fine, and was certainly in no distress.

"No...nothing else," she answered. "I've just not been feeling well lately."

The door from the waiting room opened and a man walked in, wearing a knit shirt, shorts, and running shoes.

"Sorry it took so long, honey," he said to Jenny Bristol. "The people in registration were really slow, and…" He paused and looked over at Jeff. Then, reaching out his hand, he said, "Hello, I'm Charles Bristol, Jenny's husband. Is she going to be alright?"

Then Charles put his hand on Jenny's shoulder, and Jeff thought he saw her flinch. It was a small thing, and he might have been mistaken. Then he glanced down at her record and noted the previous shoulder injury. That must be it. She must still have some tenderness there. But… he had his hand on her right shoulder.

"There's nothing seriously wrong, is there?" Mr. Bristol persisted.

Jeff looked up at him and said, "She seems fine, but we need to check out these complaints and make sure. We're going to head back into the department now," he added, standing up.

"Is it okay if I come with her?" Bristol asked.

"Sure," Jeff answered, picking up her clipboard and leading them through the triage hallway.

He glanced up at the patient board and saw that room 5 was empty.

"This way," he told the couple, and then led them around the nurses' station to the room. Amy Connors looked up from behind the counter and saw Jenny Bristol, immediately recognizing her. But she couldn't remember why she had been in the ER a few weeks ago. She knew Dr. Sims would want her old record before he saw her, and that would remind her.

Odd, though, she thought, watching her as she passed. Jenny was staring intently down at the floor. The man behind her looked over at Amy and smiled cheerfully, nodding his head.

Jeff Ryan got Jenny settled in her room, handed her a gown to put on, then said, "Dr. Sims is on duty today. He'll be with you as soon as he can."

He walked over to the nurses' station and handed the clipboard to Amy.

"We'll need her old records," he told her. "I think she was here a couple of weeks ago." He paused and then added, "Something peculiar about this one."

"Oh yeah?" Amy said, looking up at him, curious. Jeff Ryan wasn't given to making casual statements, and his gut instincts were usually correct.

"Yeah," he repeated. "Something odd."

Fifteen minutes later, Duff Sims stood at the nurses' station, looking down at the chart of Jenny Bristol.

"I remember this woman," he said to Amy. Then he picked up the top sheet and glanced at the record of her previous visit.

"Yes, this is the lady with the bruised shoulder," he announced. "Thought there might be something unusual going on, but she seemed fine, except for that contusion. What's the problem today?"

He looked again at the clinical sheet for this morning's visit and read her long list of complaints.

"Hmm," he murmured. "That's a little strange. She doesn't seem like a hypochondriac, but this is a pretty vague list of problems. Nothing very specific here."

He picked up the clipboard and walked over to room 5.

Charles Bristol looked up as Sims entered the cubicle. Then he glanced down at his watch.

"Mrs. Bristol," Sims said to the woman. "I'm Dr. Sims. I think I saw you the last time you were here."

She looked up at Duff, nodded her head, then quickly looked back down at the floor.

"Now tell me about your problems today," Sims began. "What seems to be going on with you?"

It was her husband who spoke first.

"Doctor, do you think this is going to take very long? I've got a golf match at one o'clock, and I'm hoping we can be through here by then."

Sims's face reddened a little at this, and his lips pressed together slightly.

"We'll be as efficient as we can," he told the man. "But we need to be sure your wife is alright, and that there is nothing serious going on."

"Well, Dr. Jeffers couldn't find anything wrong," Bristol said impatiently.

"Dr. Jeffers?" Sims asked, surprised. Bill Jeffers was a family practitioner in Rock Hill. "Is that her family doctor?"

"Yes," Bristol answered curtly. "She saw him a couple of days ago with all of the same complaints, and he couldn't find anything wrong. I doubt if you will either."

Jenny Bristol turned her head away from her husband and continued to stare silently at the floor.

"Well, let's start at the beginning," Duff said, pulling over a chair, sitting down, and placing Jenny's clipboard on his lap. Out of the corner of his eye he saw Charles Bristol check his watch again.

Two hours later, the battery of tests that Sims had ordered were attached to Jenny's chart, and he was studying her chest X-ray, which was hanging on the view box. Charles Bristol had left the ER over an hour ago, determined not to miss his tee time.

Jeff Ryan walked out of triage and over to where Duff stood.

"Anything there?" he asked the young doctor.

Duff looked over his shoulder at Jeff and then back at the X-ray.

"No, everything looks okay. No pneumonia and no enlarged heart. I don't see any enlarged lymph nodes or anything."

He was about to pull the X-rays down when the big nurse stepped beside him and pointed to the film.

"What do you think that is?" he asked.

Sims moved closer to the view box and studied the area at the tip of Jeff's finger. Overlying two of Jenny's left ribs were swollen areas of what appeared to be new calcium deposits. Healing fractures.

"Well, I didn't see those," he remarked. "Thanks. I'll need to ask her about this."

"Hmm," Jeff muttered, then walked back out to triage.

Duff studied the X-rays for another minute. Then he took them down from the view box, carried them over to the nurses' station, and put them down on the counter. He asked Amy to get them around to X-ray for one of the radiologists to look at.

"I need to go talk with Mrs. Bristol some more," he said, walking over to room 5.

He explained to Jenny that all of her lab work was completely normal. There was no obvious explanation for her symptoms and nothing ominous with anything they had found.

Then he asked her about her rib fractures. When had she injured her chest? And how had it happened?

"These fractures are no more than four or five weeks old," he told her.

Jenny Bristol's face flushed when he mentioned this. She had already dressed, and now started to stand up from the stretcher.

"I've…I've never injured my chest," she stammered, picking up her purse and stepping toward the door. "I don't know what you're talking about."

Duff Sims stood at the end of the stretcher, blocking her way. He didn't move.

"I've got to be going," she said to him. "If you'll—"

"Mrs. Bristol, something caused those rib fractures, and you must remember when it happened. Those injuries are very painful and—"

"If you'll excuse me," she interrupted. "I really must be going."

She gently but resolutely put her hand on his arm and moved past him into the hallway. Glancing around, she quickly got her bearings and headed for the ambulance entrance.

"Mrs. Bristol!" Duff called out, standing in the entrance of room 5, not knowing what to do.

Amy Connors looked up as the young woman walked through the automatic doors and out into the bright sunlight of the parking area. The doors closed behind her, and she was gone.

"What was that about?" Amy asked Duff as he walked over to the nurses' station.

"I'm not sure," he mumbled. His face was a little flushed, and he was tapping his pen on the counter. "I'm just not sure."

Saturday, 8:45 p.m. Three days later, the mystery surrounding Jenny Bristol began to be resolved. This time she came to the ER by herself, clutching her right arm against her chest as she walked into triage.

Lori Davidson looked up from the log she was working on and immediately saw the look of pain and fear on her face. The nurse jumped up from her chair, took Jenny by the shoulder, and helped her sit down.

"Mrs. Bristol," she said, remembering her name. "What happened to you tonight?"

Jenny grimaced with pain as her arm was jarred in the process of sitting down.

"It's my arm," she groaned, indicating her right forearm with a downward tilt of her head. "I think it's broken."

Lori checked her vital signs, made some notes on her chart, and gently examined Jenny's injured forearm. It was swollen and very tender, but the skin wasn't broken, and her wrist and elbow seemed to be all right.

"How did it happen?" Lori asked, closely studying her patient's face.

A cloud seemed to pass over it as she considered her response.

"I…I fell in the…I fell in the shower this afternoon," she stammered, wincing a bit as she talked.

"Just like last time?" the nurse gently prodded. "Jenny, how did it happen? This usually doesn't occur with a fall."

Jenny Bristol slowly shook her head and repeated, "I fell in the shower."

Lori wasn't going to push her anymore at this point. She wanted to get her back to be seen.

"Is your husband with you?" she asked.

Jenny's head jerked up and her eyes met Lori's. The pain was suddenly gone, and now there was only fear. "No!" she almost shouted. "No, he's not here." Then she glanced nervously over at the door leading out to the waiting room.

"Okay, Jenny," Lori said, helping her up from the chair. "Let's get you into the department and taken care of."

They walked through the triage hallway and toward the ortho room.

Standing at the nurses' station was Phil Warner, the ER doctor on duty this evening. Warner was in his early fifties and had been at Rock Hill General for the past twenty years. He was calm and steady, and Lori was glad he was working tonight.

"Dr. Warner," she said quietly as they passed. He turned around at the sound of his name and their eyes met. Without Lori's saying anything, he stopped what he was doing and followed the two women.

Lori helped Jenny Bristol up onto one of the stretchers, gently protecting her injured extremity. Phil Warner studied the chart that the nurse had laid on the countertop in the corner of the room.

He looked carefully at the complaint and at Lori's notes. She had mentioned the two previous visits and had underlined the words "bruised shoulder." It was followed by several question marks. Then she had underlined "fell tonight and hurt forearm." Her concern wasn't lost on Phil.

"Mrs. Bristol," he said, turning and stepping toward the stretcher. "I'm Dr. Warner. Tell me how you hurt your arm tonight."

She cradled her right arm with her left hand and said, "As I told the nurse, I fell in the shower, and I think I've broken it."

Lori glanced up at Dr. Warner and raised her eyebrows.

"Okay, well, let's take a look," he said, beginning to examine her right shoulder and elbow and then her wrist. "Everything here seems okay," he told her. "Now let's take a look at this forearm."

Jenny held it out for him as best she could, but even a slight effort caused her a lot of pain.

Warner held her arm and began to examine it. Lori noticed that the swelling was worse now, and the bruise was spreading. It looked awful.

After a few minutes, Warner said, "We'll need to get some X-rays, Mrs. Bristol, but I think you've broken one of the bones here, if not both."

Jenny nodded silently, expecting this news.

What she didn't expect was what Dr. Warner said next.

"This would be what we call a nightstick fracture," he began to explain. "It doesn't happen with a fall, but from a direct blow, usually

from a blunt object. It's a defensive injury, from holding up your arm
to protect your head. That's why it's called a nightstick fracture—from
getting hit by a stick or club of some sort."

He paused and studied the young woman.

"Now, Jenny," he said gently. "How did this happen?"

She seemed ready to say something but then hung her head again
and muttered, "I fell in the shower."

Warner wasn't going to press her on this—not just yet.

"Let's get those X-rays," he told her. "And then we'll see where we are."

Forty-five minutes later, Jenny Bristol's X-rays were hanging on the
view box. Phil Warner was studying them as Lori Davidson walked up.

"Wow," she exclaimed. "You were right."

She pointed to the obvious fractures of Jenny's forearm and asked,
"What do you think caused *that*?"

"I'm thinking a baseball bat or a golf club—something along those
lines," Warner answered. "But she's lucky, at least as far as the fractures
go. Both bones have breaks, but they're not displaced, and she probably won't need surgery. We can just put her in a plaster splint tonight
and let ortho see her on Monday."

Lori was thinking beyond these fractures and said, "Whoever did
this must have been serious about hurting her. He must have been
swinging mighty hard."

"You said, 'he,'" Warner observed, turning to the nurse. "I would
agree with that, but do you have someone in mind?"

Lori told him about her previous interactions with Jenny and with
her husband, Charles.

"Something hasn't been right there from the very beginning," she
added. "And Jeff did say something about him being a golfer," she said
nervously, suddenly remembering their conversation.

"If you're right," Warner said, the tone of his voice suddenly becoming very serious, "Then this thing is escalating, and the next time could
be something much worse."

He and Lori had seen this happen too many times. Once this pattern started, it seemed to get worse until something disastrous happened. Or until somebody got help.

"Let's go talk with Jenny," he said as he turned and walked to the back of the department.

He pulled the curtain closed behind him and sat down on the edge of Jenny Bristol's stretcher. Lori stood nearby, clutching the young woman's clipboard against her chest.

He explained the X-ray findings and the treatment for these fractures. Jenny nodded her head in understanding, clearly relieved she wouldn't have to have surgery.

"Does that mean I can go home now?" she asked, sliding to the edge of her bed.

"No, not just yet," the doctor answered. "We need to get that splint on first."

Then he paused and looked squarely into her face. She still looked away and wouldn't meet his eyes.

"Jenny," he began. "When we talked a little while ago, I told you this type of injury doesn't happen from a fall. It takes a direct blow from some blunt object...like a golf club."

He watched her closely, looking for any body language that might give her away.

She didn't flinch or move at all. And even her breathing remained calm and regular.

He was trying to think of what to ask or say next when Lori spoke.

"Jenny," she said gently, moving closer to the stretcher. Then she laid the clipboard down on the bed and put her hand on the young woman's shoulder.

"I looked at the X-rays with Dr. Warner, and I know he must have hit you very hard." She was taking a chance now, but her heart was telling her what to say, and she followed it. "Charles is a big man, and strong. If he decided to really hurt you, he—"

"I know, I know!" Jenny cried out, slumping against Lori and sobbing with uncontrollable heaves. She looked up at her and then into the concerned eyes of Phil Warner.

"It was a baseball bat!" she blurted angrily. "My husband hit me with a baseball bat!"

The flash of anger in her face was quickly replaced by embarrassment, then fear, and then by a profound loneliness. Her head sagged to her chest again.

"Jenny," Warner said, laying his hand on her uninjured forearm. "We're going to get the police involved. We have to. This is becoming dangerous, and it needs to stop."

"Not tonight!" she jerked her head up, looking first at the doctor and then at Lori. "Not now! He'll—"

"We have to do this." Lori tried to calm her. "You can't go back home until we know you're safe."

"But...but...where will I go?" she stammered.

"Do you have any family nearby? Any friends you could stay with until this settles out?"

Jenny struggled to collect herself, then said, "My sister lives in Asheville. I could go stay with her for a while."

She seemed to relax a little with this plan, and with the hope she wouldn't have to face her husband again tonight.

"Good," Lori told her. "I'm going to make a couple of phone calls and then we'll help you get in touch with your sister and—"

"Code blue—cardiac!"

It was Amy Connors calling urgently over the department intercom.

"Code blue—cardiac!" she repeated.

Phil Warner jumped down from the stretcher and looked over at Lori.

"Must be Mr. Sheavers," he said. "Let's go!"

Bill Sheavers was a sixty-year-old man who had come in less than an hour ago with chest pain. He was having a heart attack, but had seemed stable. Something had gone wrong.

"Okay," Lori answered, grabbing Jenny's chart as she hurried after the doctor. At the doorway she turned and said, "We'll be back in just a minute, Jenny."

Over the next thirty minutes, they were able to stabilize Bill Sheavers and get him on his way to the cath lab. Lori had called the police about Jenny Bristol's situation and had gone to check on her. After less than a minute, she walked back up to the nurses' station and stood beside Warner.

She didn't say anything for a moment, but then took a deep breath and sighed. "She's gone."

"What?" he asked her, incredulous.

"Jenny Bristol is gone."

Two weeks later, 6:55 a.m. Phil Warner had just walked up to the nurses' station. He was coming on duty and had his first cup of coffee in hand. Lori Davidson was standing a few feet away, and Amy Connors sat behind the counter, getting her logbook ready for the coming twelve-hour shift.

"I guess you heard what happened to the Bristol woman," Amy said, not looking up from her work.

"Bristol?" Warner repeated, not yet fully awake.

"Yeah, the woman with the broken arm," she patiently explained. "The one who slipped out of the back of the ER a couple of weeks ago."

"Jenny Bristol?" Lori asked, concerned about this young woman who had seemingly vanished into thin air.

"I think that's her name," Amy said, looking up. Obviously the two had not heard any of this. She could see the concern on their faces.

"What about Jenny Bristol?" Warner asked.

"Well," Amy began. "It seems she left here and went up to Asheville to stay with her sister."

"Good," Lori interjected with relief. "At least she got away from her husband."

"No, not exactly," Amy said slowly. "It seems her husband found out where she went and followed her up there. He broke into her sister's house. And he shot and killed Jenny. Tried to kill her sister too, but only wounded her in the shoulder before he got scared and took off runnin'. They found him somewhere on the Blue Ridge Parkway a couple of hours later. Had him locked up ever since."

Phil Warner and Lori Davidson looked at each other. Neither of them spoke, but both wondered what else they might have done. What else they *should* have done. They both knew that some people just won't allow themselves to be helped. They had seen that happen too many times.

But what else could they have done? What else?

6

Seizure Alley

*What seems like the right thing to do
could also be the hardest thing
you have ever done in your life.
It's always worth it.*

Author unknown

Joel Carver reported for his shift at 6:30 a.m. As usual, he was early. As he walked into the station's lounge, Randy Green, director of the EMS, pulled him aside.

"Joel," Randy said, putting his hand on the young man's shoulder. "It's time to change things up a little."

Carver looked at his boss, becoming a little nervous and wondering what that might mean. He waited for Green to explain himself.

"Now don't get worried," Randy continued, smiling. "You're doing a great job. And I know you've had a good time riding with Sharon Brothers. Everybody does. Remember, the idea is to put you with experienced paramedics and see how they do things. Now you're going to be riding with Denton Roberts, another veteran paramedic."

Joel nodded his head. He knew that was the plan, but he had really enjoyed his time with Sharon. She sometimes had an unusual way of doing things, but she knew everybody and every street in Rock Hill. He thought about some of their experiences and started to smile.

"So anyway," Green went on. " Like I said, I'm going to pair you up for a while with Denton. You've met him, I think."

Joel knew him, though only barely. They had been working different assignments and had seen each other only briefly during shift changes.

Denton Roberts was in his early forties and had been a paramedic with the EMS for almost twenty years. He had been one of the first on the scene when the big jet went down between Rock Hill and Charlotte in 1974. That experience had forever changed his life.

"I've met Denton," Joel said. "When do you want to start this?"

Green looked down at his watch. "How about right now?"

As if on cue, Roberts walked into the lounge, a large duffel bag slung over his shoulder. When he saw Joel standing with their director, he walked over and dumped the bag on the floor. Holding out his hand, he said, "I guess we're partners now."

Carver shook his hand. Denton had a strong grip and steady eyes that never left Joel's. This was going to be okay.

"Alright, guys," Randy said, clapping his hands together. "You'd better get at it. You're assigned to Station 4 today."

"Station 4?" Denton's voice had just the slightest hint of perplexity.

Randy caught this and quickly answered, "Yes, 4. I thought it was time Joel was broken in to that side of town."

"Okay," Denton said, picking up his bag.

He turned to the younger paramedic and said, "Let's go."

As they walked out of headquarters and over to their ambulance, Joel asked, "What's the problem with Station 4?"

Without looking over at his new partner, Denton simply said, "Seizure Alley."

The name wouldn't be found on any city map, but everyone with EMS, the police department, and the fire department knew the area around Franklin Street as "Seizure Alley." It hadn't always been that way. Not too many years ago, the area had been respectable and safe. It wasn't safe now. Seizure Alley had become the home of drug dealers, alcoholics, and a good bit of the criminal activity in Rock Hill.

Someone had given it the nickname Seizure Alley because of the frequent 9-1-1 calls for drug overdoses, alcoholics in full-blown DTs, and seizure patients who for one reason or another stopped taking their medication. The name stuck, and Denton would be introducing Joel Carver to this interesting part of town.

Denton was walking toward the driver's side of the ambulance, and Joel toward the other, when Roberts stopped and called out to his partner.

"Joel, come over here a minute."

Curious, the young man turned around and headed to the other side of the vehicle. Denton was standing beside the rear tire, waiting on him.

"I want you to feel this," Roberts said, "and tell me what you think it is."

He was pointing to an area just above the wheel, near the opening of the gas tank. The surrounding paint was smooth, dark red, and flawless. The area Denton was pointing to was oval, slightly indented, and obviously patched.

Joel leaned in close, inspected it from different angles, and then ran his hand across the uneven spot.

"I don't have any idea, Denton," he answered finally. "What is it?"

Roberts leaned over and gently rubbed the place himself.

"That, Joel Carver, is what remains of a bullet hole."

Joel stared down in disbelief.

"A bullet hole?" he stammered. "Somebody shot at an ambulance?"

"That's exactly what I mean," Denton replied, turning toward the driver's door. "Now get in, and I'll tell you about it."

When they were both belted in, Roberts turned to the younger man and said, "Over in Seizure Alley, right in the middle of Franklin Street, my partner and I had responded to a stabbing—some sort of domestic violence. When we pulled up to the house, there was a big crowd of people millin' around, and as I got out of the ambulance, I heard a gunshot."

"What did you do then?" Joel asked excitedly. This was incredible to him.

"Well, I looked around and didn't see anyone with a gun. Didn't even know the ambulance had been hit. I might have behaved differently had I known that."

"What do you mean?"

"My partner and I went on into the house and took care of the lady who'd been stabbed. We got her stabilized and into the ambulance without any trouble, and then to the hospital. If I'd known someone had put a bullet hole in my ambulance, I might have…well, I would have gone into the house anyway, but that's one time I would have thought about waitin' for the police to arrive."

Joel Carver scratched his head and stared out the front window.

"I thought it was routine for us to wait for the police before going into a house," he said. "Especially if it's a domestic."

"You're right," Denton replied. "That's policy. But it only became policy after that incident. The bullet hole got everyone's attention."

"I can't believe someone would intentionally shoot at an ambulance," Joel said, shaking his head. "What would make someone do that?"

"Sometimes it's alcohol," Roberts explained. "Sometimes people are just upset and want someone to take it out on. And sometimes…well, sometimes it's just plain meanness."

"I'm just glad nobody got hurt."

"Me too," Denton agreed. "And my partner would say the same thing. I guess that's the closest I've come to really being injured."

"You mean other stuff has happened to you?" Joel turned again to face his new partner.

Denton fired up the ambulance and began backing out of its parking space.

"Oh sure," he said matter-of-factly. "I've been yelled at, cursed out, spit on. Even had a pair of shoes thrown at me once. And one of our guys got hit with a pizza not too long ago."

"A pizza?" Joel echoed in disbelief. "What the—"

"Yeah, a pizza. And that was after the beer bottle barely missed his head."

The young man sat quietly for a moment as the ambulance headed out onto Herlong Avenue.

"Where did all this happen?" he asked. "Wait—let me guess. Seizure Alley."

Denton smiled broadly. "That's right. Seizure Alley. Right where we're headed."

When they arrived at Station 4, the crew they were relieving was outside, hosing off their ambulance. Joel knew the two paramedics, and they talked for a few minutes before they headed home for some much-needed sleep. It had been a busy night, and they had been on the road for most of it.

He looked around the outside of the station and was struck by how neat and clean it was. Granted, it wasn't on Franklin Street—it was located a half mile away on the bypass—but he had expected something different. This was impressive. And the inside of the facility looked just as good. It must have been relatively new—it had new furniture, comfortable-looking sleeping areas, and a well-supplied kitchen. *This couldn't be that bad*, he thought. Then he noticed something he hadn't seen when he was outside. There were heavy iron bars on all of the windows. And when he looked again at the front door, he saw the three sturdy dead bolts.

Maybe it *could* be that bad.

"You take that bunk," Denton told him, pointing to the room closest to the kitchen. "Maybe we'll get lucky tonight and get some sleep. You never know."

The next couple of hours were quiet, with no calls from dispatch. They could hear other units being called out to other parts of town, but nothing over here.

"We'll start getting busy when everyone else is settlin' down," Denton explained. "Most of our clients won't be wakin' up till five or six in the evening."

He was right. At 7:15 p.m., their radios started beeping, and the EMS dispatch instructed them to respond to an unknown emergency on Slater Street, just off Franklin.

"Let's go!" Denton said, grabbing the ambulance keys off the kitchen table and heading toward the door.

"Make sure it's locked when you close it," he told Joel, pointing down at the handle. "Don't want any surprises when we get back."

In the four months he had been working with the EMS, Joel could remember feeling excited and a little nervous every time his radio went off. There was always that immediate adrenaline rush, it seemed. But this time…this time, there was something else. He thought it might be fear, but he wouldn't give it that name.

He checked the door behind him, made sure it was locked, and followed his partner over to the ambulance.

As he climbed into the seat, Denton said, "The good thing about this assignment is that most of our calls will be within four or five minutes. That's where the action is. Close to home."

He was right again. They were at the scene of the "unknown emergency" within a few minutes, and had pulled over to the curb in front of a weathered and neglected house.

A crowd had gathered on the lawn outside and was spilling out into the street.

"Keep your eyes open," Denton told the young paramedic, with an edge of seriousness in his voice.

"Where are the police?" Joel asked, looking up and down the street for their reassuring presence.

"We usually arrive on the scene before they do," Denton answered. "But they should be here in just a minute or two."

He stepped out of the cab and around to the back of the ambulance, where Joel quickly joined him. They opened the back doors and were about to lift their stretcher to the ground when…*bam!*

Something hit the door just a few feet from where Joel stood.

Then another *bam!* And a rock thumped down onto the thin mattress of the EMS stretcher.

The young paramedic ducked his head and was about to jump into the back of the ambulance.

Bam! Another rock, this one bouncing off the rear fender.

Denton Roberts turned around, stood up straight, and faced the crowd gathering around them. There was a low murmuring, but nothing discernible was being directed at them. He scanned the crowd, looking for someone with a raised arm.

Seeing none, he quietly said, "Guys, we have work to do."

Then he turned back to the stretcher, glanced over at Joel, and whispered, "Let's get moving—and quick."

As they unfolded the stretcher and set it on the ground, the sound of a police siren wailed up Franklin Street. Then it turned onto Slater.

Relieved and impressed with his partner's bravery, Joel leaned over and quietly said, "You must have heard them coming."

"Yep," was all Denton said.

He hadn't, but Joel would never know that.

Inside the house they found the "unknown emergency." Two thirty-year-old men had gotten into an argument over the ownership of some drugs, and one had stabbed the other in the forearm with a needle. The stab-ee didn't appreciate this, and proceeded to club his friend with a baseball bat. Fortunately, neither was seriously hurt. Denton and Joel took the Louisville Slugger victim to the ER while the other man followed them in a police car. An hour later, the two paramedics were back at Station 4, locked in and waiting.

8:45 p.m. "EMS 2, respond code 3 to 107 Franklin Street. Shortness of breath."

The dispatcher didn't have to repeat herself. Denton grabbed his radio from the table by his recliner, depressed the send button, and said, "10-4, dispatch. EMS 2 responding to 107 Franklin."

"Roger, EMS 2." And the radio fell silent.

"Let's go," Roberts spoke, looking over at his partner.

They were out the door and in their ambulance in under two minutes. As they snapped their seat belts in place, Denton turned to Joel and said, "I think 107 is where the Burgesses live."

As he flipped the ignition of the ambulance, he nodded his head and added, "Pretty sure about that. Noah and Nannie Burgess. That's their place."

The engine roared to life, and with lights flashing and siren blaring, they headed out of the parking lot and down the bypass.

"Who are the Burgesses?" Joel asked.

"They're really a couple of great people," the older paramedic answered. "Must be in their seventies, maybe eighties. Don't know why they still live on Franklin Street, though. I guess they can't afford to leave the place. They've been there as long as I can remember."

"The people in the area don't bother them?" Joel was thinking about the residents of Seizure Alley, and its history of crime and violence. "Looks like they would be easy targets."

"You'd think that," Roberts mused. "But I can't think of a time when anyone ever bothered them. Maybe it's a matter of respect. Or maybe it's a matter of them not having anything much worth stealing. Whatever the reason, they seem to get along okay over there, but I'd still like to see them move out. You'll understand when you meet them."

He turned onto Franklin, and Joel immediately sensed an uneasy feeling in the pit of his stomach.

He had never been in a war zone, but he thought this must be pretty close to what one looked like. House after house seemed to be falling down, decaying in obvious neglect. Screen doors hung at odd angles on doorways that led into dimly lit living rooms. The yards, if you could call them that, were strewn with trash, broken bikes and toys, and the occasional automobile tire. They passed a driveway where an old Chevy sat on concrete blocks, stripped down almost to the point of being unrecognizable.

Every couple of houses or so, there would be a group of people standing around, mostly teenagers and young men. All of them stared at the ambulance as it sped by.

Joel couldn't help it, but he found himself hunching down a little in his seat. Roberts glanced over at him and chuckled. Then he looked beyond his partner, into the yard of a passing house.

It was getting close to nine o'clock, and it was dark. Four young children, none more than two years old, were running around on the bare red dirt that served as a front yard. They were filthy, and they wore only flimsy, dirty underwear. They looked up at EMS 2 as it sped by, and they waved.

Denton shook his head, then looked down the street again, slowing as they approached 107. He remembered it as being on the left side of the street.

Out of nowhere, a man lurched from behind a tree on their right and almost stepped directly in their path. He was barefoot, and had on a T-shirt and tattered blue jeans. He was staggering, trying to maintain his balance, and waved a half-empty bottle of malt liquor over his head.

Roberts swerved, barely missing him, and barely avoiding a pickup truck that was parked too far out in the street on their left.

"Whew!" he whistled. "That was close. We almost had a twofer."

Carver was about to ask what this meant, when Denton put on the brakes and smoothly wheeled into a driveway just beyond the pickup truck.

"Here we are," he said. Then he picked up his radio and reported to dispatch.

"EMS 2 on the scene at Franklin. No police backup yet."

Joel had been looking up and down the street for a police patrol car but hadn't seen one. He was staying put.

"EMS 2, they should be there in a minute," the dispatcher replied. "Two units responding. Just wait till they get there."

Denton Roberts looked down at the radio in his hand. Then he asked, "Dispatch, is this call for Noah Burgess?"

A moment passed as the dispatcher checked her notes.

"Roger that, EMS 2. Noah Burgess. Shortness of breath."

Denton looked up and quickly scanned what he could see of Franklin Street. Still no patrol cars.

"10-4, dispatch. EMS 2 out."

He slipped his radio into the holder on his waist and then released his seat belt. Turning to Carver he said, "Noah needs our help, and I'm going in. You can wait on the police units to get here. No problem with that, Joel. I'll understand."

Without waiting for a response, he jumped out of the cab and hurried to the back of the ambulance. Joel heard the doors opening and the stretcher being released.

What was he waiting for? He wasn't about to let his partner do this alone.

He unsnapped his seat belt, opened the door, and joined Denton. He helped him get the stretcher down and then grabbed the emergency kit.

"Let's do this," Joel Carver said, surprising himself with the resolve in his voice.

Denton Roberts looked over at him and smiled.

The EMS stretcher was light, and they easily lifted it up the wooden steps leading to the front porch. There was a difference between 107 Franklin and the other houses Joel had seen on this street. Its outside was built of the same material, clapboard, but had recently been painted, and the chairs on the porch were cushioned and in good repair. In the pale light from a nearby streetlamp, he noticed that the yard actually had grass, and well-kept boxwoods surrounded the porch.

Standing in the doorway and holding the screen open for them was Nannie Burgess. She was a tall woman, with a full, white head of hair pinned up in a bun. Her blue linen dress hung loosely on her slender frame, and a red gingham apron was tied around her waist.

"Better hurry up, son," she told Denton. "Noah's not doin' so well." Then she glanced over at Joel and asked, "Who's your young friend here?"

Denton reached over and held the screen door.

"This is Joel Carver," he told her. "Just started with us a couple of months ago."

He and Joel slipped by Nannie with the stretcher and stopped in the living room.

"Where's Noah?" he asked her, glancing toward a hallway that led to the back of the house.

"In the bedroom," she answered, pointing in that direction. "Last room on the left. I'll be back there in just a moment. Got to check on somethin' in the kitchen."

She turned and walked out of the room, leaving the two paramedics alone. Without saying a word, they wheeled their stretcher toward the hallway.

Noah Burgess was reclining in the queen-sized bed that took up most of the space in the small bedroom. He was propped up on four or five pillows and leaning a little to one side. His breathing was labored, and his eyes were partially closed. He did manage to see Denton as he came into the room, and weakly raised his right hand in recognition.

"Noah," the paramedic said to his friend as he stepped quickly to the side of his bed. "What kind of trouble have you gotten yourself into tonight?"

He reached down and held the old man's hand, checking his pulse while he did so.

Noah just shook his head, unable to say anything. With his other hand, he managed to pat his chest a few times, right over his heart. He looked up into his friend's eyes, imploring him.

"You just relax," Denton told him, patting his cool, damp, shoulder. "Just let us help you."

Noah Burgess was in congestive heart failure again, and he was probably in the worst shape Denton had ever seen him. He was in trouble.

Joel was opening the emergency kit when he heard the screen door squeak open. The sound was followed by the thumping footsteps of a group of people, making their way down the hallway and toward Noah's bedroom.

He continued to work, taking out the blood-pressure cuff and tossing it onto the bed. Then he started getting out the things necessary to start an IV. He didn't look up when he heard muffled voices approaching them, and then the sound of more feet. But he moved a little closer to the bed and away from the doorway.

Denton grabbed the BP cuff and was putting it around Noah's right arm as several men burst into the room. The stench of cheap alcohol quickly filled the small space.

"Well, well. What have we got here?"

It was the man closest to the foot of Noah's bed, and he was looking back and forth from one paramedic to the other. He was big, at least six-and-a-half feet tall, and his belly hung way over his pants belt. His soiled T-shirt was several sizes too small and only managed to cover the upper part of his protuberant abdomen.

He appeared to be in his forties, but the dozen or so men with him, and who were now spreading around the room, were all in their twenties—maybe younger.

"What do you guys think you're doin'?" he blustered. "This ain't no place for you two to be." The man was obviously their leader.

Denton kept working and never looked up.

"Blood pressure's 70 over 50," he told Joel. "We need to get that line in and check his rhythm strip. His pulse is irregular, and he may be in atrial fib."

"Did you hear me, buddy?" the man asked, getting louder. "This ain't no place for you guys."

Joel was trying to start the IV, and also trying desperately to keep his hands from shaking. He glanced behind him when he sensed some of the others beginning to crowd in. Then he felt someone bump into his back.

"Excuse me," someone mumbled sarcastically behind him. Then there was another bump.

"Listen," Denton said, standing to his full height and squarely facing the man at the foot of the bed. "We're trying to help Noah here, and we need some room. If you will take your friends back to the living—"

"Whoa now!" the big man said derisively. "Just who do you think *you* are, givin' us orders? We don't need you people here, understand? Every time you come down here, the police come too, and there's always trouble. When are you goin' to learn to stay away from our neighborhood?"

"Maybe they need some educatin'," said one of the men standing behind Joel.

"Yeah, maybe they do," another joined in. He was standing just behind Denton. He stepped forward a little, barely inches from the paramedic. Joel looked over and saw a large hawkbill knife in his hand.

"Denton…" he warned his partner.

Roberts turned and looked down at the menacing weapon. Then he looked up at the face of the teenager who was holding it.

"Son, you don't want any part of this," he told him calmly. "Why don't you put that away and let us help Mr. Burgess."

"You ain't my daddy!" the boy said, puffing out his chest and bumping into the paramedic. He glanced around the room for approval, and someone in the back yelled, "Stick him!"

What is going on? Joel thought. *And where are the police?*

"Yeah, stick him!" somebody else hollered.

The big man nodded his approval and folded his arms across his belly. Suddenly he was pushed forward, causing him to lose his balance and stumble. The men behind him were scattering, looking for somewhere to move.

Joel shook his head with relief. The police must finally be here.

Into the rapidly opening space at the foot of the bed stepped Nannie Burgess. She was indignant, and stood with her hands on her hips.

At first she didn't say a word, but only stared around the room, studying each face and shaking her head. When her eyes came to rest on the big man, she pointed a gnarled finger at him and said, "Sammy Jones, what has gotten into you? I'm gonna tell your momma, and we'll see what she has to say!"

Then she looked over at the young boy still holding the knife.

"And you, Johnny Stevens! How dare you pull a knife out in my house! I've a mind to give you a frammin' right here, right in front of your friends! You aren't too old or too big for that!"

Johnny looked down at the blade in his hand and quickly slid it into his pocket. There was a sudden shuffling of feet as people hurried out of the room and headed for the front door. Johnny Stevens quickly followed them.

The big man, Sammy Jones, just stood there, not knowing what to do. He stared malevolently at Denton, and then sheepishly at Nannie.

"Go on, git!" she demanded.

That was all it took. Sammy turned and almost ran out of the room.

In the distance, Joel could hear police sirens approaching. Then he looked down at Noah Burgess.

Noah hadn't missed any of this. He was looking up at his wife and smiling. Without a word, he held his hand out to her. She stepped across the room, her face softening as she took her husband's hands in hers.

"Now Noah, you just try to relax here," she soothed him. "Mr. Roberts and this young man here are gonna take good care of you."

The old man glanced up at Joel and winked. Then he looked at his wife, sighed comfortably, and gently patted her hands.

"Let's get you squared away and to the hospital," Denton told him, getting back to work.

Randy Green sat behind his desk, drumming his fingers loudly on the wooden surface.

"What am I going to do with you two?" he asked Joel and Denton. They were standing in front of him, not having been asked to sit down.

"Joel had nothing to do with this," the older paramedic began to explain. "It was my idea to go into that house before police backup got there."

"That doesn't surprise me," Randy said, shaking his head. "But you both know our policy. You don't put yourself at risk. Ever. You wait on police backup. Understand?"

Joel looked down at his feet, still upset over last night's experience. Noah Burgess had made it to the ER, but just barely. Following that, he had been admitted to the CCU in critical but improving condition. But if they had followed the policy…if they had waited…if they had delayed in getting to him…

"Randy, I hear you," Denton said calmly. "And you know I try to go by the book. But this has always been more than just a job. And it's not about me. That's why I'm a paramedic."

He paused briefly, struggling with his thoughts, and with his emotions. "Look," he went on. "I understand the importance of police backup, especially in that neighborhood. And I know you're always lookin' after us and tryin' to keep us safe. But I knew it was Noah Burgess, and I knew he needed help."

Joel looked over at his partner. This was a tough one. Rules and policies were important, but sometimes saving a life meant breaking the rules. Denton understood that. This was about taking care of all the Noahs out there, and the Nannies—and even the Sammys and

Johnnys. And if that came with rocks and bullets and knives—well, that would just have to be part of it.

He was about to speak up when Randy Green leaned back his chair, sighed loudly, then spun around with his back to the two paramedics. He was shaking his head a bit ruefully.

"You guys are off today, so I'll see you in the morning," he told them.

"What's our assignment?" Denton asked him, stepping toward the door.

"Do I have to tell you?" Green responded. He turned around, faced the two men, and smiled.

"Seizure Alley."

7

The Eye of the Storm

Even though I walk through the valley
of the shadow of death,
I will fear no evil,
for you are with me.

PSALM 23:4

Every eye in the room was on him, and C.L. knew it. He stood there for a moment, calmly meeting their stares, and then he quietly closed the back door behind him.

Artie's Billiard Parlor was a single-room establishment located just off Main Street. There were five pool tables crowded into its long and narrow space, and on this Tuesday afternoon, each of them was occupied. Artie's was a favorite hangout for the men working the first shift at the Jackson Bleaching Plant, located a few blocks away, and they came here to unwind after their eight hours.

This was the early 1970s, and while the color barrier in Rock Hill had officially been beaten down, it hadn't been too many years since another kind of beating had taken place just down the street at the town's bus station.

In 1961, thirteen civil-rights activists had boarded buses in Washington D.C. and headed south. One of the national leaders of the civil-rights movement, John Lewis, had been among them. When the group had arrived in Rock Hill, their first stop, Lewis and another man had stepped off their bus and been beaten by a white mob.

Those had been turbulent years, and while the memories and hostilities were fading, some of the men who had crowded the sidewalks of Rock Hill on that dark afternoon were now sitting in Artie's pool hall.

All of the customers in Artie's were white. And C.L. was black.

He made his way through the maze of tables and cue sticks, nodding his head and smiling each time he met someone's eyes. And then he was at the front door. Artie Ballard was sitting there behind the small counter, smoking a cigarette and reading the local newspaper.

He lowered the paper and looked up at C.L. "Thanks for comin' by, Officer Jamison," he said.

C.L. Jamison had been on the Rock Hill police force for a little over two months. There were a few other black officers in the department, but it seemed C.L. had been given the toughest duty, or at least he thought so. The downtown beat started at one end of Main Street, made its way through some alleyways and parking lots, circled back through Artie's Billiard Parlor, and then back on to Main Street. It wasn't a physically tough assignment. In fact, most officers in the department thought it was a pretty good way to spend a day. But for C.L., it was emotionally difficult and potentially dangerous.

His captain had clearly and honestly spelled out his intentions.

"C.L.," John Rice had told him, "things are changing, and we need to help the people of Rock Hill see that. I need a black officer downtown, patrolling Main Street and interacting with everyone over there. It's a tough assignment, I know, but you're the man for this job. I wouldn't put you out there if I didn't think you could handle it."

The young officer had studied Captain Rice intently as he said this. He believed him, and more than that, he trusted him. He just hoped he was right.

Artie's cigarette dangled from the corner of his mouth as he said, "Things goin' okay?"

C.L. mustered a hesitant smile and replied, "Sure, Mr. Ballard. Everything's great."

"Call me Artie," Ballard told him. "Just Artie."

A man sitting at a table near the door looked up at hearing this. His eyes studied the policeman, and then Artie Ballard. He shook his head and turned back to his coffee cup.

The reaction wasn't lost on C.L., and he just nodded his head a little. Then something made him look toward the back corner of the room, to a small booth just past the last pool table. Two men were sitting there, one with his back to C.L. The other man cradled a coffee cup in his hands and studied the police officer carefully. He was probably in his early forties—slender, balding, and with a furrowed brow that was the sign of a man given to dark moods. He wore a white dress shirt, its sleeves rolled up to his elbows. In its breast pocket was a pack of cigarettes.

C.L. met his eyes, but there was something uncomfortable there, something threatening, and he turned back to Artie Ballard.

"Yeah, everything's going fine, Mr.—Artie. I'll probably be back through later on this evening."

"Good," Artie said, not looking up from his newspaper this time.

C.L. stepped toward the door, then hesitated. He turned to Ballard and said, "Artie, who is the guy in the back booth over there—the one in the white shirt?"

Artie laid the newspaper on the countertop and slowly turned on his stool. Peering over the top of his reading glasses, he glanced back to the far corner of the room. Then he pursed his lips and turned again to C.L.

"Bubba Hendricks," he said quietly.

C.L. thought a moment, then asked, "Is there anything I need to know about him?"

"About Bubba?" he mused. "Just stay clear."

He picked his newspaper up again and adjusted his glasses, signaling the end of this conversation.

The man at the table near the door stood up and walked over to Artie, handing him a dollar and some change.

Abruptly he spun around and faced C.L.

"Did you say somethin'?" he asked brusquely.

Artie cleared his throat but didn't look up. This was up to the young officer to handle.

"Nope, just standing here, sir," C.L. answered with all the politeness he could muster. Then he turned to Artie and said, "See you later."

He stepped out the rickety screen door and onto the street. He let out a long sigh and just stood there for a few minutes, waiting for his heart rate to return to normal.

I sure hope Captain Rice was right, he thought.

Before long, C.L. was mostly settled into his routine, and the downtown beat was actually starting to feel comfortable. All except the daily passage through Artie's Billiard Parlor. He thought about the gauntlet run in Cooper's *The Last of the Mohicans,* and sometimes wondered what it would have felt like had the Indians been armed with cue sticks. He hoped he would never find out.

Every time he walked through Artie's, he would glance back into the corner to see if Bubba Hendricks was there. Usually he was, and he always sat in the same booth, in the same seat. And his eyes were always on C.L., studying him with that same furrowed brow and dark, threatening expression on his face.

Sometimes C.L. thought he might just go over to the booth and introduce himself to Bubba. But then he would remember Artie's advice—"Stay clear."

And so he did.

A month passed, and nothing exciting had happened on his beat. In fact, things in Rock Hill were relatively quiet. There were the usual domestic problems, of course, and the drunk-and-disorderly arrests. But nothing really serious.

Then one morning Captain Rice made an announcement during early report. The department was clamping down on the city's repeat offenders and those citizens who had not responded appropriately to legally tendered warrants and invitations to appear before one of the local judges.

"We've got some bad actors out there," he had told his group of officers. "And we need to get them served and before the court."

He began passing out pieces of paper with the names and pictures of about twenty of these individuals. He came to the last one and held it up in the air.

"This is Junior Bishop," he informed them, to the knowing groans of many in the room. "It's time we bring him in."

He glanced down at the paper and added, "Fifteen outstanding warrants on this guy."

"Yeah," one of the officers near C.L. called out. "Just make sure you have some help if you serve him. And be ready for anything."

C.L. was studying the rap sheet on Junior Bishop. Multiple assault charges—one on a police officer—and other alleged violent criminal actions.

"Officer Truesdale is right," Captain Rice agreed. "If you come across Bishop, make sure you have some backup. He's dangerous and unpredictable. But if you get the chance, bring him in."

C.L. carefully studied Junior Bishop's face, then folded the sheet of paper and slid it into his shirt pocket. He wasn't too worried about running into Junior on his beat—too populated downtown, and too open.

The next couple of shifts he worked were routine. The only exciting thing that happened was finding that the back door of one of the jewelry stores on Main Street had been jimmied, but unsuccessfully. Whoever the perpetrator, they were scared away by something, or just got frustrated with the multiple locks on the door. The owner thanked C.L. for pointing out the attempted entry and asked his locksmith to add two more dead bolts.

"Can't be too careful," he told the policeman.

That same afternoon, a strange thing happened when C.L. made his rounds through Artie's place. He entered through the back door as usual, and then slowly made his way through the middle of the room. As always, he made it a point to nod his head if anyone looked up at him. He was hoping for some breakthrough, some connection with one of these men. But it hadn't happened yet. If one of the customers looked up and caught his eye, they quickly looked away. *It'll happen one day*, he thought. And if not, well, he'd just keep on trying.

He reached the front of the store and spoke to Artie.

"Looks like you're pretty busy this afternoon," C.L. observed, glancing behind him at the crowded pool hall. There were a lot of men in here today, unusual for a Wednesday, and unusual for three o'clock.

"Yeah…well, that's a good thing," Artie mumbled, studying his fingernails. He barely glanced up, and he seemed to be nervous about something.

C.L. was about to say something more, when his attention was drawn to the back corner of the room. There sat Bubba Hendricks in his usual spot. And as usual, he cradled a coffee cup in his hand and stared at C.L. Then he did something *un*usual. He broke his eye contact with the officer and looked across the table at the man sitting in front of him. Then he put his coffee cup down, shifted his body away from C.L., and said something to the other man.

C.L.'s back stiffened and he reflexively put his hand on the night-stick hanging from his belt. The man across from Bubba seemed somehow familiar, though he could only see the back of his head and occasionally one side of his face.

It was Junior Bishop! Had to be! There was no mistaking the flat-top and big ears, and those huge, hunched-over shoulders. Nervously he reached for the piece of paper in his pocket. Turning toward Artie to conceal his actions, he quickly unfolded it. He felt his heart speed up as he confirmed his suspicion. It *was* Junior Bishop.

Now what was he going to do? This would be a tough place to make an arrest, but maybe he could quietly call for backup. After all, Captain Rice had said—

"I'd put that away if I was you," Artie whispered, an ominous warning in his voice.

C.L. glanced over at him, but Artie just continued to study his nails.

Now what? He wasn't going to be intimidated by Junior or any of the men in the pool hall. Yet this could get real ugly real quick.

Without thinking, he folded the paper in half and turned again to the table in the far corner.

Junior Bishop was gone!

And so was Bubba Hendricks.

C.L. spun around to Artie and was about to say something, but Artie spoke first. "C.L.," Artie began, this time looking up at him and straight into his eyes. "You'd better be careful."

Two men walked up to the counter with their tabs in their hands, ready to pay Artie and head home.

The police officer didn't have a chance to say anything more. He touched the front rim of his hat and stepped out onto the street. He looked both ways, but there was no sign of either Bishop or Hendricks. They had vanished through the back door and were gone.

Two days later, he had a chance to tell Captain Rice about this encounter.

"That surprises me," Rice said. "I didn't think Bishop would show up downtown, and not in the middle of the day. And I don't know what Hendricks is doing hanging out with him. Bubba is a tough character, but he generally stays out of trouble. That would be a dangerous pair, if they're up to something."

C.L.'s mind raced through his beat, and he thought about the jewelry stores on Main Street. And there were other shops there that were always busy, and probably always had a fair amount of cash on hand.

"Captain," he started to ask. "If I see Bishop again—"

"If you see Bishop again," Rice interrupted him, "You call for backup right away! Understand, C.L.? We don't need any heroes in the department."

"But—" C.L. stammered.

"There're no 'buts' here," Rice stated firmly. "I doubt if you'll see Junior again, but if you do, you call for backup. Understand?"

"Yes, sir," the young officer answered. He was surprised by the relief he felt when the captain had said he probably wouldn't see Junior Bishop again. Somehow, that would be alright with C.L.

But Captain Rice was wrong.

On Friday afternoon at a little past three, officer C.L. Jamison stepped through the back door of Artie's Billiard Parlor and began to walk slowly across the floor, just like always.

Nobody looked up at him, and he quietly made his way toward the front. His eye caught some movement just outside the pool hall, and then he noticed four men getting ready to come inside. One of them had reached for the handle of the door and was about to open it. Then Artie, having glanced up and seen the policeman come into the place, made a slight motion with his left hand. It was a wave, some kind of signal, C.L. thought, and the men standing outside quickly turned and started walking up the street.

Odd, C.L. thought. Then he became suspicious. Quickening his step, he reached the front counter, where Artie stood, and glanced over his shoulder, out onto the sidewalk.

Four men were walking away from Artie's, and one of them—a tall, stout, mean-looking guy, glanced back, straight into C.L.'s face. He turned around and leaned his head toward the man walking beside him, telling him something, and pointing back at the officer with his thumb.

The man beside him half-turned, and then faced forward again, leisurely making his way down Main Street.

But C.L. had seen him. It was Junior Bishop.

He immediately reached for his radio and pressed the *send* button.

"Dispatch," he spoke into the receiver. "This is Officer Jamison. I'm at Artie's on Main Street, and I need some backup."

The radio made a funny, squawking sound as C.L. released the button. He glanced down at it, and his heart sank. The battery light was flashing red, indicating it was getting dangerously low. And then it stopped blinking altogether.

He shook the radio a few times and mashed the send button again. Nothing. Then he turned it off and back on. Still nothing. Frustrated, he jammed it into the holder on his belt.

"Artie, I need to use your phone," he quickly said, hearing the nervousness in his own voice.

"Back in the corner," the owner replied, motioning to the far end of the room.

The police officer turned and looked in that direction. There sat Bubba Hendricks, studying him just like always.

"But it doesn't work," Artie nonchalantly added. "Not in a couple of years."

C.L. spun around and faced him. "Is there another phone here?" he asked, doubting that he would get a truthful answer. He needed to call the department, but time was running out, and Junior Bishop was getting away.

"Nope, that's it," Artie answered, leaning lazily back in his chair.

C.L. had to make a decision, and he had to make it fast.

He glanced back once more at Bubba Hendricks and then he turned and stepped toward the door.

"Be careful," Artie muttered, barely above a whisper.

But C.L. had heard him as he walked out through the door. And he felt his face flush.

He glanced up and down the street, hoping that luck would bring him another patrol car, or another officer happening to be down in this part of town. There was no help to be found. Then he caught sight of Junior Bishop and his three friends turning a corner and disappearing into an alleyway. C.L. knew it well. It was part of his beat, and connected with Hampton Street after making a few tortuous turns. It was narrow and dark, and he usually enjoyed its coolness. But today there was nothing enticing about it.

The screen door to Artie's Billiard Parlor rattled closed behind him as he hurried down Main Street, his eyes fixed on the entrance to the alley.

He reached the corner and stopped, listening. He didn't hear any voices or footsteps. Perhaps the four men might already be on Hampton Street. He thought about trying to cut them off by hurrying up Main and turning down another side street, but decided against it. He would follow them into the alley, and hopefully catch up with them from behind.

C.L. reached down and felt the butt of his revolver in its holster. He knew it was loaded and ready for use, but he hoped it would remain where it was. But just to be sure, he unsnapped the small leather strap securing it in place.

The young officer stepped around the corner and down the alley. It was dark here, and it took his eyes a moment to adjust after being out in the bright afternoon sun. There was no one in sight, and he quickly walked the thirty feet or so to the next turn.

The air was cool in here, but he felt sweat on the back of his neck. *Nerves,* he thought.

As he rounded the next corner, he froze, and his breath caught in his throat.

Just a few yards up ahead, Junior Bishop and his three friends had stopped. They were casually leaning against the windowless brick walls of the alley, smoking their cigarettes, and they looked up at C.L. as he came into view.

"Well, well, well," the tall, stout guy uttered with disdain. "Look what we got here."

The young officer quickly sized up the situation and didn't particularly like the odds. But then again, he was a policeman, he had a firearm, and…and he was scared to death.

"Mr. Bishop," he called out to Junior, who was standing in the middle of the group. He had one foot on the pavement, with the other planted on the wall behind him.

"That's right," he sneered. "I'm Bishop. And don't ever forget the *Mister* part."

His three friends chuckled derisively and waited.

"Mr. Bishop, I'm Officer Jamison, and we have some business to attend to down at the station," C.L. calmly stated. "I need you to come with me, and your friends can stay here."

"Some business?" he said, feigning curiosity. "Now I wonder what that might be."

"Yeah," one of his buddies echoed. "I wonder what that might be."

C.L. was about to ask him again when Junior said, "Well, Officer Jamison, why don't I just save us all some time, okay? I'm not goin' down to the station with you, so you can just take yourself right back where you came from…if you know what's good for you."

The stout fellow standing beside Junior took a menacing step toward the officer, flicked his cigarette ash to the ground, and stared at him.

"Boys, I don't want any trouble here," C.L. said quietly. He was trying to remember all the tips he'd been taught to use when trying to defuse a tense situation. "Talk calmly" was one of them. "Maintain eye contact and don't make any threatening moves."

What else was there? He was going to need more than that.

"Boys?" Junior scoffed. "It's *Mr.* Bishop, remember? Now why don't you just run along and we'll forget this happened."

"That won't be possible," C.L. replied, straining to maintain a calm voice. "You and I will need to take a walk down to the station."

He took a few steps forward and was suddenly surrounded by the four men. How it happened, he would never be able to remember. But before he knew it, he was face-to-face with Junior Bishop, with Junior's friends at his sides and behind him. He tried to sidle to his left, to get to the wall of the alley, but they would have none of it.

"Now, where were we?" Junior asked. "Oh yeah, you and I were going somewhere…to the station, I think."

He stepped closer to C.L. and began to thump the officer's chest with his index finger.

"Seems to me you need to learn a few manners, Jamison," Bishop snarled, stale beer and cigarettes strong on his breath.

"Mr. Bishop—" C.L. began. But before he could say another word, Junior jumped at him and had him in a headlock. Jamison reacted immediately, grabbing Junior by the waist and swinging him to one side with all of his strength. Then he tucked his head down and managed to pull himself free of the shorter man. The other three had stepped back, allowing Bishop to handle this green and foolish police officer.

Junior spun around, surprised at the ease with which the policeman had broken what he thought was a stranglehold.

"Well, well…" he said, wiping the sweat from his forehead. Then he lunged at C.L. with a vicious right hook, hoping to catch him off guard. Jamison was ready, and dodging the blow, he reached out with his own right hand, grabbed Junior's, and spun him around with his back to him. Then he wrapped him in a bear hug, pinning his arms to his sides.

"Get him to ground," C.L. remembered his instructor telling him. "As soon as you can, get him to ground."

The young officer picked up his opponent and slammed him to the pavement, knocking the breath out of him.

Jamison didn't want to hurt this guy—he just wanted to get things under control and somehow get him out of this alley. They were starting to make a good bit of noise, but no one had ventured off Main Street yet to see what was happening. And then there were the other three men. He didn't know what they were doing, or what they would do. He just knew they were standing right behind him, and he was worried.

Bishop struggled to free himself from C.L.'s grasp, but without success. Jamison was well-conditioned, and he knew how to wear this guy down.

It didn't take long, and Junior's arching and jerking slowly subsided. He was getting tired.

Then he said, "Aren't you guys gonna do something?"

C.L. felt a wave of panic pass over him. He was helpless, and he knew it. He had Bishop under control, but the other guys in the alley could do anything they wanted, and he couldn't stop them. He was powerless. All he could do was hold on desperately to Junior.

"Frankie, you hear me?" Bishop called out to one of his friends. "Get this guy off me!"

C.L. braced himself for a blow, tucking his head down as much as he could into his shoulder. But nothing happened. He continued to tense, and he waited.

Then he felt it, and his heart sank once again.

Someone was fumbling with his revolver, and before he could free one hand and try to stop them, he felt it slide out of its holster. Then he felt the cold barrel of the gun against the back of his neck.

"Don't ever get shot with your own gun." How many times had he heard that? And every time he'd heard it, he couldn't help but laugh. It was just plain…

And here he was—the end of his own firearm was pressed into his neck, at the base of his skull.

"Don't move, buddy," the man standing behind him said. "Just ease up on Junior there, and let him get up."

C.L. had to make a decision. He hadn't been trained for this circumstance, and he knew his life would depend on what he did next. He grabbed Junior Bishop even harder, and pressed his face into the back of his head. If the man behind C.L. pulled the trigger, there was a good chance the bullet would pass through his neck and into the head of Junior Bishop. He prayed the man would know that and would give him some time to come up with a plan. But these guys weren't that smart, and anything could happen.

"I told you to ease up on him," the voice behind him repeated. And then the barrel came off his neck. C.L. somehow knew what was coming next. There was a terrible crunching sound, and a knifelike pain tore through his scalp. The man had struck him with the barrel of his gun, dazing him, but not causing him to lose his grip on Junior. He felt the gun against his neck again, and then felt something warm running down the side of his face. He shook his head, trying to clear it, wondering how many more blows he could take.

It was then he realized he was going to die. The thought somehow didn't bother him. What bothered him was that his life was going to end in this dark alleyway, at the hands of these trouble-making ne'er-do-wells.

He grabbed Junior Bishop even tighter, causing him to gasp with pain. Whatever happened, he would hold on to him as long as he could.

"Listen, buddy," his assailant yelled at him. "I told you to—"

Then the barrel of the gun came off his neck again, and C.L. flinched, readying himself for the blow.

It never came. And what happened next was hard for him to comprehend. A body flew off to his right somewhere and struck the brick wall, causing the human missile to let out a painful grunt. Then there was the sound of footsteps desperately running away from him down the alleyway. It sounded like a couple of people, and they seemed to be tripping over each other in their haste to escape.

And then there was a hand on his shoulder, patting him gently.

"It's okay," a voice said behind him. "You can get up now."

It was calm and reassuring, and C.L. Jamison felt himself releasing his viselike grip on Junior Bishop.

Thank heavens! C.L. thought. Some of his fellow officers had happened down the street and heard the ruckus. And they had saved his life.

He slowly got to his feet, unsteady from the blow to his head. Junior Bishop lay flat on his face, his palms on the ground. He was worn out, and didn't know what to do.

C.L. stood up and stretched painfully, gingerly feeling for the wound on the back of his head. Then he turned around to thank his rescuers.

"Officer…" his voice trailed off into silence, and he stood there, staring in disbelief at the man in front of him.

It was Bubba Hendricks. And he was alone.

They looked into each other's eyes for a moment, and then Bubba nodded his head. He reached out with his right hand and grabbed C.L.'s shoulder.

"Come on, let's get you some help," he said, stepping beside him and putting his arm around his waist. Together they walked down the alley and out onto the street. They stood there as a patrol car sped up and then screeched to a stop. Bubba must have called for help as soon as he realized what was happening.

Two officers jumped out of the car. One grabbed C.L. Jamison, and then helped him into the backseat.

Hendricks pointed back down the alley with his thumb, indicating the whereabouts of Junior Bishop, and the other officer hurried off in that direction.

C.L. sat back gingerly in the cushioned seat of the patrol car, grateful for the comfort.

"Wait a second," he called out to the officer. "Where's…."

He leaned out of the car, searching for Bubba Hendricks. Then he saw him on the other side of Main Street. Hendricks was quietly walking away. Before C.L. could call out to him, he disappeared around a corner.

> *There are no strangers here;*
> *Only friends you haven't yet met.*
>
> WILLIAM BUTLER YEATS

8

It Wasn't Me

*True merit, like a river, the deeper it is
the less noise it makes.*

SIR GEORGE SAVILE, FIRST MARQUIS OF HALIFAX (1633–1695)

Tuesday, 8:25 a.m. Eric Larson looked over at his partner, Andy Wilson. "Now don't that beat all," he remarked, chuckling.

The two men had climbed into the front seat of Engine #2 a few moments ago and were headed back to the station. They had just left a residence in the middle of Rock Hill, having responded to a 9-1-1 call.

"Yeah, Swede," Andy replied. "We'll be talking about that one for a while."

An hour earlier, they had been on Herlong Avenue, returning to Station 3 on Cherry Road. The communication from the 9-1-1 dispatcher had sounded urgent.

"Respond code 3—302 Clarendon—missing child."

Swede Larson didn't hesitate. He switched on the lights and sirens of the fire engine and made a U-turn in the middle of Herlong. As he sped down the four-lane road, the heavy early-morning traffic cleared out of the way, making room for the emergency vehicle.

Larson knew the neighborhood and didn't have any trouble finding the address. The two firemen were the first to arrive, but they knew that EMS and the police would soon be there.

As they climbed out of the cab and headed toward the front door, Swede told Andy, "Dr. Daniel lives here. He's one of the ER docs, and

113

I think he and his wife have three or four young kids. I wonder what the problem is."

The front door of the house suddenly burst open and a distraught young woman came running into the front yard. She still had her pajamas on and was wearing pink slippers.

"Hurry! Please! I can't find my baby!"

The two firemen rushed up to her and tried to calm her.

"Mrs. Daniel," Swede said. "Tell us what's going on."

From the open front doorway, a girl who looked about six excitedly called out, "Mama, Lucy and I looked upstairs again, and can't find him! We looked everywhere!"

From behind her, a younger girl peeped out into the yard.

Barbara Daniel spun around and ran back into the house. "We've got to find Damon!" she called over her shoulder to the firemen. "I don't know where he could be!"

Swede and Andy were trying to keep up with the frantic mother. She stopped in the foyer and excitedly began to explain.

"The children don't have school today, and they wanted to play hide-and-seek. This is a big house, and there are a lot of places to hide. Anyway, we've been playing for a while, and now we can't find Damon. We've looked everywhere. He couldn't have gotten outside, because all the doors have been locked."

"Mama, Lucy took my Barbie doll!"

The indignant exclamation had come from the kitchen, immediately followed by "It's mine! And she wouldn't give it to me!"

"You two behave!" With an exasperated shake of her head, Barbara dismissed the uproar in the kitchen and continued. "We've looked everywhere. We've been calling his name, and listening, and…but we haven't heard a peep. I don't know where he could be!"

"What's his name again?" Andy asked.

"It's Damon," Barbara answered. "Sometimes we call him Doodle, but he'll answer to 'D.'"

"And how old is he?" Swede asked this time.

"He just turned two last month," she told him.

"And when was the last time you saw him?" asked Andy.

"It's been almost an hour," she explained. "We were all in the kitchen, and then everyone took off to hide. Elaine was 'it,' and...and we haven't been able to find him since. I just know something's happened. It's not like him to—"

"Mama! Lucy threw my doll in the sink!"

Swede stood silently, giving Barbara a chance to handle the commotion in the kitchen.

She just shook her head and called to the girls, "Barbie can wait!"

Suddenly a blur of red and blue came rocketing through the dining-room archway and into the foyer.

"Mama! Mama!"

It was Elliott, the Daniels' four-year-old son. He stopped in front of his mother, gasping for breath. Tall for his age and slender, he had on a long-sleeved Superman pajama top and matching briefs.

"Did you find Damon?" Barbara asked excitedly.

"No, no!" he answered, jumping up and down. "There's a fire engine in the front yard!"

Then he looked over to the fireman standing at Barbara's side, and his mouth fell open, his brown eyes wide and staring.

"Wow!" was all he could say.

Swede patted Elliott on the top of his head.

"Good morning, Superman," he told the young boy.

"Wow!" Elliott exclaimed once more, then bounded into the dining room and out of sight.

There was a knock on the front door. Andy opened it, and two paramedics and three police officers walked into the house.

The two firemen explained the circumstances, and the group split up, some going upstairs and the rest spreading out downstairs.

For the next twenty minutes, voices calling out "Damon!" could be heard throughout the house. Every few minutes, Swede would throw in a "D!" just to see if the toddler might respond to that.

Nothing. There was no response anywhere inside. The men looked in every closet, under every bed, in every cabinet. They even looked in every dresser drawer. All the while, Barbara Daniel ran from room to room, searching for her boy.

She returned to her bedroom for the fifth or sixth time and ran into Swede and Andy. They had searched the bathroom again, and once more under the bed.

"What about the closet?" Swede asked.

"I've looked in there three times, at least," Barbara answered, growing increasingly frantic.

"And I looked in there too," Andy said. "He's not in there."

Swede glanced into the closet and decided to check it out himself. The light was on, and he leaned in, quickly glancing around. Then he stepped in and began feeling among the hanging clothes, pulling them aside and checking the floor underneath. He even looked up on the shelf above the racks, though he couldn't imagine how a two-year-old could get up there. Still...

Nothing. No sign of the boy. He was about to walk out when he happened to look down and see a small overnight case. It was over in the far corner, up against the wall, and seemed too small to hold a child. But they had looked everywhere else, so why not at least try?

He stepped to the back of the closet and stood over the suitcase. The bag had a zippered closure, which was partially open. Without saying anything, Swede reached down and lifted the top of the case.

"Hmm, hmm," he murmured. "Come here and look at this," he called out loudly.

"What is it? Did you find him?" Barbara ran into the closet and stood beside Swede. There, curled in a ball in the suitcase and fast asleep, was Damon.

Barbara Daniel burst into tears and grabbed her son, holding him tight against her, turning and rocking from side to side.

"Thank you! Thank you! Thank you!" she cried.

Damon's eyes slowly opened and he looked straight at Swede.

Then in a clear, calm voice he said, "Am I 'it' now?"

Swede and Andy had turned onto India Hook Road and were getting closer to the station.

"Yeah, we'll be talking about that one for a while." Andy chuckled again.

Then both firemen fell silent. They knew that emergency calls for young kids didn't always end like this. Swede Larson was thinking about Myrtle Beach.

Swede and his wife, Shelly, had just checked the family into the Trade Winds, an oceanfront hotel in Myrtle Beach. Their five-year-old son, Jake, and three-year-old daughter, Taylor, were jumping up and down on one of the beds, screaming with excitement and begging to be taken swimming. It was late afternoon, getting close to six, and Shelly had patiently told them a dozen or more times they would all go out on the beach in the morning. It was too late today. They needed to get something to eat and then have a good night's sleep.

Jake jumped off the bed and ran over to the window, wistfully looking down at the beckoning ocean. His dad walked over and stood behind his son. He put his huge hands on the two small shoulders and looked down at the beach. Then he looked over to his right. Part of the hotel's swimming pool was just barely in sight.

"No beach today, but what if we go down to the pool for a few minutes?" he asked the children.

Shelly glanced over at her husband and raised her eyebrows. She was still unpacking everybody and trying to get them settled.

"That would be *you*, honey," she said to him, the tone of her voice allowing no mistake about her intention.

The kids started squealing.

"Yeah! Let's go to the pool!" Jake hollered.

"Yeah, the pool!" Taylor parroted, heading toward the door.

Shelly reached into a duffel bag and tossed some brightly colored swimming suits onto the end of the bed.

"And don't forget to put the swimmies on Taylor," she reminded her husband.

"Got it," he responded while helping the children change clothes.

"I don't need swimmies anymore, Daddy," Jake told him proudly, twisting and squirming while his father tried to lace up his suit.

"I know, son. You're really a good swimmer," Swede told him. "But your sister still needs to wear them, don't you think?"

Taylor was dressed and trying to get the flotation devices on her upper arms, impatient to get out the door and on the elevator.

When everyone was ready, Swede Larson took a deep breath and looked over at his wife.

"We'll be back soon," he told her hopefully.

A few minutes later, they walked out of the hotel and up to the fence that surrounded the large kidney-bean shaped pool. There were twenty or thirty people in the water, mostly children, and there was a lot of splashing and squealing.

This is going to be fun, Swede thought, nodding his head.

They made their way through the gate and headed toward the shallow end. Shelly had given him a towel as they left the room, and Swede tossed it onto an empty chair near the fence.

"Let's go, Daddy!" Taylor called out, grabbing his hand and tugging him toward the pool.

She bumped into a man sitting on the concrete edge, his feet dangling in the water and his large abdomen dangling over the unseen top of his bathing suit. He looked up at Taylor and smiled. She quickly said, "Excuse me, mister."

"No problem, honey," he told her. "Just call me Leon. And this is Darius," he added, patting the head of a two- or three-year-old boy who was bouncing up and down in the water at the man's feet. The pool was shallow, maybe only two-and-a-half-feet deep at this end, and Darius could easily stand on the bottom. He smiled up at Taylor and kept jumping up and down while trying without success to splash his father.

"1...2...3..." and Jake was in the water. Fearlessly, Taylor followed him.

"I guess that means it's my turn," Swede said to Leon, slowly lowering himself into the chilly water.

"You'll get used to it in a few minutes," the fellow dad said, his grin large and genuine.

Swede feigned a shiver, waved at him, then turned to follow his children.

Twenty minutes later, it was time to leave. Larson had just herded the kids out of the pool, and thankfully, both were now tired and hungry, ready to head back to the room.

"Help me! Somebody help me!"

Swede spun around in the pool, searching for the source of this loud and anguished cry. It sounded like a man, and someone in trouble.

"Help me! Please!"

It was Leon, and he was in the pool now, awkwardly probing the water in front of him.

Where's the little boy? Swede thought, thrashing through the water as fast as he could. Without missing a stride, he turned to Jake and Taylor and called out, "Stay right there! Don't move!"

Leon's head went under the surface, and his arms flailed ineffectually, churning the water all around him.

The big fireman quickly got to his side and looked down and around them. The water was four feet deep here, and with all the foam the panicked father was creating, it was difficult to see much below the surface.

Then Swede thought he saw something—just a shadow to the right of where Leon stood. He plunged down into the water and, with outstretched arms, grabbed Darius's motionless body.

Bursting up and out, he ponderously made his way to the side of the pool, holding the little boy close to his chest.

"Somebody call 9-1-1!" he called out.

There were screams now from all around the pool, and a crowd started to gather as he gently laid Darius on his back on the hard concrete. With unexpected grace for a man his size, he swung out of the pool and knelt at the boy's side. Glancing up, he saw Taylor and Jake huddled together on the far side of the pool, out of the water and safe. They just stared at their father. He nodded to them, and then went to work.

Leon was climbing up a ladder, desperately trying to get out of the pool and to his young son.

"Darius!" he called out. "Darius!"

He ran up behind Swede and stopped just at his shoulder. Then he got down on his hands and knees.

"Is he all right?" Leon pleaded, his voice trembling.

The fireman was checking the boy for a pulse but couldn't find one.

"How long was he under?" he asked without turning around.

"Just a…it must have been just a second…" Leon stammered. "One minute he was there, and the next he was gone…"

Water was foaming out of the boy's mouth, and Swede turned him on his side, letting it drain out freely. Then he rolled him on his back again and began CPR. He knew what to do, and his efforts were smooth, controlled, and sure.

The boy's eyes had rolled up in their sockets, and he was making no attempt to breathe. His arms and legs lay lifelessly at his sides. He seemed to be dead.

"Did someone call 9-1-1?" Swede called out between mouth-to-mouth breaths.

Someone in the back of the crowd yelled, "They should be here any minute!"

The big fireman continued his rescue breathing and chest compressions. How long had it been? He knew it didn't matter. He wasn't going to stop. He wasn't going to lose this boy.

By now the crowd had swelled in number, but there were no more screams or frantic outcries. Everyone watched in silence while Swede worked with the child.

Then he heard, "Move out of the way! Let us get through."

He looked up and saw two paramedics coming toward him. The crowd was quickly parting, making space for them.

"What ya got?" one of the men asked while putting his emergency kit down on the concrete and opening it.

"I'm a fireman," Swede told the men. "And I need a number 5 tube and a curved blade."

The paramedic glanced over at Larson and quickly studied him. This was their turf, but something in this man's bearing told him he needed to listen and do as he asked. And fast.

He reached behind him and into the emergency kit. Then he brought out a child's endotracheal tube and a laryngoscope. Meanwhile, the other paramedic took out an ambu bag, connected it to a small oxygen tank, and knelt at Darius's side.

"Let me give him some O2," he told Swede, placing the mask over the boy's face and expertly ventilating him.

Swede unwrapped the trach tube, waited while the paramedic delivered the much-needed oxygen, and then said, "Okay, hold on a second."

As if he had done this a thousand times, Larson used the scope to visualize Darius's tiny vocal cords and then quickly passed the tube into his windpipe.

"Let's get that taped in place and start bagging him again," he said.

Then he put his hand over the boy's heart and felt for any indication of activity. Nothing. With one hand over the sternum, he continued chest compressions while one of the paramedics continued bagging. Somewhere in the distance, they could hear the sound of approaching sirens. More help was on the way.

Swede stopped his compressions and put his hand over the boy's heart again. Still nothing.

Then...maybe just the slightest pulse. He leaned closer, as if that would somehow help him feel Darius's chest more precisely.

There it was again, and this time stronger. He put his fingers on the boy's neck.

"He's got a pulse," he spoke quietly to the paramedics.

Leon heard this and raised his hands toward the sky. "Praise God!" he cried out.

There was a murmured response to this in the crowd of onlookers, and then a few people began to applaud. Swede frowned slightly. He knew the boy was a long way from being out of the woods.

Then Darius took a breath, and then another. Suddenly his right arm went up in the air.

The paramedic stopped bagging and watched as the boy began taking deeper and more regular breaths through the tube.

Swede Larson leaned back on his heels and glanced up at the crowd around him. Then he looked over to the other side of the pool. Shelly was standing there now with her arms around Taylor and Jake, watching.

Two policemen hurried up, and two more paramedics. Within a few minutes, Darius was loaded on a stretcher and was being put into the back of the ambulance. He was still breathing. And he was starting to fight the endotracheal tube—a good sign.

The big fireman spoke again to the paramedics, thanking them and giving them his room number in the hotel. He wanted to hear how Darius was doing as soon as things settled out. Then he turned around and headed toward his wife and children.

Standing in front of him, blocking his way, was Leon. Without a word, he grabbed Larson, hugged him, and began sobbing.

"I..." He choked up and couldn't speak.

Swede held him for a moment, then said, "Go get in the ambulance with your son. And I want to hear from you."

Leon stepped back, wiped his eyes, nodded silently, and hurried away.

As Larson approached his wife, he suddenly realized how exhausted he was. Shelly took him in her arms, and Jake and Taylor each grabbed one of his legs. They just stood there, not saying anything—thankful to have each other.

At ten-thirty, the phone in the family's room rang, startling everyone awake.

Swede reached out in the dark, groping for the receiver.

"Hello," he spoke in a hushed voice.

"This is Dr. Childress at Strand General Hospital," a man began. "Is this the fireman?"

"Yes, this is the fireman."

"Good. I wanted to give you a report on the young boy you saved this evening."

"Saved?" Swede asked. He sat up, shoving back the covers a little. Shelly was wide awake now and leaning close to the phone, trying to hear.

"Yes, saved," Childress repeated. "Darius is doing fine now. We've been able to take his tube out, and he's sitting up in bed, asking for something to eat. He looks great, and we think he's going to make a complete recovery—thanks to you."

Shelly gently stroked her husband's arm as Swede took a deep breath and let out a big sigh of relief. "That's great," he said. "But Doc, it wasn't me—I mean, not just me. There were a lot of people there helping, and—"

"That's not exactly the way we heard it," Dr. Childress interrupted. "Anyway, he's doing great now and should be able to go home in the morning. We just wanted to let you know. And to thank you."

Then he hung up.

In the dark, Swede sat quietly, with his eyes closed. Shelly put her arms around her husband.

"Get some sleep, Mr. Fireman," she whispered in his ear.

He hung up the phone and lay back on the bed. It took him a while to fall asleep.

❧

"All available units, respond code 3—114 Wisteria Lane. Drowning. And it's a child."

Andy and Swede had almost gotten back to the station, when the radio shattered the silence. The dispatcher repeated the call, and Swede muttered, "You've got to be kidding." It was uncanny. After what he had just been thinking about—

He slammed on the brakes of their unit and swerved to the right.

"We're just down the street from Wisteria," he told his partner. "Give dispatch a call and tell them we're a minute away."

Andy grabbed the radio and reported their location to dispatch.

"Copied your call, Engine 2," she responded. "There's a swimming pool behind the house, and you go through the gate at the end of the driveway."

"10-4," Andy answered, then tossed the radio onto the seat beside him. Other fire and EMS units were also responding to the call, but no one else was nearby.

"Looks like it's us," he said, turning to his partner.

Swede shook his head and sped down Wisteria, looking for 114. He couldn't help but think about Darius in the pool at Myrtle Beach. That had been a miracle, the way the boy had responded. But Larson knew that was the exception. Usually, with a toddler in a swimming pool, things didn't work out like that. It was all a matter of timing. If you could get to the child soon enough…

He glanced down at his wristwatch, knowing that each passing second was precious. And then there it was, off to their right—114.

He slowed the huge fire engine and expertly pulled into the driveway. Strangely, there were no cars there or on the street. The whole place seemed deserted.

He turned off the engine, jumped out of the cab, and ran toward the wrought-iron gate at the end of the drive. Andy reached behind him to grab the emergency kit and followed as fast as he could.

The gate was closed but not locked, and the big fireman easily pushed it open.

He quickly looked to his left and then back to his right, trying to get his bearings. It was a beautifully manicured backyard, with a formal garden just ahead of him. There were some stepping-stones leading off to his right, toward an opening in a tall hedge. He headed that way.

As Swede cleared the opening in the hedge, he found himself at the side of a large, rectangular swimming pool. On the far side stood a teenage girl, dressed in khaki shorts and a white blouse. She was soaking wet.

She looked up at Swede with large, sad eyes, but didn't say a word. Then she looked down at her feet. There lay the motionless body of a two-year-old girl. Her arms and legs were splayed out at odd angles, and her wet, matted hair covered most of her face.

The fireman dashed around the pool toward the child, and yelled back over his shoulder, "Andy, I'm over here!"

As he reached the two girls, he glanced behind them. There was a telephone sitting on a poolside table. The teenager must have been the one who called 9-1-1.

Swede went to work on the little girl. Just like Darius, she wasn't breathing and had no pulse. But she was still warm. That was something.

Andy was soon beside him, and he dropped the emergency kit to the ground and opened it. As Swede started CPR, Andy turned to the teenager and began asking her what had happened.

Her name was Meredith, and the little girl, her sister, was Lizzie. Their mother had run to the store and left Meredith in charge. That was usually no problem, and she knew to keep an eye on the little girl. This morning though, one of her friends had called. She had been in the kitchen making sure Lizzie finished her breakfast, and as she talked on the phone, she had lost track of her sister. She had happened to glance out the dining-area window and had seen ripples in the swimming pool.

"I dropped the phone and looked around the kitchen for Lizzie, but she wasn't there," Meredith said, her voice flat and unemotional, still in shock. "Then I ran outside and…and…she was at the bottom of the pool. I jumped in and pulled her out, and then I…called 9-1-1. I didn't know what else to do."

"How long do you think she could have been in the pool?" Andy asked her gently.

Meredith stood there, staring down at her little sister, and slowly shook her head. "It couldn't have been long, but…I just don't know."

Swede glanced up at his partner. This wasn't going well. Lizzie's airway was full of water, and though they kept suctioning it out, there always seemed to be more. She still wasn't making any effort to breathe, and there was still no pulse.

But they continued to work on her.

Suddenly there was a commotion coming from the entranceway in the hedge. A group of paramedics and policemen were hurriedly making their way into the pool area and toward the two firemen. Andy hadn't heard any approaching sirens and was surprised by their sudden appearance. But he was thankful for the help.

The paramedics knelt beside Larson and asked, "What can we do, Swede?"

Andy filled them in on what was happening while one of the police officers took Meredith aside and began asking her some questions. The other officer, when he heard their mother had gone out to the store, headed back to the driveway to meet her.

As Swede talked with the paramedics, he continued ventilating Lizzie, praying for some change in her condition, some response to his efforts.

One of the paramedics had gone to the ambulance to get the stretcher. As he came through the hedge with it and began rattling toward them over the uneven stone pavers, it happened.

Swede had paused with his ambu bag and was staring down at Lizzie, examining her intently for any sign of life. At first, he thought it was just some air and water escaping from her stomach. It was a gurgle, and there was some foam coming out of her endotracheal tube. But she seemed to be trying to take a breath…and then another.

"Look!" the paramedic called out. "She's starting to breathe!"

He was right, and Swede began timing his ventilations with the girl's own efforts.

And then a pulse became detectable. It was weak, but it was definitely there.

"Let's get her on the stretcher and to the ER!" Andy spoke excitedly behind Swede.

Larson nodded, and without interrupting his rescue breathing, he helped Andy gently lift the little girl to the stretcher. The paramedic covered her tiny body with a blanket, leaving only her head exposed.

An hour-and-a-half later, Swede and Andy stood at the nurses' station in the ER. They waited, hoping for some news about the little girl in the cardiac room.

Lori Davidson walked out of cardiac and over to the two firemen.

"How is she?" Andy asked her before she could say anything.

"It's amazing," Lori began. "She's going to be all right."

"She's what?" Swede asked, hoping he had heard her correctly.

"She's breathing on her own, and has a good pulse and blood pressure. And she's looking around the room. When she saw her mother standing beside the stretcher, she reached out her arms for her."

"Wow, that's wonderful," Andy whispered, overcome by this news. He hadn't thought Lizzie was going to make it.

"And her mother wants to speak to you guys before you leave," the nurse added. "So don't go anywhere."

She turned and walked back to the cardiac room. The two firemen just looked at each other, not knowing what to say.

The door to cardiac opened again, and Les Daniel, the ER doctor on duty, walked over to where they stood. He gave them the same report on Lizzie's condition, and told them he was pretty confident she would make a full recovery.

"She's really starting to come around," he said to them. "You two got there just in time. Another minute or two, and who knows…No. Another minute or two, and she wouldn't have made it. You guys were in the right place at the right time. And you were the right people. You saved Lizzie's life."

The firemen didn't say anything.

"And Swede," the doctor added, "I want to thank you for finding Damon this morning. Barbara was terrified."

Larson chuckled a bit huskily, thankful for the change in topic that let him get control of his emotions.

"No problem, Doc," he said. "Glad we could help. And ya know, it's not every day you get to meet Superman."

Les smiled and shook his head, knowing that in the Daniel home, another drama was waiting just around the corner.

A few days later, Chief Rick Stevens was talking with his crew, making sure everyone knew their assignments for the day. And then he started talking about little Lizzie, and how Swede and Andy had responded and saved her life.

Larson looked down at the floor and shook his head.

"Just like that little boy in Myrtle Beach," Stevens added.

Andy reached over and without a word, patted his partner on the shoulder.

"You know," the chief mused, "the guy who said, 'Lightning never strikes twice in the same place, 'cause the first place ain't there anymore,' never met Swede Larson."

A warm and knowing laughter rippled through the room. Stevens was about to add something else when Swede interrupted him.

He was sitting up straight now, his words calm and measured.

"Chief, I think I know what you're going to say, and I appreciate it. But this is what I know to be true. The Lord put me there in the pool at the beach, and he put me and Andy just a little ways from Lizzie's house."

He paused for a second. "And it wasn't my hands that saved those little children."

9

Righteous Anger

*The only person who does not believe
that the devil is a person
is someone who has never attempted
to combat him or his ways.*

ISOBEL KUHN (1901–1957),
MISSIONARY TO CHINA

D on Brantley had just fixed himself a cup of coffee and was sitting
down at the table in the break room when the county dispatcher
changed his plans.

"EMS 2, respond code 3 to 118 James Street. Possible SIDS."

Don looked over at his partner Randy Lutz, carefully put the steam-
ing mug on the table, and then bolted toward the door and their waiting ambulance.

Randy jumped up clumsily from his chair, almost knocking the
table over, and followed his partner out into the warm afternoon air.

Any call for possible SIDS—sudden infant death syndrome—
grabbed their attention and got their hearts pumping. Both of these
men had children of their own and had learned to be thankful—grateful—for every day they had with them. They had seen enough to know
that things, and lives, can change in a hurry.

"Possible SIDS," Randy muttered as he climbed into the passenger
seat of the ambulance. "Maybe they got it wrong, and whoever called
it in was just excited or something," he added hopefully.

"Maybe," Don said quietly, but in a voice that left little room for
hope.

With lights flashing and siren blasting, they wove their way through the heavy traffic of Cherry Road and then onto Charlotte Avenue.

"James Street, right?" Don asked Randy.

"118," he answered. "It's the next left, I think."

They pulled onto James and slowed down, searching for their street number. Up ahead, about thirty yards, a young man ran out into the street and started waving his arms wildly.

"There!" Randy said, pointing ahead. "That must be it."

The distraught man stood in the middle of the road, barefoot and shirtless, wearing only grimy blue jeans. His hair was long and scraggly, and he sported a small, patchy goatee.

Then he started doing something that surprised the two paramedics. With his right hand he began motioning them to come forward while with his left hand he directed them to turn to their right—just like a traffic cop.

"This guy must have been pulled over a few times," Don quipped. He brought the ambulance to a stop and the two men jumped out. Randy grabbed the emergency box from the back and then ran to catch up with his partner. Their traffic director had been ahead of them and was holding the front door open.

"He's in the back bedroom, on the right!" he shouted excitedly. "You guys need to hurry!"

They made their way past him and into a small, dark living room. The place was filthy, with worn-out furniture and an orange shag carpet that was stained in several places with who knows what. Dirty clothes were scattered around the room, and an armless doll sat all alone on the sofa.

There was a smell in the room—something not quite rancid, but getting close.

Food was spoiling somewhere, and Don glanced briefly through a doorway as they passed it on their way to the back of the house. It was the kitchen, and what he could see of it was a mess too. Food was scattered on the floor and on the tabletop, and a yellow Cheshire cat looked up lazily at them as they walked by.

"Last room on the right," the man behind them called out.

Don and Randy reached the back bedroom and were met by a young woman who appeared to be in her mid-twenties. She was slender, maybe five-foot-six, with short dirty blond hair. Her large blue eyes were frantic.

"Please, do something!" she screamed, grabbing Don by his shoulders and shaking him.

"Let me get by, ma'am," he said to her gently while shrugging and twisting to release himself from her grasp.

Randy was already past him and into the room.

"Oh my…" he stammered, stunned by what he saw.

On the far side of the room, a crib was angled awkwardly against the wall. Its sides were up, and on the section facing the door, a child's head protruded between two of the white, wooden rails. The child, a little boy, looked to be about eighteen months old. His arms hung limply through the rails, dangling lifelessly, it seemed.

Randy raced over to the crib and grabbed the rails that were trapping the boy's head. He spread them apart as Don came up behind him, reached over the top, and gently pulled the toddler back into the crib and onto the mattress.

The child was dead. His color was a dusky blue, and his skin was cool to Don's touch. His limbs had already begun to stiffen. He had been this way for a while.

"Is he going to be okay?" the woman asked from behind them.

Don turned to her, mystified that she could ask such a question. Maybe it was denial. Yet something…

"Are you the boy's mother?" he asked her.

"Yes, I'm Ali Cooper," the young woman answered. "Is Jesse going to be alright?"

Don glanced over at Randy and then back to the woman.

"Yeah, is he going to be alright?" The echo came from the young man who had led them into the house. He was standing in the doorway of the bedroom, his hands in the pockets of his jeans. Then, nonchalantly, he leaned against the door jamb.

"And you are?" Don asked the man.

"That's T.C. Mason," Ali answered for him. "He's my…he's my boyfriend."

Mason nodded his head and just stood there.

"Is he the boy's father?" Don asked her.

She looked down and shuffled her feet, seeming to forget her dead child lying across the room.

"No, he's…Jesse's…that's my boy…his father is in prison in Columbia," she reluctantly answered.

Randy turned from the crib and with rising anger said, "This boy has been dead for a while. When was the last time you two checked on him?"

"Dead?" Ali Cooper screamed. "He can't be dead!"

She started sobbing hysterically and ran over to the crib. She was about to reach over the rail and grab her boy when Randy stopped her.

"I'm sorry, but we need to leave him where he is, ma'am," he explained. "We need to call the police and the…the coroner. They'll need to investigate this, and we'll have to leave things sort of like we found them."

When T.C. Mason heard this, he quietly slipped from the room and, as they later discovered, out of the house.

"You can't do anything for Jesse?" Ali pleaded.

"I'm sorry," Don said to her. "He's been dead for a couple of hours."

Randy radioed dispatch, and twenty minutes later the small house was filled with police officers. A group of curious neighbors was beginning to gather on the sidewalk, attracted by all of the emergency and police vehicles.

Frank Campo, the county coroner, was in the back bedroom, alone with Don and Randy.

"Not a SIDS, is it?" Don said, understating the obvious.

"Hardly," the coroner replied, making some notes on the legal pad in his hand. "Looks like an accidental death to me."

Randy shook his head and said, "Frank, something's just not right about this one. I mean, that guy T.C., he seems a little squirrelly to me."

"Where is he, anyway?" Campo asked, looking past the two paramedics and out into the living room. "I'd like to talk with him about this before I close the books."

"Good luck with that," Don quipped. "He took off outta here like a bat outta…well, he took off."

Campo flipped the pages of his legal pad closed and put his pen in his shirt pocket.

"Well, probably doesn't matter," he pronounced officially. "Seems straightforward to me. Accidental death is what I'm going to call it. Darned shame, too. A real tragedy for that young woman. At least she's got her other children."

Don Brantley bristled at this remark. His sister had lost a child a few years earlier, and he knew Frank Campo was the furthest he could be from the truth. But Don had known Frank a good while, and he trusted his heart. He was sure this was a lack of understanding and not of compassion. However, this was not the time or place to correct him in this mistake. He was more concerned about something else the coroner had said.

This was the first he and his fellow paramedic had heard of any other children in the house. They looked at each other, puzzled, and then Randy grabbed his emergency bag and they followed Campo out into the living room.

Several police officers were standing in the middle of the room, talking with Ali Cooper. She seemed much calmer now, and only had to dab her eyes occasionally. She looked over at Don, and then nervously looked away.

"Don," Randy whispered to his partner, nodding his head in the direction of the worn and stained sofa against the far wall.

Both men were startled at first by what they saw. Sitting on the sofa, wearing only a diaper, was…it was Jesse!

"Twin brother," one of the officers remarked behind them. "Gave me the creeps too." He had noticed their reaction when they saw Jonah Cooper, Jesse's identical twin. "Really something, isn't it?"

The paramedics stared in disbelief at the little boy. He was sucking his thumb and carefully studying the group of men in his living room.

"And that's Scarlett," the officer added, pointing to a four-year-old girl sitting next to Jonah. She had long, brown curly hair and was dressed in pink panties and a cotton T-shirt. She held the armless doll tightly against her chest. "She's their sister."

"Thanks for your help, boys."

It was Frank Campo, and he waved to the two paramedics as he walked out of the house.

They followed him a few minutes later and climbed into their vehicle. Don sat behind the wheel of EMS 2 for a minute, staring at the woeful dwelling in front of them. It was a depressing and decaying house, filled with a sadness and…something else Don couldn't name.

"Hopeless," Randy said quietly, completing Don's thought. "It's hopeless."

The next day, they read in the paper about the tragedy on James Street and of the accidental death of Jesse Cooper. He was buried in the downtown cemetery, destined to be quickly forgotten.

Two months after that call to the Coopers's house, Don and Randy were in the ER, having just brought in an elderly woman with a broken hip. They were standing at the nurses' station, talking with Amy Connors, the unit secretary.

The radio at Don's belt crackled to life, and he lifted it up so they could both hear the call from dispatch.

"EMS 1, respond code 3," the voice spoke.

Good, Don thought, grateful for a chance to catch up on their paperwork before going out on another run. EMS 1 would be able to handle this call.

"118 James Street," the dispatcher continued. "Possible SIDS."

Don and Randy looked at each other in surprise, then disbelief.

"Oh no," Amy said, shaking her head upon hearing the nature of the call. "That's awful."

"Did she say 118 James Street?" Randy asked his partner.

"I…surely not," Don stammered. "Can't be."

"Yeah, it was 118 James Street," Amy said with certainty. "Why?"

Don looked down at Amy and shook his head. "Just something that happened…" he began hesitantly.

"That's too much of a coincidence," Randy said. "If it's the same house, it must be little Jonah."

"Who's Jonah?" Amy asked with growing curiosity. "What's going on here, guys?"

"Nothing, Amy," Don said to her. "I hope."

He motioned for his partner to follow him through the ambulance doors and out into the parking area.

"What do you think?" Don asked.

"I think we need to go over there," Randy said emphatically. "Medic 1 could use the help, and we don't have anything to do right now, and… and I just remember that T.C. guy. There was something about him that really bothered me."

"Just hold on," Don tried to calm him. He didn't like T.C. either, but he knew his partner, and he was starting to get riled up. "We don't know anything for sure yet. And it might not even be the same place."

"No, it's the same place," Randy said, shaking his head. "I've got a bad feeling about this."

They jogged over to their ambulance, jumped in, and headed toward James Street.

This time when they turned off Charlotte Avenue, they knew just where to go. And this time there was no T.C. standing out in the middle of the street to direct them. The ambulance and two police cars confirmed their fears. They were parked in the driveway and front yard of 118 James Street—the home of Ali Cooper and her two children.

Randy looked over at his partner and without a word, shook his head. As they climbed out of the ambulance, two teenagers stepped out from another gathering crowd. One of them approached the pair and asked, "Hey dudes, what's goin' on here?"

Don just glanced at him briefly then turned and walked toward the house.

Two police officers were standing on the front porch, talking. They looked up as the paramedics climbed the rickety wooden steps, and one of them said, "I think everything is under control in there. Medic 1's been here thirty minutes or so. Nothing to do."

The other officer shook his head with finality.

"We're just, uh…we'll just check with them," Don muttered, moving quickly by the officers and into the house.

The living room hadn't changed since their last visit. The same worn and stained sofa was over against the far wall, and the same orange shag carpet was on the floor. If anything, the place might be even more littered than they remembered.

A group of police officers stood in the middle of the room, talking with the deputy coroner, Scottie McDaniel.

"Hey, boys," he called over to the paramedics. "Don't think we'll be needing you this morning. Medic 1 is back there and it's…well, there's nothing they could do."

"Who is it?" Randy asked nervously.

"Who is it?" McDaniel repeated, wondering why the paramedic would be curious about this. "It's a little boy—Jonah, I think, is his name." He glanced down at the slip of paper in his hand. "Yeah, Jonah Cooper."

Randy turned quickly and headed to the back bedroom, brushing the arm of one of the officers as he passed.

"What's up with him?" McDaniel asked Don.

"It's just that…" he began to answer, but thought better of it. "What happened to the boy?" he asked the deputy coroner. "We heard the call go out for a possible SIDS."

"Nope, not a sudden infant death," McDaniel explained. "This was an accidental death. And a real tragedy too, after what this mother has gone through. She said she lost another child not too long ago."

"Wait a minute! Did you say accidental?" the paramedic asked with growing concern. "What kind of accident?"

"Just a bizarre thing," McDaniel said, shaking his head. "Really bizarre. I mean, for two little boys, identical twins, to both—"

Before he could finish, Don turned away and hurried out of the room, down the small hallway to the back bedroom.

He found his partner standing over the same crib, talking with the two paramedics of EMS 1. Don walked over to the men and stopped, staring down into the crib with sudden horror.

Lying on his back on the mattress was Jonah Cooper. He was blue and mottled, obviously having been dead for at least a few hours. Don looked closer, and noticed the indentations on both sides of his head, just above his ears.

"Same thing." Randy spoke quietly, through clenched teeth. "Same darned thing."

Don looked up at his partner, and in his eyes saw a dreadful anger beginning to grow.

"Yeah, apparently the same thing happened a couple of months ago to his brother," one of the other paramedics explained. "Got his head caught between the rails, and must have suffocated. Terrible accident."

"It's terrible all right." Randy sounded ready to explode. "But this is no accident."

"What do you mean?" the other paramedic asked. "McDaniel is ruling this an accidental death."

"He's what?" Randy bellowed, turning to the doorway and striding toward the living room. Don hurried to follow, knowing he needed to calm his partner down.

"Scottie," Randy called out to the deputy coroner. "I need to have a word with you."

He motioned McDaniel aside, took a deep breath, and said, "You're calling this an accidental death?"

"Yes, Randy," McDaniel calmly replied. "It's pretty obvious what happened here."

"Have you talked with T.C. Mason yet?" the paramedic asked, barely able to control himself.

"Who?" McDaniel asked.

"T.C. Mason, the mother's boyfriend," Randy explained, looking around the room for the scruffy young man.

"Nope, haven't talked to anybody by that name, only the mother. And she's pretty upset, as you can imagine."

"What did she have to say about this?" Don put in.

"Well," the deputy coroner answered patiently, "she says the boy was fine last night when she put him to bed. And then again early this morning when she checked on him. No problems, nothing. And then when she went back a little while ago, she found him like that," he said while pointing to the bedroom. "Must have gotten up and tried to get out of the crib and got his head caught between the rails. And that was that."

Randy was red-faced and about to say something when Don gently grabbed his arm. He looked at McDaniel and asked, "You're aware of how his brother died? His twin brother, about two months ago?"

"Well, I…" McDaniel stammered. "I remember hearing something about another accidental death here…or somewhere on this street… but I don't remember the exact circumstances."

Scottie McDaniel was one of the county's part-time assistant coroners. His regular job was as a used-car salesman, and he filled in occasionally when the full-time coroner was unavailable.

"Have you talked with Coroner Campo?" Don persisted.

"No, Frank's out of town this week, and I'm in charge."

"Well, you'd better—" Randy began. But again Don stopped him with a gentle squeeze of his arm.

"Scottie, I think there's a real problem here," Don began to explain. "We responded to a call here two months ago, when Jonah's brother, Jesse, was found dead. Same exact circumstances. His head was jammed between two rails and he had apparently suffocated. He had been dead a while before his mother called 9-1-1. Just like this time. And then there's this guy T.C. He's bad news, and he must be around here somewhere."

"What are you trying to say, Don?" the deputy coroner asked with growing concern.

"I'm trying to say…" the paramedic answered, then paused. "Are you planning on having an autopsy done?"

"An autopsy?" McDaniel asked, obviously not having considered this possibility. "Why would we need an autopsy? We know what—"

"You don't know anything!" Randy blurted. "This child was killed, and so was his brother!"

"Now hold on a minute!" McDaniel cautioned the impassioned paramedic. "Don't go making those kinds of accusations lightly."

"I'm not making anything lightly," Randy angrily replied. "I'm just telling you those boys were killed, and you need to find out how."

"Now just hold on," the deputy coroner stammered.

"Scottie," Don interjected calmly. "Why don't we try to get in touch with Frank Campo and ask him what *he* thinks? There's a lot at stake here, and we don't want to miss anything."

"Well, I suppose I could call him." McDaniel rubbed his chin as he considered this request. Actually, it looked like he was greatly relieved by the suggestion. "I've got his cell phone number, and he did say to call him if anything unusual came up."

"I'd say this was unusual," Don told him. "Why don't we try to call him now?"

Frank Campo answered his phone after only two rings. Scottie McDaniel explained what was happening on James Street, and went over the circumstances of Jonah Cooper's death. Then Don Brantley got on the phone and told Campo of his and Randy's concerns. After a moment of silence, the coroner asked to speak to McDaniel again and instructed him to order an autopsy.

"Good," Randy Lutz muttered. "Now maybe we'll find out what happened here."

McDaniel called one of the police officers over and said, "I think we need to find this T.C. Mason person. We might want to ask him a few questions."

As Don and Randy walked out of the house, they noticed Ali Cooper standing in the front yard. An older woman was standing there with her arms around her. Behind Ali, clinging anxiously to her mother's leg, was Scarlett Cooper. She looked over as the paramedics walked by, wide-eyed and innocent.

It didn't take long for the pathologists at the hospital to determine the cause of Jonah Cooper's death. His neck had been broken, and not by catching his head between the rails of the crib. Someone, somebody stronger than Ali Cooper, had snapped the boy's neck and then wedged his head in the side of the crib, trying to make the death look accidental.

The next day, the district attorney ordered the exhumation of Jonah's brother, Jesse. An autopsy revealed the same cause of death—a fractured neck. The boys hadn't died from horribly coincidental accidents. They had been murdered.

The police found T.C. Mason and were able to connect him to the murder of Jonah Cooper. A jury of his peers agreed, and he was convicted of first-degree murder and sent to death row in Columbia. T.C. never confessed to killing the boys, and would only smile when asked about them.

Ali Cooper pleaded to a lesser offense. She claimed she didn't have anything to do with the deaths of her sons, but her lawyer was convinced that no one would believe she hadn't known what was going on. And he was right. She was sentenced to fourteen years in prison.

As for Scarlett Cooper, she became a ward of the state and was soon adopted by a family near Greenville.

A few weeks after all of this had settled out, Randy Lutz and Don Brantley were returning to the EMS station after taking a patient to the ER. It had been a little boy with a broken arm, about the same age as the Cooper twins. The sad story of 118 James Street had come to Randy's mind, and he sat quietly, staring blankly down the road ahead.

After a few minutes, he turned to his partner and said, "You know, Don, if we hadn't pushed Scottie McDaniel that day…and gotten that autopsy done…" His voice trailed off and he sat in silence, unable to deal with the painful realization of what might have been.

"I know." Don spoke quietly. He knew Randy's heart. His partner had been right to be angry then, and to demand that the police and the deputy coroner open their eyes and see what was happening on James Street. And he had been right in his obstinate determination that the two of them should get involved, even if it meant going out of their way.

Don looked over at his partner and said what they both knew. "If you hadn't insisted on us going over to James Street, that little girl was going to be next."

The LORD is known by his justice;
the wicked are ensnared by the work of their hands.

PSALM 9:16

10

All Units Respond

*He has honor if he holds himself
to an ideal of conduct
though it is inconvenient, unpredictable,
or dangerous to do so.*

WALTER LIPPMANN (1889–1974)

Summer 1975. 10:35 p.m. Elon Roth sat at his kitchen table. Actually, it was only a rickety card table covered with old and yellowed newspapers. He stared down at what remained of his dinner—a half-eaten can of beans and franks. The palms of his hands were down on the table, and he absently edged the can forward a little at a time with his thumbs.

Then he sat straight up, folded his hands together as if praying, and stared up at the single lightbulb hanging from the ceiling.

"Yes," he said quietly. "Yes, I understand."

He stood up, walked to the front door, glanced quickly behind him, then stepped out onto his porch. The door closed behind him on an empty house.

Elon Roth was headed to Rock Hill.

10:45 p.m. "Blow the horn," Steve Adkins dared his wife.

"I'm not about to do that," Sherry answered him. "I don't want to wake up the neighborhood."

Steve chuckled and glanced out his passenger-side window. His partner, Jerry Perkins, was walking down the sidewalk toward them. In one hand he carried his radio, and in the other a small paper bag—his customary roast-beef sandwich, Granny Smith apple, and chocolate-chip cookie.

Jerry and Steve had the 11 p.m. to 7 a.m. shift tonight, just as they'd had all week. Steve's wife, Sherry, and their daughter, Callie, would drop them by the police department on their way to Steve's parents' house. Sherry didn't like staying alone overnight when her husband was working.

"Uncle Jerry!" Callie squealed with excitement as Jerry slid into the backseat beside her. She squirmed out of her seat belt and grabbed him around the neck.

"Hey, sweetie." Jerry struggled to get out the words. Callie's bear hug made it difficult to speak.

"Honey, get back in your car seat," Sherry told her, twisting around and encouraging her five-year-old daughter to release their friend.

"Aw, Momma," Callie weakly protested. But she loosened her hold on Jerry, planted a big kiss on his cheek, and settled back into her seat.

Sherry backed the car out of the driveway and headed down Oliver Street. It was only a five-minute trip to the station, and then another five or so to Steve's parents'.

"Last night for a while," Jerry said from the backseat.

"Yeah, thankfully," Steve answered. "Off for a couple of days, honey," he added, patting his wife on her shoulder. "Maybe we can take Callie somewhere. How about Carowinds?"

"Yea! Carowinds!" Callie agreed with excitement.

Steve grinned. The giant amusement park near Charlotte, with its many rides and large water park, was Callie's favorite place to spend a summer's day.

"Now you've done it," Sherry said, glancing into her rearview mirror at her bouncing daughter. "I guess it will be Carowinds," she agreed, smiling.

Before they could get to the station, Callie had fallen asleep, her head resting on Jerry's arm. He carefully repositioned the little girl in her car seat before getting out, managing not to awaken her.

Steve leaned over in the front seat and kissed his wife.

"See you in the morning," he told her.

"You two be careful," Sherry replied, again feeling that twinge of fear in her stomach. It was always there when he left for work, and she knew it would pass.

"Okay?" she added, making sure Steve had heard.

He was sliding out of the car, and he quickly glanced back at her over his shoulder.

"Sure. We'll be careful."

Steve Adkins and Jerry Perkins had been close friends since high school. And now they were rookie police officers together. They had been with the department for a little more than six months and had been assigned the graveyard shift with Ted Hunt. He was a seasoned sergeant with more than twelve years of experience.

The two men walked into the dayroom to get their assignment. As they sat down in a couple of the front chairs, Lieutenant Flanders walked over.

"Looks like you two are going to be on your own tonight," he told them. "Hunt called in sick this afternoon, and there's no one to take his place."

"That's fine," Steve said, looking up and smiling. "We can handle it. Where have you got us?"

Flanders looked at his clipboard and flipped the top sheet over, looking for their names.

"Charlotte and Oakland," he informed them. "That's where one of you will be on car patrol. And the other will have the Main Street beat to walk."

Jerry looked over at Steve and nodded his head. These were quiet areas in the city, and shouldn't be too challenging. He knew Flanders had done this on purpose.

"That sounds okay," he told the lieutenant. "Thanks."

They sat in the dayroom for another fifteen minutes, listening as Flanders told the night-duty officers of things that had been happening in town, and people to be watching out for. There was nothing very exciting going on, and "it should be a pretty quiet eight hours," he told them. "But keep your eyes open."

They got up and walked outside. Their patrol car, #4, was parked nearby. Jerry pulled his keys out of his pocket, and then reached in again, this time taking out a bright, shiny quarter.

"Heads or tails?" he asked Steve.

"Doesn't matter to me," Adkins answered. "If you want to drive first, that's fine."

"Nope," Jerry answered resolutely. "We're gonna flip."

He tossed the coin in the air, and Steve called, "Tails."

"Tails it is," Jerry said, glancing down at the coin. "Here," he added, tossing the keys to his partner. "You're driving."

On a routine shift with three officers, one would be assigned to drive the entire eight hours. One of the other officers would stay in the patrol car with him for two hours, while the other officer would walk the assigned beat. Then the two would alternate, with the driver always remaining behind the wheel.

Ted Hunt, since he had seniority, had been the designated driver the past week, while Jerry and Steve would alternate walking and riding every two hours. Tonight, they would just alternate walking the beat and driving the assigned patrol area. And Steve would take the first two hours in the car.

"Just drop me off here," Jerry said as they stopped at a red light on White Street. "Then I'll head over to Main."

He patted his radio, making sure it was on his belt, and then he felt for his duty weapon. He was ready. He opened the door and stepped out.

Steve leaned over and said, "See you in two hours. Stay in touch."

Jerry looked down at his partner, touched the brim of his hat, and started to walk down the street.

The light changed, and Steve drove off, heading toward Charlotte Avenue, about a mile away.

The night was muggy and warm. *Must still be close to 80,* Jerry thought as he made his way down the sidewalk, checking door handles and shining his flashlight into storefronts as he walked.

A car drove by every ten minutes or so, but other than that, the downtown area was deserted and eerily quiet. Jerry liked it that way, and liked the solitude. It gave him time to think.

1:10 a.m. Jerry trained the beam of his flashlight down an alleyway, making sure there were no overnight guests in this frequently visited refuge. Empty.

He turned back down the sidewalk and his radio crackled.

"Jerry, this is Steve." His partner spoke quietly.

He took the radio out of its holder and pressed the *send* button.

"Steve, this is Jerry. Go ahead."

There was more static, and then Perkins heard his partner say, "I'm over on Charlotte Avenue, headed toward Cherry Road, right across from Winthrop. There's a beat-up Oldsmobile station wagon pulled over by the curb. Blue, with a missing taillight. Looks like an out-of-state tag, but I can't quite make it out. And there's a guy standing over in the grass. Looks like he needs some help. I'm gonna see what's going on."

"10-4, Steve," Jerry answered. "Let me know. I'll see you in about twenty."

"Roger that," came Steve's reply. It would soon be time for them to trade off, and Jerry would need to keep an eye out for his partner, who would be driving over with the patrol car.

He put his radio back into its belt holder and walked on down the street. It continued to be a quiet night.

1:45 a.m. Jerry came to a sudden stop when he reached a streetlamp and looked down at his watch. He had lost track of time, and realized Steve should be heading over to Main Street.

"Wow!" he said out loud. He needed to give his partner a call. He reached down for his radio, but before he could press the *send* button, it squawked to life.

"This is Corporal Sutherland," a voice said in an urgent tone, shattering the quiet of the dark night. "All units respond to Charlotte Avenue, corner of Myrtle. We've got an abandoned patrol car. No sign of the officer."

Jerry Perkins stared at the radio, stunned. Steve was over on Charlotte, but…

"Steve! This is Jerry," he spoke into the receiver, apprehension quickly giving way to fear. There was no answer.

"Steve!" he repeated. "Do you hear me?"

Silence.

"Andy!" Jerry spoke into the radio, this time calling his corporal. "This is Jerry Perkins, and I'm on foot over on Main Street. Can somebody pick me up? I need to get over to Charlotte Avenue. Steve is patrolling over there, and he won't answer me."

"Sure, Jerry," Sutherland responded. "I'm on my way."

Perkins wasn't sure what to do. He wanted to start walking…running…to Charlotte Avenue, but he knew he needed to stay put and wait on Sutherland. It was the longest two minutes the rookie officer had ever spent.

Sutherland's patrol car screeched to a stop right by him.

"Get in!" the corporal called unnecessarily. Jerry was already piling into the front seat, slamming the door behind him.

"What do you know, Andy?" he asked.

"Not much. I left my two officers over on Charlotte while I came to pick you up. They're lookin', but so far nothin'. No sign of a struggle, or anything. Just Unit 4 parked at the curb, with its motor running and the driver's door open."

Jerry's heart sank in his chest.

"Unit 4. Are you sure?" he asked, hoping Sutherland was somehow mistaken.

"Yeah, Unit 4," Andy answered without looking over. "Why? Is that—"

"Yeah, that's Steve, and the last time I talked to him…"

They pulled up behind the abandoned patrol car and jumped out.

By now, there were five police vehicles scattered at different angles in the four-lane street, each with their lights flashing.

Jerry ran over to the car and looked inside. Steve's nightstick was lying on the passenger seat, and everything seemed to be in order. Then the picture on the dash caught his eye. It was Sherry and Callie. Steve always had it with him when he was on duty.

As he looked into Sherry's smiling eyes, he suddenly shuddered. Something was terribly wrong.

Sutherland had walked over to a group of officers who were huddled in one of the nearby front yards. They were looking at something on the ground as Jerry walked up.

Sutherland leaned over and used a gloved hand to carefully lift a handgun partially hidden in the fescue grass of the recently mowed lawn.

"That's Steve's!" Jerry called out, immediately recognizing the weapon.

The officers silently looked over at him, and then Sutherland asked, "When was the last time you talked with Steve?"

Jerry looked down at his watch, but didn't focus on the dial. He was thinking.

"I guess it was forty-five, maybe fifty minutes ago. He said he was going to check on a—Wait a minute! There was a station wagon pulled over here somewhere, and he was going to check it out!"

Jerry gave the description of the vehicle—a beat-up blue Oldsmobile—and Corporal Sutherland relayed the information to the dispatch officer at the station. From there, it would be spread over several counties. Now they would have to wait.

"Hey, over here!"

One of the officers was standing in a natural area full of waist-high azaleas. He was shining his flashlight down onto a thick bed of pine needles where its beam was being reflected by a shiny metal object. A pair of handcuffs.

Corporal Sutherland hurried over, and with Jerry Perkins peering over his shoulder, he again carefully picked the item off the ground. He held the cuffs in front of him as the other officer continued to shine his light. They were police issue. No one said a word.

They continued to search the area, hoping to find some other piece of evidence, some other sign of Steve or the driver of the Oldsmobile. Nothing. It seemed that Steve Adkins had disappeared into thin air.

All they could do was wait and hope that something would turn up, or that someone would see something.

Every four or five minutes, a dozen police radios crackled, and they all heard the dispatcher announce, "All available units…" Then once again the description of the Oldsmobile.

Jerry stood motionless, staring down at the sidewalk in front of him. He was helpless, powerless to do anything to help his friend, and he slowly began to shake his head. Andy Sutherland walked up to him and put a hand on his shoulder. He didn't say anything.

The rookie officer kept shaking his head, and finally whispered, "We tossed a coin, Andy. We just tossed a coin."

2:25 a.m.—Highway 322, western York County. Sheriff's deputy Danny Smith turned off Blanton Road and onto 322, headed back toward Rock Hill. He had just finished his second loop of the southwesternmost tip of the county, and as on most nights, had seen nothing unusual. There *had* been that possum scurrying across the road ahead of him back on Blanton, and the two deer standing just off the highway, but that was about it.

And then there had been all the excitement over in Rock Hill. For some reason, they had everybody searching for an old station wagon. Danny would keep on the lookout, just like he always did. But this time of night, he was usually the only one on the road. This was a sparsely populated part of the county.

Smith pulled off the highway at Jake's Minute Market, just like he always did this time of the morning. The store was closed but the lights were still on, and it was a good place to stop and eat the ham-and-cheese sandwich his wife had made for him.

As he drove around the three gas pumps in the island near the road, he glanced inside the store, making sure everything was secure. No problems there. Then he parked off to one side, close to the highway and facing it, and cut off his motor and lights.

As he grabbed the paper bag in the seat beside him, he was a little startled when his radio went off again.

"All available units, be on the lookout…"

Still trying to find that car, he thought to himself. *Must be pretty—*

Something off to the left got his attention, and Danny squinted his eyes, focusing.

A couple of hundred yards away he saw the lights of a car heading in his direction, and toward Rock Hill. The bag remained unopened in his hand as he watched the vehicle approach.

Whoever it was wasn't speeding, and there was nothing suspicious about the way he or she was driving. As the car passed Jake's, Danny could see that the driver was a man. Even though the deputy was parked in the dark, something made the driver look over and straight into his eyes. Danny didn't recognize him, but there was something strange about the man's face, and the way he just stared at the officer. No wave or acknowledgment, just a blank, empty stare. Then the driver turned back to the road ahead of him and disappeared into the night.

Danny Smith suddenly shivered, and just sat there for a moment. *There was something odd about that guy,* he thought.

He was about to take a bite of his ham and cheese when it occurred to him, *That was an old station wagon. I wonder…*

He put his sandwich back in the paper bag and picked up his radio. The car was way down the road by now, and he probably wouldn't be able to catch up with it or even find it. But he was going to give the police in Rock Hill a heads-up anyway.

He made the call to dispatch at the police station and put the radio back in its holder.

Probably nothing, he thought.

Russ Kemper and Craig Yoder got the call. They were out on Cherry Road, and like all the other police officers in Rock Hill, they were looking for an old station wagon and for any sign of Steve Adkins.

"What do you think?" Russ asked his partner.

Craig shook his head. "No one's seen anything yet, so we need to check this out. But it doesn't make much sense. If this is the car, and if it's the people involved with whatever happened to Steve, why would they be way over on the other side of the county but heading *back* into town?"

"Beats me," Russ agreed. Then with growing frustration and anger he added, "But we're gonna find the people who did this, and this is the best tip we've had."

A few minutes later, Craig stopped his vehicle in the parking lot of a grocery store just on the edge of Rock Hill. Highway 322 was right in front of them, and he switched off his lights and they waited.

There were a few vehicles on the road, but no older-model station wagon. Russ looked down at his watch. Based on the time the call had come in from the county deputy, the car should have been here by now, if in fact it was headed this way. He knew that would be too much to hope for. First, that it was the vehicle involved with Steve Adkins, and second, that they would be—

"Look!" Craig exclaimed, reaching over and grabbing his partner's arm. "Station wagon!"

Russ couldn't determine the make of the vehicle, but he could tell it was old and beat-up. It passed them heading into town, and they could see a lone driver, with apparently no one else in the car.

Craig flipped the switch on the dash, and his blue lights began flashing. He pulled out into the highway behind the station wagon.

For a moment, the car ahead didn't slow down. Russ Kemper shook his head and was about to turn on the siren, when the driver decided to pull off the road. The car came to a stop in some loose stone, but with its motor still running.

Kemper picked up his radio and notified the police dispatch that they were making a stop on Highway 322, out near the Bi-Lo. The officers got out of their car, each reflexively patting the butts of their handguns. Craig pointed his flashlight at the back of the car in front of them. The tag was rusted and bent, and impossible to read.

As they walked toward the vehicle, the men could make out the silhouette of the driver. It was a male, and he seemed to be pretty tall. Craig couldn't see anyone else in the car. Without saying a word, he motioned for Russ to circle around to the passenger side while he continued on to the left side of the station wagon.

When he came up beside the driver's door, he tapped on the window, trying to get the driver's attention. The man was just sitting there, staring straight ahead.

Slowly, the driver turned toward Craig and rolled down the window.

"What's the problem, officer?" he asked. He wore a yellow, collared shirt, and Yoder noticed the two top buttons were missing. His hair was thinning and matted.

Craig shined the flashlight into the car, making sure he could see the man's hands.

"How are you doing this morning?" Craig asked him. "I need to see your driver's license and registration."

"What's the problem, officer?" the driver asked, still looking straight ahead. "Did I do something wrong?"

"Just routine, sir. I need to see your license," Yoder repeated, this time with more of an edge of authority in his voice.

While the driver fumbled with his wallet, Russ had reached the other side of the station wagon and was shining his flashlight into the backseat. It was empty, except for some scattered, rumpled newspapers.

Then he noticed some dark splotches on the seat cover. He leaned a little closer, his mind beginning to form around what his eyes were telling him.

It was blood. Or at least it sure looked like it. Russ glanced again at the driver through the partially open passenger window. The man was now leaning over the front seat and starting to open the glove compartment. Kemper reached down and unsnapped the strap of his holster. Keeping his hand on the butt of his handgun, he asked, "What are you doing, sir?"

"I'm trying to find my registration, officer. Just like your partner asked."

Over the roof of the car, Russ got Craig's attention, and motioned with his head to the backseat.

Suddenly the glove compartment fell open, and some papers dropped to the floor of the car. Startled, Russ stepped back from the car and drew his handgun. "Take your hand away from the dash and give me your driver's license," he told the man.

"But what about the—"

"You heard me, sir. Keep your hands where I can see them."

The driver sat up straight and handed his license through the passenger window. Then, loose and relaxed, he put both of his hands on the steering wheel.

Russ glanced down at the South Carolina license, but something made him peer down farther, to the floor of the passenger's side. One of the things that had fallen out of the glove compartment looked familiar. It was a small white notebook of some sort. He looked closer and could make out the name "Jeffers Funeral Home."

It was a pocket calendar, and it was for this year. Russ Kemper stiffened. He again glanced back over the top of the car at Craig, a growing concern now in his eyes. Yoder sensed that something was bothering his partner. He unsnapped the strap over his handgun.

Each year, the owners of Jeffers would give a pocket calendar to every member of the Rock Hill Police Department, as well as to the officers of the York County Sheriff's Department. Russ had gotten his just last week. And just like his, the one on the floor had "Thanks for all you do!" embossed in gold letters on the cover.

It was starting to come together for Kemper. He looked down at the side of the car, and then over at the hood ornament. This was a blue Oldsmobile wagon! And it matched the description of the vehicle the entire department was looking for.

"Sir, would you step out of the car," Kemper told the driver.

"What's the problem, officer?" he asked. "I wasn't speeding, was I?"

Russ looked down at the driver's license.

"Mr. Roth, please step out of the car, on the driver's side."

Craig heard the command in his partner's voice, and he reached down and opened the driver's door. At the same time, he drew his handgun.

"Now!" he ordered Roth.

This time there was no mistaking the officers' resolve, and Elon Roth slowly got out of the Oldsmobile.

Craig held his gun on the man, stepping back a little. He put his flashlight on the top of the car, then took the radio out of his belt holder. He called police dispatch again and asked for backup as Russ walked around the front of the wagon.

"And make it fast," he added.

Roth was a tall, lanky man, with long arms and huge hands. He towered over the two officers.

"Officer, if you'll only—" he began, stepping toward Yoder.

"That's enough, Mr. Roth," Russ interrupted him, now standing just to the man's side. "Turn around, face the car, get your hands on the hood." He tightened his grip on the handgun.

Russ Kemper was getting angry, and cautiously tense. He knew Roth was considering his options, considering whether to resist these officers or give up. And Kemper knew anything could happen.

They stood there for what seemed an eternity, none of them moving.

"You heard me—now do it!" Russ barked at the man.

There was another taut moment, then Roth's shoulders slumped, and he slowly turned to face the Oldsmobile. Off in the distance, Craig could hear the wail of a patrol car's siren. It was coming from somewhere downtown and getting closer.

"Spread your legs and don't move," Russ told Roth. "Are you carrying any weapons?"

Kemper stepped closer and began to pat down the suspect.

"I don't have any weapon, officer," the tall man answered quietly. "And if you'll just let me—"

"Just stand still and be quiet," Russ instructed him. The siren was getting closer, and Craig could see some flashing blue lights approaching.

He continued to check the man for hidden weapons, but found nothing suspicious. When he patted down his right pants pocket, he felt something round and firm, about the size of a golf ball.

"What's that?" he asked.

Elon Roth started to turn around, but Kemper stopped him.

"Stay where you are and don't move!" he told him. Then he carefully reached into the man's pocket and pulled out a balled-up handkerchief. As he did so, a police car pulled up, its lights shining brightly on the three men and the Oldsmobile. Two officers jumped out of the car, drew their weapons, and hurried over to where Russ and Craig stood.

Kemper looked down at the handkerchief in his hand, and slowly opened it.

As the stained cloth fell away, revealing its contents, Russ gasped. It was an eyeball.

An hour-and-a-half later, Elon Roth sat at a desk in the Rock Hill Police Station. He was calm and relaxed, with his cuffed hands folded together on the table. And he told his story.

He had been driving down Charlotte Avenue earlier that night and decided to pull over to the curb and get out of the car. A few minutes later, Officer Steve Adkins had come up and asked if he could help him.

"I knew what I had to do," the arrested man explained matter-of-factly.

He distracted Steve, pulled a .38 out of his pants pocket, and shot him once in the chest. Then he carried him over to the Oldsmobile and put him in the backseat.

"Must have been dead right off," Roth told the investigator. "He didn't say anything, and wasn't moving. Didn't cause me any trouble."

Then he had driven all the way out to Bullocks Creek, miles from Rock Hill and in one of the remotest parts of the county. There he had shot Steve Adkins sixteen more times and dumped his body in some bushes near a creek.

"Why the eye?" the detective asked with growing disgust. "Why did you do that?"

"Oh, that," Roth responded dismissively. "I was told to do that."

The detective just stared at him and waited.

"I hear them a lot," the man continued, slowly nodding his head. "And tonight the voices were really clear. No question."

And that was the end of his statement.

In the light of day, an army of police officers scoured the area Roth had described and confirmed everything he had said. They found three handguns in the spare-tire well of the Oldsmobile. One was the murder weapon.

It took the jury thirty minutes to return a guilty verdict of first-degree murder. Elon Roth was given a sentence of life in prison—and with good behavior, a chance of parole in 18 years.

And Roth behaved. In 1993, he was up for parole, and Steve Adkins's wife, daughter, and other family members made the trip to Columbia to protest his release. Jerry Perkins was with them, always sitting beside Callie, always with his arm around her shoulders.

Parole was denied, thankfully. But every year, for thirteen years, they would all make the trip down I-77 to appear before the board and sit in the same room with the man who had viciously murdered their husband, father, loved one, and friend. And every year his parole was denied.

Then, unexpectedly, Elon Roth died. It was over. No more trips to Columbia. No more fearing that one day this murderer would walk free. No more worrying that justice would be undone.

None of that changed the reality that Steve was gone. He would always be with them, but so would the memories of that terrible night back in the summer of 1975.

At the end of all those years, Jerry Perkins had come to understand that there might not always be justice in this world. But Steve had taught him there could be honor.

And Jerry made sure that Callie knew the kind of man her father had been. He had loved his wife. He had cherished his daughter. He was a brave man—not foolish, but knowing when to take a stand and when to do his duty. He had known that his job was dangerous, but that it was important.

And he had been Jerry's friend.

"See you in the morning."

And then the toss of a coin.

11

The Shirt off My Back

"What should we do then?" the crowd asked.
John (the Baptist) answered, "The man with two tunics
should share with him who has none,
and the one who has food should do the same."

LUKE 3:10-11

The weather was perfect—clear skies, 82 degrees, and only a slight breeze. Adam Locke, a twenty-six-year-old from Cleveland, was flying the single-engine Cessna 182 Skylane while his younger brother, David, studied the map spread out on the panel in front of him.

David had graduated from Ohio State a few weeks ago, and he and Adam were heading to Florida to celebrate. Their flight plan called for them to stop at the small airport in Rock Hill and refuel, and David's job was to make sure they found it. Charlotte was just ahead, so they were getting close.

"How about a landmark, David?" Adam asked. "There's Charlotte off to our right, and we need to stay away from that airport."

David glanced up from the map and looked over at the city's skyline.

"There's the Panthers stadium," he said, pointing to the distinctive structure in the middle of a cluster of large buildings. "We just need to find the 77 Interstate and follow it south."

He searched the surrounding landscape until he located the wide and winding gray ribbon.

"Look, Adam—there it is." He pointed. "Follow it south until we come to a big river. Then we'll head east. We're pretty close."

The Cessna made a smooth correction and the city of Charlotte was soon behind them.

"That must be it, the Catawba River," Adam said, nodding down at the dark green meandering waterway. "Can't be far now."

He turned east, and as the plane settled again, they both heard it.

It was only a tiny pause in the otherwise smooth and constant hum of the engine. But it had been there, and they looked at each other. Then the plane trembled slightly, and Adam quickly glanced at the control panel.

"Oh no!" he exclaimed, staring with shocked disbelief at the fuel gauge.

"What's the matter?" David asked, following his brother's horrified stare.

Sharon Brothers and her partner, Charlie, were pulling out of the ER parking area when the call came in.

"EMS 2, respond to a plane crash off Mt. Gallant Road, near the intersection with Twin Lakes," the dispatcher excitedly instructed.

"A plane crash?" Charlie repeated incredulously. "That can't be right."

Sharon picked up the radio and said, "Dispatch, this is EMS 2. Did you say 'plane crash'?"

"That's right, Sharon. A small plane came down. Single-engine, apparently. Don't know anything about survivors, just that someone out there saw it go down and called 9-1-1. You and Charlie need to get out there. I'm notifying the fire department and police as well."

"10-4," Sharon said, looking over at her partner. "We're on our way."

She flipped a couple of switches on the dash, and the ambulance screamed out onto the highway, its lights flashing.

When they arrived at the scene of the crash, a few cars were pulled over on the side of the road, and a young boy was excitedly motioning to them. Then he began pointing out into a large, open cow pasture.

Charlie grabbed the emergency kit from the back of the ambulance, and they hurried to where the boy was standing. The pasture was enclosed by a rusty barbed-wire fence, and Sharon stopped in front of it, looking down at the waist-high top strand.

"Now how am I…" she began, wondering how she was going to negotiate this obstacle.

"Come on—here," Charlie said, putting his hand on the top wire and using his weight to push it down as far as he could. "Just try to step over it."

"Well, this won't be too ladylike…" Sharon muttered, indelicately swinging her leg over the fence, straddling it, and then somehow making it over to the other side.

Charlie hopped over after her, and they began jogging toward the middle of the field.

"Look at this," he said, pointing to the ground as they hurried through the field. They were running beside a straight line of newly plowed earth that was leading them to a group of people standing fifty or sixty yards away.

"Over there!" Sharon pointed off to their right, where a wing of a small plane lay crumpled in the foot-high fescue.

They reached the group and now saw what had recently plowed the field. The freshly turned furrow ended at what remained of the rest of the plane, which was mashed and folded almost beyond recognition.

No survivors in this one, Sharon thought as they stopped at the edge of the wreck, gasping for breath.

"They're over here!" someone called, motioning them to the other side of the plane.

Charlie glanced over at Sharon and shook his head as they quickly made their way around the plane.

There on the ground, with his back against what had once been part of the fuselage, sat a young man. He was holding his head in his hands, and a trickle of blood was making its way down his left cheek and onto his neck.

Charlie was stunned there could be a survivor after such a terrible crash, and he raced over, dropped the emergency kit to the ground, and quickly opened it.

"Son, can you hear me?" he asked.

Sharon looked beyond where Charlie was and saw the outstretched body of another young man. He was lying on his back, motionless, with blood covering his face and chest.

As she stepped toward him, something unbelievable happened. He raised his right hand, and his head began to turn from side to side.

"David…" he weakly mumbled. "David, are you there?"

Within minutes, two rescue vehicles and a fire engine were in the field. The two young men had been stabilized. And Charlie had made sure there were no other passengers. He ran back to the ambulance and drove it up the road and through a now open gate, back to his waiting partner. He and Sharon loaded the boys into the ambulance and sped off to the hospital.

"Those Locke boys are pretty lucky," Lori Davidson told Sharon. She was the ER nurse taking care of them, and she'd finally been able to take a break. She wanted to let the two paramedics know the status of the two brothers. "It looks like they're both going to be fine."

"Whew!" Sharon exclaimed. "I'd say they're more than lucky, Lori. You should see that plane. There's not much left of it."

"Yeah," Charlie added. "I don't know how they got it down. It was a good thing they came up on that field, with no trees and all. And a good thing they ran out of fuel. If there had been a fire…well, they wouldn't have survived that."

"Well, I wouldn't say it was a *good* thing they ran out of fuel," Sharon goaded him.

"You know what I mean," he shot back, quickly taking the bait. "I just—"

"Here comes Dr. Williams," Lori interrupted them. "Let's see what he has to say."

Jay Williams walked up the hallway toward them, shaking his head. As he reached the nurses' station, where they were standing, he tossed two patient clipboards onto the countertop.

"Wow, Sharon," he exclaimed to her. "Now *that's* something that needs to go into your 'I can't believe it happened' file. Those two young men should be down in the morgue and not here in the ER."

"How are they?" she asked him. "They seemed to be okay when we brought them in. Has anything turned up?"

"David, the young one," Williams began to explain. "He's got a few stitches above his left ear, but he's fine and I'm sending him home. Adam, on the other hand…well, he's going to be okay too, but he probably lost consciousness for a while. Doesn't remember much of what happened. He has some cuts and bruises, and his CT scan is good, but we're going to put him in the hospital overnight just to be sure. Should be able to go home sometime tomorrow."

"That's a relief," Sharon sighed. "You should see their plane, Doc—or what's left of it."

Jay Williams looked straight at her again. "Like I said, Sharon, you need to put this one in your file."

He turned and walked back down the hallway.

"Lori." Sharon spoke quietly to the nurse. "Dr. Williams said he was sending the younger brother home. Well, the problem is, they're from Cleveland, and David Locke doesn't have a home to go to. They were on their way to Florida, and the sheriff's department has locked up all of their luggage and stuff out at the airport. They won't be able to get any of that until there's been an investigation into the cause of the crash. I don't know where David will go tonight. No ID, no money…"

"You know he can't stay here in the hospital." Lori was beginning to understand where the paramedic was taking this. "The hospital administration has really been cracking down on family members staying overnight in the room with patients. That won't be a possibility."

"Well, we'll see about that," Sharon muttered, stroking her chin. "Do you know where they're planning on admitting him? I'm sure it won't be the ICU."

"No, not the ICU. Probably 4-B. He'll need a monitored bed overnight, but that's about all."

"Isn't Jackie Fletcher the charge nurse up there?" Sharon continued. Jackie had worked in the ER for more than ten years before transferring upstairs, and she and Sharon were good friends.

"Sharon," Lori said accusingly. "You don't want to get—"

"Well, she *is* the charge nurse now, isn't she?" the paramedic persisted.

"Yes, but—"

"Good," Sharon stated with finality. Then she turned to the unit secretary and said, "Could you hand me the phone and dial 4-B? Thanks."

An hour later Adam Locke was upstairs, being moved from the ER stretcher over to his hospital bed. David Locke was standing on the other side of the bed, a folding cot propped up against the wall behind him.

Sharon stood near the doorway alongside her husband, Mike. He and his partner on EMS 3 had brought a chest-pain patient to the ER, and Mike had come upstairs to find his wife.

When Adam had been comfortably positioned in his bed, Jackie Fletcher made sure he had everything he needed and then left the room. The two brothers were alone with Sharon and Mike.

Adam spoke up first.

"I just want to thank you for everything you did for us," he began, looking up at their rescuer. "We would have—"

"Now hold on there," she interrupted. "Charlie and I were just doing our jobs. You were the one who somehow brought that plane down and managed to land it in that field."

"You call that a landing?" David quipped. "And would *he* be the one who also ran us out of gas?"

"Come on now, boys," Sharon said in her best motherly tone. "Don't get into that. The main thing is that the two of you are safe and you're going to be fine. Are you sure you don't want us to call your folks and let them know what's going on?"

"No, don't do that!" they exclaimed in unison. "We'll let them know in a few days," David continued. "But right now, we don't want them to get upset. They'd just hop in a car and drive straight down here. And the only thing they'd do the whole time is worry."

"Okay," Sharon said. "I think I understand. But if you change your mind, you let me know and we'll get in touch with them."

"Sure," David said. "But let's just leave it at that."

She was a little uncomfortable with this, but these young men were able to make their own decisions, and if they didn't want their parents to know what had happened to them—well, that was up to them.

Mike stepped over to the side of the bed and put his hand on Adam's shoulder.

"The two of you have been through a lot, and being in a strange place just makes things worse. If you need anything, or any help, I want you to give us a call."

He took a pen out of his pocket and looked around for something to write on. An unopened package of 4x4 cotton gauze was lying on the bedside table, and he picked it up and scribbled his phone number on the back of it.

Handing it to Adam, he said, "Here—and I mean it. If something comes up or you need anything, call this number."

David stood up, and in a voice a little rough from emotion said, "We know you mean it. You guys have been great to us. And if you're ever in the Cleveland area, please give us a call."

Sharon shook her head and smiled. "Well, if we're in that neck of the woods, we'll be driving and not flying. I can promise you that."

Adam managed a smile, and the couple turned toward the door.

"You guys take care," she called back to them as they walked out into the hallway.

The next morning, Sharon and Mike were sitting at their kitchen table, drinking coffee and planning what they would do on this, their day off.

The phone rang.

Mike reached behind him and picked up the receiver.

"Hello, Mike here."

He was silent, and then slowly began to nod his head. He looked over at his wife and raised his eyebrows.

"I see," he spoke into the phone. "No, you did the right thing. And don't worry about it."

He listened to the caller for another minute or two, and then said, "I understand. And what exit was that again?"

Sharon looked at him questioningly, but Mike kept listening, and then finally said, "Okay, exit 4. Let me make a couple of phone calls, and we'll be there as soon as we can. Don't go anywhere."

He hung up the receiver and slapped his palms down on the table-top, smiling.

"Well, I guess I know what we'll be doing today," he told his wife.

After Sharon and Mike had left Adam's hospital room, David Locke had called his girlfriend in Cleveland, sworn her to secrecy, and told her of their predicament. Jill didn't hesitate. After hanging up with David, she and Kathy, her apartment-mate, grabbed a few things and jumped into her car.

"Do you know how to get to South Carolina?" Kathy had asked as they headed toward I-77.

"Sure," Jill answered. "But just to be sure, why don't you get a map out of the dash pocket."

They made it to Rock Hill in a little under nine hours, and didn't have any trouble finding the hospital. It was a little after eight o'clock when they loaded Adam carefully into the back of the small Toyota.

As David jumped into the driver's seat, Jill asked, "What about your luggage? Your clothes and everything?"

He shook his head and said, "The sheriff's deputies said they would mail everything to us once the investigation was finished. Since it's Saturday, I don't think there's much of anything we can do."

He looked down at his khakis and noticed the grease and blood stains. He had washed most of the blood from his face, but there were still some matted areas in his hair. He was a mess. But Adam was worse. The hospital staff had offered to let him take one of their gowns with him, but he had declined. The front of his shirt was stained a dark red, and his pants were spattered as well. The bandage around his forehead was the finishing touch, making him look like a character out of *Saving Private Ryan*.

"Anyway," David continued. "We'll be home soon enough. Just let us know if we start smelling too bad."

"Too late," Jill said playfully.

"Hmm…well, I guess you'll just have to roll down the windows," he responded, smiling at her.

They had just made it past the Catawba River when they first began to smell something burning. A few miles later, they saw the smoke. It began to pour out from beneath the hood of the car. Then the engine alerts on the control panel began flashing, and David knew they were in trouble.

The steering column started to lock down, and he barely got the car off the interstate and onto the grassy shoulder before they came to a smoking, grinding stop. They were near an exit ramp, #4, and David walked up the hill looking for a gas station and telephone. That's when he had called Mike.

Forty-five minutes later, Mike pulled up behind the broken-down Toyota. He was followed by one of his friends in a tow truck. Then he had everyone pile into his car while his friend hooked up the Toyota and began towing it back to Rock Hill. The man had a repair shop, and was going to take a look at it and see if anything could be done.

"Mike," David began. Then he paused, shaking his head. "Thanks."

"Don't worry about any of that," Mike interrupted him. "I told you to call us if you had any trouble, and you did. And I'm glad we could help. I just hope Jimmy Mack can do something with that car and get you back on the road."

"I don't know," Jill said, not very optimistically. "I was afraid something was going to blow up, with all that smoke and everything."

"Well, we'll just have to see," he told her. "Jimmy Mack is a pretty good mechanic, and if anybody can fix it, it's him. Right now, though, we're going to the house and get you guys something to eat. And it looks like you could use some cleaning up too," he added, looking over at David's soiled clothes and mussed-up hair.

When they reached the house, Sharon greeted them as they all piled out of the car.

She immediately noticed the state of Adam and David's clothes. "I can't believe the people at the hospital would let you leave looking like that! Didn't they at least let you take a shower or something?"

Without waiting for an answer, she went on, "Well, never mind. You boys get on in here and we'll get you cleaned up. And Mike, you're about their size, so get some extra clothes out for them to wear."

"Sharon, you don't have to—" David began.

"I'll have none of that," she insisted. "And you two young ladies can give me a hand in the kitchen."

She turned and went back into the house. Mike looked over at his guests and the expression on his face clearly indicated that his wife's requests were to be obeyed.

"Let's go," he said to them.

After the young men had showered and changed clothes and everyone was seated around the kitchen table, Adam remarked on the food Sharon had prepared.

"I don't think I've ever had chicken like this before," he ventured.

"Well, I hope you like it," Sharon said, with mock threatening in her voice. "This is *real* Southern fried chicken, with all the fixin's."

"No, don't get me wrong!" he quickly explained. "This is delicious. I've just never had anything like it before."

"Well, then I'd say it's about time," she commented knowingly. "And help yourself to some more."

They ate in silence, a testimony to their hunger and to Sharon's good food. Then the older Locke boy said, "Mike, while I was changing clothes, I couldn't help but notice your hat collection. Tell us about that."

"Yeah, tell them about that," Sharon teased him.

"Well, you see—" her husband started.

"No, *I'll* tell them about it," she interrupted. "This has been going on for about ten years now. Everywhere we go, Mike has to buy a ball cap, or some hat with the name of the place on it. And football teams. He's got a bunch of those. And hunting hats. He's got a bunch of those too."

"And what about your T-shirts?" Mike broke in. "Why don't you explain *those* to our new friends?"

"I did notice a lot of T-shirts with some pretty funny stuff written on them," Adam volunteered. "Especially the one with the skinny kid on it and the words 'Chick Magnet' under him."

"Oh, I got that one for Mike in Pigeon Forge," Sharon explained. "Sorta looks like him, doesn't it?"

Before anyone could agree, Mike interjected, "She has T-shirts from all over. Can't walk into a store without buying one. But I have to admit, she eventually wears every single one of them."

Adam chuckled at this, then grabbed the side of his head, which seemed to have given him a twinge. "There's nothing wrong with collecting stuff if it means something to you. Like these coffee mugs," he added, pointing to several racks on one of the kitchen walls. They were laden with forty or fifty cups, each with its own unique painting and printing.

"Yep, you're right about that," Mike agreed. "See that one on the top rack in the middle? The blue one with the white printing? We got that one on our first trip to San Francisco."

"*First* trip?" Sharon asked, surprised. "It was our *only* trip!"

"Well, you never know," her husband sheepishly replied. "We've always wanted to go back there, and someday...well, you never know."

The phone rang.

He got up and walked over to the counter and picked up the receiver.

"Jimmy Mack," he said, looking toward the group at the table and nodding his head. "What ya got for us?"

David pulled his chair out and turned toward the phone.

"Yeah?" Mike said into the receiver. "You think that should do it? They've got to be able to get back to Cleveland, you know."

He listened in silence to Jimmy Mack's response.

"Okay, if you're sure about that. Just bring it on over, and I'll drive you back to your house. Headin' over there anyway. And thanks."

He hung up the phone and spoke to the expectant group.

"Jimmy thinks he's got your car fixed," he announced. "Apparently it had hardly any oil in the engine and was just about to burn completely up. A few more miles and it would be a different story."

Jill blushed at this and looked down at her fingernails.

"My father always reminds me to have the oil changed every three thousand miles or so, but I sometimes forget," she confessed.

"Sometimes?" Kathy asked her. "How about *always*?"

"Well, that doesn't matter now, does it?" Sharon put in. "The important thing is that your car is fixed and you can head back home. I bet your folks are getting pretty worried right about now."

Adam and David looked at each other and nodded.

"We need to get home," David agreed.

Sharon had washed their clothes and put them in a paper bag. Another bag contained food for their trip back to Ohio.

"Here you go, guys," she said, handing these to Jill and Kathy. Just then, they heard Jimmy Mack drive up in Jill's car. Sharon glanced out the window. "Mike and I need to take Jimmy back to his house, and then we need to go across town to see our daughter. You can stay as long as you want to, and can spend the night if you want to get some rest. Just make yourselves at home."

The couple headed for the door. The she turned and said, "You all take care of yourselves. And if you ask me, you could all do with some automotive classes." She pointed at Jill and said, "You with oil maintenance, and you," pointing at Adam, "with fuel gauge reading."

They all laughed at this, and Sharon and Mike stepped onto the front porch, closing the door behind them.

Three weeks later, Sharon came home to find a large box on her front porch. It was addressed to Mike and Sharon Brothers, and the return address was Cleveland. She had difficulty waiting to open it until her husband got home, but somehow she managed.

Together, they opened the box, and Mike found the letter on top of its contents. He opened the envelope and began reading.

"Well, I'll be…" he stammered. "I had no idea…"

"What?" Sharon asked him impatiently. "Give me that," she said, snatching the sheet of paper from his hands.

"Well, what in the world…" she exclaimed.

The letterhead on the single sheet of paper read, "The Locke Cor-poration—Family-Owned Since 1904." Suddenly it all came together. Adam and David were the heirs to one of the largest corporations in America. The letter was addressed to Mike and Sharon, and it was signed by the young men's mother and father. In it, they profusely thanked them for taking care of their sons, and for "going out of their way and far beyond any reasonable expectations" in seeing that they made it safely back home.

"And listen to this," Sharon said, reading the last paragraph of the letter. "'We've enclosed a few things that we thought you might like.'"

She looked down as Mike began emptying the contents of the box. He started to laugh, and soon his wife joined him. Inside the box were a couple of dozen caps, some signed by members of the Cleveland Indi-ans, and some by the Ohio State Buckeyes football team. There were even a few with the Locke logo on them.

And then there were dozens of T-shirts, multicolored and each with a different message or logo. The one at the bottom simply read "Sha-ron."

She picked up the shirt and held it to her chest. "Well, I'll be. Those boys…"

"And look at these!" Mike said, unwrapping an object from the very bottom of the box. It was a coffee mug, one of about thirty. Each one was different, each one unique.

"I'm going to need a new shelf," Mike said proudly.

Another two weeks passed, and they were still talking about the gifts from the Locke family. One evening the doorbell rang, and Mike opened the door to find a Fed-Ex man standing on the porch with a large and heavy box. He signed for it and brought it into the kitchen.

"This one is from Cleveland too," he told Sharon. "Don't they know they've done enough?" he said, smiling.

She opened the box and found another letter. This one was not on the Locke Corporation letterhead, but was signed by Adam and David's grandmother and two of their aunts. In it, they thanked them for taking care of their "rascally boys" and hoped that the couple would make good use of the contents of the box.

Inside, carefully folded, were Mike's clothes, the ones Adam and David had borrowed for their trip home. Under the clothes were jars of homemade jams and jellies, and tins of four or five different kinds of cookies.

"Wow, would you look at this stuff!" Mike exclaimed. "What a wonderful family."

"What's this?" Sharon asked, digging down to the bottom of the box and pulling out another envelope.

She opened it and her mouth dropped open. She looked at her husband, unable to speak, and handed him the envelope.

"What's the matter?" he asked her. Then he read the letter, looked up at Sharon, and just stared.

Neatly folded in a plain piece of paper were two airline tickets and a reservation for a week's stay in a five-star hotel. In San Francisco.

Blessed are those who can give without remembering,
and take without forgetting.

UNKNOWN

12

You Just Never Know

A farmer went out to sow his seed.
As he was scattering the seed,
Some fell along the path, and the birds came and ate it up.
Some fell on rocky places, where it did not have much soil...
Other seed fell among thorns,
which grew up and choked the plants.

MATTHEW 13:3-5,7

9:48 p.m. "Shots fired. 144 Stone Avenue. All units in the vicinity respond."

T.J. Sanders was slowly patrolling down Mansfield Street, when he heard the call from dispatch. He was only a few blocks away from the address but was headed in the wrong direction. Flipping the switch for his lights and siren, he made a U-turn and headed back toward downtown.

He knew Stone Avenue all too well. It was the home of many of Rock Hill's drug dealers and too often the scene of much of its violence. As he sped down Mansfield, he reflexively reached to his side, making sure his handgun was holstered and ready. Then he thought of his wife and two small children, and he said a quick prayer.

Turning onto Stone and needing to decide which way to turn, he started to search for house numbers. Fortunately, the choice was made easy. Another officer had already arrived at the scene, and his flashing lights were easily visible just up the street on the right, about five houses away. Sanders peeled his patrol car in that direction and pulled up behind the other vehicle.

"Officer Sanders at the scene," he spoke into his radio, tossing it

back onto the seat. He didn't wait for a response, but grabbed his flashlight and bolted out of his car.

It was chaos. He could see two officers standing on the sidewalk in
front of 144, talking with a woman who looked to be about forty, and
whose face wore the years hard. She was wearing a loose-fitting night-
robe that would partly open as she waved her arms wildly in the air.
T.J. thought he saw a pink, oversized hair curler fly off her head as she
wailed to the officers. Standing behind her, and crowding her and the
two officers, was a group of about twenty people. Several of them were
yelling at the policemen and pointing in different directions. One man,
barefoot and dressed in blue jeans and a dirty T-shirt, stepped forward
and pointed to the ground in front of the officers.

That's when T.J. first saw the young woman lying in the grass, clutching her left thigh and staring up at the dark sky. She looked to be about
twenty, and was screaming incoherently and violently shaking her head
back and forth. He couldn't make out anything she was saying, except
for the occasional expletive.

Chaos.

Officer Smith looked up as Sanders approached. "Glad you're here,
T.J.! This place is crazy. Can't get much sense out of this lady, other
than that she's the mother of the victim." He pointed to the shrieking
woman lying in the yard.

"How is she?" T.J. asked, taking a few steps into the lawn and kneeling beside the apparent gunshot victim.

"She's stable," Smith responded. "Large-caliber gunshot to the thigh,
and it looks like she's lost a lot of blood. But her pulses are okay, and
we got the bleeding stopped with some pressure. Didn't see any other
wounds. EMS should be here any minute, and more backup is on the
way."

T.J. tried without success to calm the woman while he quickly
examined her injured leg. She was holding pressure over the wound,
and the bleeding seemed to be under control. Smith was right—her
lower leg was warm and he could feel good pulses. But she had lost a
lot of blood—her lower leg and shoeless foot were stained a dark red.

It was when he glanced toward the growing crowd of people

surrounding this girl's mother and the police officers that he noticed it. In the glare of a nearby streetlight, he saw what looked like footprints heading up the sidewalk. Or more correctly, one footprint. There was only one of what should have been a pair, and from a distance of only ten or twelve feet it looked like the imprint of a left foot. It was red, and it faced toward him.

T.J. looked back down at the young woman and quietly asked, "Ma'am, what's your name?"

She didn't answer him but just kept staring up into the night and rocking back and forth. And now she was moaning, and murmuring something about Jesus.

"Yolanda Beeker." The voice came from behind T.J.'s right shoulder. He jerked around and found himself looking into the face of a young man who was leaning over next to him, his hands on his knees. As he stared down at the woman on the ground, he repeated, "Her name is Yolanda Beeker."

At the sound of her name, Yolanda let out a loud shriek and began wailing more shrilly than before, rocking with even more energy now. "My leg! My leg! I've been shot! Somebody help me!"

The man behind T.J. stood up and motioned him to follow. He moved back a few steps, and when the policeman came up to him, he said, "I was sittin' on my front porch when I heard the shots. Must have been seven or eight—I lost count. Not unusual around here, ya know. Gunshots, I mean. But then I saw Yolanda runnin' down the sidewalk, screamin'. Or more like she was hobblin', I guess. She was holdin' her leg and wavin' her other arm and yellin' somethin' about 'They shot me.' I came off the porch and got her to lie down in the grass, and then her momma came out of the house, and then…well, it didn't take long for the whole neighborhood to be out here."

T.J. was trying to put the pieces together.

"She said, '*They* shot me'?" he asked the man.

"Yeah, that's what I heard," he answered, shaking his head a little. "Or what I thought I heard. Didn't make much sense to me, but that's what I think she said."

They. That was going to mean trouble. There might be two or more shooters out there somewhere. T.J. and the other officers were going to need more help.

As if on cue, two more patrol cars sped up the street, lights blazing and sirens blaring. They screeched to a stop in front of the house, angling themselves to block the road.

T.J. looked again at the young man. "Which way was she coming from?" he asked.

Pointing over his shoulder and up the sidewalk, he answered, "That way. Yolanda came from up there somewhere."

T.J. turned and looked up the sidewalk. He could now see a line of single bloodstained footsteps that disappeared into the dark.

He took out a notepad and pencil and faced the young man again. "Can you give me your name and address?" he asked him.

"I...uh...uh..." he stuttered. "I've got to be going..."

"Just give me your name, son," T.J. persisted.

The young man hesitated, and then muttered, "Andy. Andy Smith."

The policeman wrote this down, knowing it was bogus.

"I've gotta go..." the young man said. Then "Andy" turned and quickly walked off, disappearing into the crowd.

T.J. didn't have time to pursue him, and he stuffed the pencil and notepad back into his pocket. Then he walked over to where Officer Smith stood.

"Jason," he said to him. "Come with me. I need some help."

Jason Smith glanced around him, noting the four additional officers who had just arrived. They were starting to quiet the crowd and move them back from the injured woman. And they all saw and heard the fast-approaching EMS unit up the street.

"Okay, T.J. What ya got?" Smith asked.

Sanders took him by the elbow and led him from the middle of the crowd to the sidewalk. They were standing beneath the streetlight, and T.J. motioned with his head, looking down. Smith followed his lead and saw the bloody footprints. He was standing on one of them.

"Good Lord!" he exclaimed, jumping back. Then his eyes followed the prints up the sidewalk. He reached for his revolver with one hand and his flashlight with the other.

"Just a minute, Jason," T.J. cautioned him. "There might be more than one shooter out there. The victim said something about 'they.'" He drew his own revolver as he said this.

Together they walked up the sidewalk, shining their lights into the blackness of the yards bordering the street. The beams bounced off porches and windows as the two officers searched around and under untended shrubbery.

The footprints led them on, and then suddenly they disappeared. The last print angled into the unmown yard of a deserted and run-down house. There was an alley on the far side of the house, connecting Stone Avenue with Archdale, the street behind it. Smith looked over at T.J. and silently nodded. They separated a little, by maybe ten feet or so, and headed slowly toward the alleyway.

They were more careful now, each sensing something just ahead. T.J. held out his hand and motioned Smith to stop. Then with his flashlight he pointed down at some broken concrete in the alley. There, clearly visible though distorted by the uneven surface, was another bloody footprint.

Smith nodded and they started off again. Without realizing it, they were both crouching slightly, their weapons pointed out in front of them at some unseen and unknown threat.

Just then, a car drove down Archdale Street, approaching them from their left. Its headlights played over the houses on the street and briefly illuminated their yards. And then the car was gone. But not before they had both seen it.

They stopped in the alley and looked at each other, seeking confirmation of what lay just ahead. T.J. nodded and they started off again, this time separated even more and walking more slowly.

At the entrance to the alleyway, on their right side, was a small brick house connected to the alley by a graveled parking area. In the momentary light from the passing vehicle, they had both seen a large black sedan parked close to the house. Sitting in the gravel and leaning back against the driver's door, and outlined by the light, was the figure of a large man. They could now see that he was staring straight ahead with his hands folded in his lap.

As they approached the car, a Mercedes, Smith shined his flashlight on the man while T.J. used his to search the surrounding area for anything moving or suspicious. Nothing.

Smith held out his hand, motioning T.J. to stop.

"You, over by the car!" Smith called out. "Put your hands on your head!"

They both had their weapons trained on the man, ready for any sudden threatening movement. He just sat there, staring straight ahead.

"You heard me," Smith called out again. "This is the police. Put your hands on your head."

Still no response. T.J. looked over at his fellow officer and motioned with his head that he was going to approach the car. Smith stood where he was, with his flashlight bathing the area and his revolver at the ready. The night was eerily silent.

T.J. flanked the car to the left, making sure he wasn't in Smith's line of fire. As he slowly approached, he spoke to the man. "Listen, buddy, put your hands on your head and do it real slow."

The man just sat there, and when T.J. was ten feet away, he stopped.

"Jason, come over here," he whispered hoarsely.

Now both lights were directed on the man by the car, and for the first time the two officers could see the bloodstains soaking his starched, white-collared shirt. His eyes were open and he was staring up into the night sky. They were open, but they were glazed and lifeless.

"Look at that," T.J. said, motioning with his revolver at the man's neck.

There was a large entrance wound just to the left of midline, right where the carotid artery lived. T.J. holstered his weapon and stepped over to the man. Then he knelt and checked the other side of his neck for a pulse. The pressure caused some air bubbles to escape from the victim's mouth, and the policeman reflexively jumped back, reaching for his revolver. Then the man slumped away from him and, in slow motion, fell to the gravel.

"This guy's dead, Jason."

"Kick that gun away, T.J.!" Smith told him, motioning to the .357 Magnum still in the victim's right hand. T.J. hadn't seen that, and he flinched in embarrassment. He carefully used his foot to move the weapon a safe distance from the dead man's fingers.

"We need backup in the alleyway connecting Stone and Archdale," Smith said into his radio. "And another ambulance. We've got a man down, no signs of life."

T.J. stood up and stretched. He felt something warm and sticky on his hand, and looking down, he noticed the blood covering his fingers. He cringed, and tried to wipe it off on his pants leg, without much success.

He was staring down at his fingers, when his fellow officer whispered, "Listen! Did you hear that?"

He hadn't heard anything, and now he strained, forgetting about the man's blood on his hand. He was listening carefully for whatever Smith might have heard. There was no sound except for the distant rumbling of the ten o'clock Norfolk-Southern as it made its nightly journey along the tracks at the outskirts of town.

And then he heard it too. Somewhere off to their left near the street, there had been a strange sound. It had been brief and faint, and it had sounded like a…maybe a gurgle.

He drew his revolver again, and both policemen started walking toward the source of this noise.

Smith was the first to see the sandaled foot sticking up over the edge of the shallow ditch that ran beside Archdale Street. As he put his beam directly on it, the foot seemed to move, just a little.

They looked at each other briefly, and Smith snatched up his radio again.

"We need an ambulance right away, in the alley! There's another man down, and it looks like he's alive."

As they carefully approached the ditch, T.J. called out, "This is the police! Hold your hands up where we can see them!"

The foot moved again, but no hands were visible. And there was that noise again. This time, it was clearly a gurgle.

T.J. reached the ditch first, and shined his light directly into the face of a man in his twenties. He looked up at the policeman with wide and terrified eyes, and tried to mouth something. All T.J. could hear was that same gurgling. Then he saw the bloody foam in the man's mouth, and as he quickly scanned his body with the flashlight, he saw the two huge holes in the left side of his chest.

Lying beside the ditch, out of reach of the victim, was a large handgun. T.J. couldn't make out the caliber of the weapon, but he made sure his fellow officer had seen it.

Just then, the man's right hand came up out of the ditch, reaching toward T.J. And there was that gurgling again. Then the hand collapsed back on the injured man's chest.

Thankfully, an EMS unit came screaming up Archdale, its spotlight searching for the officers who had called for help. Smith signaled them over with his flashlight.

T.J. and his companion helped the two paramedics pull the man out of the ditch and then watched as they worked feverishly to save his life.

"Rock Hill ER, this is EMS 2," one of the paramedics excitedly spoke into his radio. "We've got a gunshot victim, two large-caliber wounds to the left chest and a blood pressure of 40. No breath sounds on the left and…"

The other paramedic had been rechecking the man's blood pressure, and when he took the stethoscope out of his ears, he shook his head.

"Now there's *no* blood pressure. We've got two lines going wide open and we've got him tubed." He glanced around, trying to get his bearings. "And we're about five minutes out. Anything further?"

The ER instructed the paramedic to transport as quickly as possible and bring the victim to the trauma room.

While several other officers gathered around T.J. and Smith, the paramedics loaded the victim onto their stretcher, put him in the back of the ambulance, and sped away down Archdale Street.

Somewhere between Archdale and the ER, the young man lost any remaining sign of life. He was DOA at the hospital.

At a little after midnight, T.J. walked out of Yolanda Beeker's hospital room. He closed the door behind him and just stood in the hallway shaking his head. Incredible.

During the mayhem in the alleyway off Stone Street, a misaimed bullet had been fired in her direction, striking her mid-thigh. She had been very lucky. The bullet had torn through one of the large veins in her leg, but hadn't hit an artery or nerve or bone. She had lost a lot of blood, but she would recover.

"The doctor says I can probably go home tomorrow or the day after," she had told T.J. "But he says I'm gonna have a scar there, and that really ticks me off."

He wanted to make sure she knew there were two men dead tonight— and dead because of her. They wouldn't be worrying anymore about any scars on their legs.

Yolanda didn't seem to care. She had kept rubbing the bandages on her injured thigh while T.J. questioned her, trying to put the puzzle pieces of the night's events into some comprehensible picture.

Finally, he thought he understood what had happened.

Yolanda had been dating a middle-aged man from Charlotte—George Teague, the owner of the Mercedes. Usually they saw each other up there, away from Rock Hill. She had told him he wouldn't like her friends, and anyway, the clubs in Charlotte were a lot nicer.

The real reason she hadn't wanted this guy to be in Rock Hill was that she'd also been seeing someone else, someone much younger, who lived not far from Stone Avenue. His name was Manny Rivers. She didn't want the two to run into each other by mistake.

She'd been right to worry. Both men might still have been alive if Teague hadn't decided to surprise Yolanda this evening. Her birthday would be the next weekend, and he had bought her something special. He had been impatient to give it to her. And so he had driven the twenty miles to Rock Hill without calling her.

He knew about the alley connecting Stone Avenue and Archdale. He'd decided to park his car there and walk around the corner and down the street to Yolanda's house. He hadn't counted on running into her and Manny in the alleyway. They were walking toward him, arms around each other, as he got out of the Mercedes.

At first he didn't think it was Yolanda, though in the shadows he thought he recognized her silhouette. But when he heard her laughing, any doubt was erased.

There was a lot of shouting and some pushing, and then George had walked back to his car and reached through the open window. When he turned around, he held his .357 and pointed it at the middle of Manny's chest. Yolanda knew Manny also carried a gun, and she screamed and started running back down the alley. Then there were the shots.

It was impossible to know who had fired first and who had drawn first blood. What T.J. *did* know was that George Teague and Manny Rivers had killed each other. And after the stray bullet had struck Yolanda in her leg, she hadn't stopped to see what happened, but ran as fast as she could back to her house.

"I hope it's not going to be a big scar," she had muttered to herself.

∞

Six years had passed. T.J. was in his police car patrolling the south side of Rock Hill. His radio crackled to life, and then the dispatcher was speaking.

"Any nearby unit, respond to 144 Stone Avenue. Domestic dispute."

The address sounded familiar. For a moment T.J. struggled to place it—and then it came to him.

Surely not! What was that woman's name?

And then as if it were yesterday, he remembered everything. Yolanda Beeker. It was the same address. But this couldn't involve her. She must have learned *something* that night. And it had been six years ago. Maybe somebody else lived there now.

T.J. was near the address, and he answered the dispatcher. "Unit 42 responding. I can be there in three minutes."

"10-4, Unit 42," the faceless voice answered.

He pulled into a gas station on Phillips Street, circled the pumps, and then drove back onto Phillips in the other direction, heading toward Stone Avenue. This time he didn't have to search for the house numbers. He knew where 144 was located.

As he pulled into the driveway, he glanced across the surrounding area. It was mid-afternoon on a clear, bright October day. This time there was no gathered crowd, no curious onlookers, no bloody foot-prints on the sidewalk. The only people he saw were sitting on the front porch of 144. There, slowly rocking in a rickety wooden chair, was an older woman marked by years of care and toil. Standing on each side of her, encircled by her arms, were two small children. They were prob-ably two or three years old, and they were barefoot.

The woman didn't say anything. She looked up as T.J. mounted the steps, and with a resigned look in her eyes, she shook her head and motioned toward the front door. The policeman tipped his cap and smiled at the children. They just stared at him with round, large eyes and pressed back further against the woman T.J. assumed was their grandmother.

He stepped to the door and was about to knock, when he heard the loud and angry voices coming from inside the house. Reflexively he put one hand on the butt of his revolver and carefully opened the door with the other.

It took a few seconds for his eyes to adjust to the dimly lit living room. But as they did, he quickly figured out what was happening.

The screaming and yelling had suddenly stopped when he stepped into the house, but it was only a momentary reprieve. There were two people in the room, a man and a woman, and as soon as they realized he was a police officer, their hollering began again, this time with more insistence.

And yes—it was Yolanda Beeker standing in the middle of the liv-ing room. She was barefoot and wearing a cotton nightgown. In the pale light from a solitary overhead bulb, T.J. could see that the left side of her face was swollen and bruised. He couldn't understand what she was saying, but she was pointing to her face and to a young man sit-ting on the single piece of furniture in the room, an overstuffed and overused sofa.

T.J. heard Yolanda spit out the name "Aaron," and he looked in the direction of the sofa.

Aaron was sitting there with his legs sprawled out in front of him. He was wearing a T-shirt and boxer shorts, nothing else. And his right hand was clutching his left upper arm. The policeman glanced quickly at Aaron's arm and stiffened in amazement. He shifted to his right, trying to get a better look at what he thought he had just seen.

Yolanda was now behind T.J., screaming in his ear, saying that if Aaron ever laid a hand on her again, she would kill him.

The police officer tilted his head a little, and then just stared. A shiny metal object was protruding from Aaron's shoulder, wobbling in the air with each movement he made. T.J. stepped a little closer and suddenly realized it was a kitchen fork. Its prongs were almost completely embedded, and a trickle of blood was making its way down the young man's arm and dripping onto the sofa.

"Look what she did!" Aaron screamed. "She tried to kill me!"

"You lay another hand on me and you'll be gettin' more than a fork in your arm!" Yolanda yelled back at him.

T.J. didn't doubt that for a second, and he quickly scanned the room for other potential weapons, or a nearby place setting.

It took a while, but he talked the two of them down, or at least got them to the point where they could be handcuffed and taken into custody. He gave Aaron the chance to put his pants on, and then he took the pair downtown, where they would both be booked for assault.

As the group walked down the front steps of the house, the two young kids just silently stared at them while their grandmother looked down at the porch floor and shook her head. T.J. suddenly felt sorry for the woman and for all the years of trouble he knew she had seen. And as he looked at the children, he was sorry for the trouble they were going to see.

Later that evening, T.J. and his wife, Myra, were driving down Cherry Road on their way to one of the local steakhouses for dinner.

"You seem quiet tonight, sweetheart," Myra commented, concerned by T.J.'s brooding silence.

He drove with both hands on the top of the steering wheel, leaning forward and deep in thought.

"It's just that…well, it's just that sometimes I wonder what I'm doing this for," he answered her.

"What do you mean?" she asked him, looking over and giving him a chance to ventilate. He was upset about something.

"It just seems that we keep arresting the same people over and over, and dealing with the same problems again and again. Nothing seems to change, no matter what we do."

He never talked to her about specific people or circumstances, and he wasn't going to do that tonight. She understood this and didn't press him. She just let him talk.

He was thinking about Yolanda Beeker and her boyfriend Aaron. Or ex-boyfriend Aaron. He wondered how long it would be before he was called back to 144 Stone Avenue. But there were a lot of 144 Stone Avenues in Rock Hill, and they were all over town. Not a few of them were in some of the city's best neighborhoods.

"I just wonder if I'm doing any good," he sighed.

He was silent for a moment, and then she said, "T.J., you put your heart and soul into your work, and you care about the people in this town. That's all you can do. You can't fix everybody. Maybe you can't fix anybody. But you keep trying, and you keep doing your job. You know that better than anybody, 'cause that's what you do."

She put her hand on his arm and studied his troubled face.

He just shook his head as they drove into the parking lot of the restaurant.

The place seemed crowded, but a waitress approached them right away with two menus in her hand and said, "Follow me."

T.J. walked a few steps behind his wife as they threaded their way between the tables.

It was noisy, and if the man hadn't grabbed his arm, T.J. would have kept on walking. He hadn't heard his name being called out.

He stopped and stared down at the man seated at the table beside him. The stranger still held his forearm, and he released it as he stood up.

Myra had stopped and turned around just a few steps away. She moved a little closer, surprised by the interruption.

The man leaned forward a little and said, "You're Officer Sanders, aren't you?"

T.J. nodded warily, not recognizing the man and wondering who he was and why he had stopped him.

"Officer Sanders, I'm sure you don't remember me, but my name is Gerome White, and this is my wife, Melanie." He patted the shoulder of the woman sitting beside him at the table. She looked up and smiled at the policeman and then at his wife.

"I've been hopin' to run into you for a long time," White said. He was smiling, but T.J. was still cautious. Years of training and street experience had taught him to be that way. He felt naked without his uniform and holster.

He nodded to the man and waited.

"Like I said, you probably don't remember me and my wife, but you came to our house, probably fifteen years ago."

That didn't help T.J.'s memory, and he just stood there, studying the man in front of him, still cautious.

"My wife had called 9-1-1 because of…well, I used to do some drinkin' back then. Actually, a lot of drinkin'. And on that night we got into an argument and I had…I hit her. A couple of times. It wasn't the first time, and she had threatened to leave me if it ever happened again. That's when she called 9-1-1 and you came and arrested me."

Myra stepped over to T.J.'s side and gently put her left arm around his waist. She felt him tense a little.

"You handcuffed me," White continued. "And then you set the two of us down and started telling us about the law, and about what was going to happen. You told Melanie about the options she had. You said how she needed to protect herself from me. I remember just sitting there, drunk, but mad as fire. I was mad at you, but I guess I was mainly mad at myself."

He was nodding his head at the police officer, and he was still smiling.

"Then you said something that changed my life," Gerome told him. "It changed *both* of our lives," he added, looking down at Melanie.

"You finished talking about the law, and about what was going to happen downtown. And then you said, 'The problem here is that the law is not going to fix you. It's not going to repair or save this relationship.' Do you remember that now, Officer Sanders?" he asked.

T.J. shook his head, trying to recall this episode, but nothing came to his mind.

"Then you started telling us about the only thing that was going to help us," Gerome went on. "You told us how God expects us to live and how He wants us to live with each other. And you told us about Jesus and about how we needed to decide if He was going to be a part of our lives. You didn't say much, just a couple of things. And I have to tell you that it made me mad all over again. I didn't like it one bit, sittin' there in my own house in handcuffs with a police officer preachin' at me."

"He wasn't preachin'," Melanie broke in. "He was only speakin' the truth."

"I know, I know," Gerome agreed, nodding his head. "But it made me mad, all the same. Anyway, Mr. Sanders, I just want to thank you for that night. I spent a few days in jail, and I had time to think about what you had said to us, or mainly to me. And I had time to make some decisions."

For the first time, his voice broke a little, and he looked down at his wife. Melanie smiled up at him and took his hand in hers.

"We've been together for fifteen years," she told T.J. and Myra. "And while it hasn't been perfect, mind you, things changed after that night. Everything changed. And Gerome…well, both of us want to thank you for what you did, for what you said to us."

Gerome White looked back up at T.J. and held out his hand.

He cleared his throat and said, "Melanie's right. I've wanted to tell you that for a long time, and when I saw you walk in the door tonight, it was like…well, I knew I was supposed to speak to you."

T.J. shook his hand, and he felt Myra hugging his waist.

They said a few more things to each other, and then the impatient waitress led the Sanderses away to their table. They were both smiling as they sat down.

"You see, T.J.?" Myra leaned over and whispered in his ear. "You just never know."

Still other seed fell on good soil...

Matthew 13:8

13

Last Man Out

When a man becomes a fireman,
his greatest act of bravery has been accomplished.
What he does after that
is all in the line of work.

Chief Edward F. Croker, FDNY
February 1908

Thursday, 12:48 p.m. Mac Evans was checking his equipment for the fourth time since his shift had started at 7 a.m. He was again polishing his helmet, when he heard the sizzle. He turned around, looking for the source of the sound, and then he smelled it. Gardy Webster, the driver of Engine #3, was in the lounge, firing up his world-famous grilled-cheese sandwiches. Or at least they were famous throughout the Rock Hill Fire Department.

Gardy was a twenty-year veteran, and a couple of times each month he would surprise his crew by cooking lunch. The morning had been quiet, and he thought this might be a good time to get started.

Mac put his polished and gleaming helmet back down on top of his jacket and walked over to the lounge.

"Something smells pretty good," he said to Gardy, stepping over to his side and looking down at the oversize skillet.

"Uh-huh," Gardy mumbled, effortlessly flipping one of the sandwiches, causing the melted butter to sizzle angrily.

"Grilled cheese?" a voice called from the sleep room. It was Sandy Russell, one of the engine's firefighters. Known for his sense of humor and his dogged loyalty to his crewmates, he was everyone's friend.

Gardy looked over at Mac and shook his head, knowing that Sandy realized full well what was being cooked in the lounge.

"Nope," he called loudly over his shoulder. "Liver mush and turnips!"

"Great, that's my favorite!" Sandy answered. His footsteps quickly approached the lounge. As he passed through the engine-house bay, Mac could see him glance down at the neatly stacked pile of equipment lying on a bench against the wall, where the rookie fireman had left it. Sandy smiled and shook his head.

Walking into the lounge, he looked over at Mac and nonchalantly said, "I think you missed a spot on your helmet."

"What?" Mac answered in surprised concern, immediately turning to the door and taking a step in that direction.

"Hold on there, son," Gardy said, grabbing his arm. "Don't pay any attention to Sandy. He's just—"

Before Gardy could finish, he was interrupted by the piercing squawk of the station alarm. There were three quick blasts, followed by the familiar voice of the dispatcher. "All units respond to a structural fire at 35 Eastridge Road. Entrapment."

"Let's go, guys!" Gardy hollered, cutting off the range top and sliding the skillet to an unused burner.

They were all moving purposefully now, and Sandy called out to Mac, "See what I mean?"

Mac already had his overalls on and was fastening the buttons of his fireproof jacket. He knew what the older fireman was referring to.

Earlier that morning, Sandy had asked Mac to name the most important piece of equipment for a fireman. After a few unsuccessful attempts, he had given up, and finally said, "I don't know, Sandy. What is it?"

"It's the microwave," he had answered matter-of-factly.

"The microwave?" Mac responded doubtfully. "Why the—"

"Because..." Sandy interrupted him, "the dispatcher always seems to know when we're getting ready to eat. That makes the microwave indispensable if you're going to have a warm meal around this place. Sometimes we have to nuke our food three or four times. You'll see."

Sandy had been right, at least this time. As Mac tightened the strap of his helmet, he wondered how grilled-cheese sandwiches would taste after being microwaved.

"Come on, men, let's go." It was Captain Ben Fuller calling out to them as he climbed into the front passenger seat of Engine #3. Gardy Webster was cranking up the engine as Sandy and Mac piled into the back.

With lights flashing and siren blaring they pulled out onto Highway 72.

"Know where you're going?" Fuller asked Gardy.

"I know Eastridge like the back of my hand," he answered. "Used to live not too far from there."

The dispatcher informed them it was a single-structure fire and two other engine companies were responding. The call had come in from a neighbor after he saw smoke coming from some back windows.

"A couple lives there with their two small children," the dispatcher reported. "And their grandmother."

Sandy Russell was standing in the back of the engine, leaning out of one of the doors as they approached a busy intersection. The traffic light was still red, and Gardy Webster blasted the alarm a couple of times, notifying everyone around that they were coming through. Nonetheless, a middle-aged man in a late-model Cadillac pulled into the intersection, almost colliding with the fire engine.

He was only a few feet from Sandy and yelled something at him. It must not have been very nice, because the driver quickly followed it with a universal gesture of displeasure.

Sandy leaned out of the doorway as far as he could and slowly mouthed the words, "We're going to *your* house!"

The jaw of the Caddie's driver dropped, and his eyes opened wide in disbelief and shock. Then the engine sped through the intersection and was gone. Sandy turned to the flabbergasted Mac Evans and winked at him.

Within a few minutes, Engine #3 arrived at the scene of the fire. They were the first unit there, and Captain Fuller quickly had them organized and storming the blazing house. Twenty or thirty neighbors were crowding the yard, and curious passersby were stopping their cars in the street to take in the scene.

The man who had called in the fire trotted over to Captain Fuller. "The mother and one of the kids are out of the house." He turned his head and pointed to a cluster of people gathered under a large oak tree in the front yard. Fuller could see a woman sitting on the grass, cradling a three- or four-year-old in her lap.

"Who else is in the house?" he asked the neighbor.

"Johnny, the father, went back in after his little girl," the man answered excitedly. "I heard him say he thought she was in the back bedroom with Granny."

Fuller saw that Sandy Russell and Mac Evans were on the front porch and were heading through the open front door. There wasn't much smoke in this part of the house, and the captain didn't see any open flames. He called out Sandy's name. When he stopped and turned around, Fuller directed Sandy and Mac with hand signals to the back of the house, then let them know there were three more people in the structure.

Sandy nodded his understanding and disappeared through the doorway.

"How old is Granny?" Ben asked the neighbor, needing to know what to expect about her condition and how much help she might need.

"I'd guess she's pushin' eighty," the man replied. "She's in good shape, though, and gets out in the yard most afternoons with the kids. Just moved in a few weeks ago. Johnny and Fran have been doin' some remodeling for her, and…well, this is just a shame. They were all excited and everything."

Ben Fuller looked back at the house and could now see flames leaping through large holes in the back of the roof. There wouldn't be much left when this was over.

Two other engines had now arrived, and their crews were getting organized. Water was being poured onto the flaming house, but the fire seemed to be gaining momentum. For the first time, Ben could see flames through the front door.

Those guys don't have much time, he thought.

He walked over to check on the mother and little girl. Fran was coughing a little but looked okay, and her daughter was fine.

He was about to say something, when the mother jumped up and started running toward the front of the house.

"Johnny! Betsy!" she screamed, rushing to her husband and other little girl. Mac Evans was carrying the child with Johnny staggering behind him. He was coughing and rubbing his eyes, trying to get his bearings. The little girl seemed okay, and she only started crying after she caught sight of her mother.

Mac hurried over to Fran and placed the girl in her arms. She sat down on the grass, rocking her daughter gratefully. Johnny made it over to her and collapsed beside them.

"Betsy! Betsy! Are you alright?" Fran asked the sobbing two-year-old. She stroked her hair and hugged her tightly. Ben Fuller led the other little girl over to her family and then turned to Mac.

"Where's Sandy?" he asked him, looking over the firefighter's shoulder and back toward the house.

"He was right behind me," Mac answered, turning around. "We were looking for the grandmother, but we couldn't find her."

"Closets? Under the bed?"

"Yeah, everywhere," Mac answered, not offended by the captain's questioning. "It was getting pretty smoky, and parts of the ceiling were starting to collapse."

Just then, Sandy Russell burst through the front door and scanned the growing crowd of people. When he found Fuller and Evans, he hurried over to them. He was alone.

"What about the grandmother?" the captain asked him.

Sandy pulled off his mask and just stood there, breathing heavily. Then he leaned over with his hands on his knees.

"Never saw her," he said between gasps. "I looked everywhere."

Mac Evans could see the charred sleeves of Sandy's coat and the smudged and reddened parts of his face and ears that had been exposed to the fire. He had placed himself in too much danger as he tried to find the elderly woman.

The rookie fireman glanced up at the captain, wondering what he was thinking and what he would do next.

Fuller looked down at the father and said, "Are you sure Granny is still in there? Could she have possibly gotten out a back door or window?"

Johnny shook his head and stared at the ground. "Nope, no back door. And she couldn't have gotten through any of those windows. They're too small and too high off the floor." He looked up at Fuller with pleading eyes and said, "No, she's still in there. She's…"

He stopped abruptly when the captain jerked his head around and took a step toward the house.

"Smell that?" he asked Evans.

Mac stepped over beside the captain and sniffed the air. He could smell smoke, but that was all. He closed his eyes and tried again, focusing all his attention on his sense of smell.

"There! Smell that?" Fuller said again.

This time Mac *could* smell something other than the acrid wood smoke. It was faint, but there was definitely something that was…He struggled, not quite recognizing it yet. It was sweet and almost pleasant. Then he knew what it was—the smell of burnt almonds.

"It's cyanide!" the captain exclaimed.

Then he turned to Johnny. "Are there any chemicals in the house? Any paint or stuff you're using for the remodeling? Anything unusual you can think of?"

Johnny scratched his head and said, "No, we're just getting started, and we don't have any chemicals or anything like that. What makes you think it's cyanide?" he asked, having heard Fuller's alarming declaration. "Where would that come from?"

Mac Evans was trying desperately to remember what he had seen in the house that might have been unusual. Cyanide gas can be produced from the combustion of a lot of ordinary products, but he couldn't remember if... The rolls of new carpet! There had been rolls of carpeting stacked against a wall in the back hallway, and he remembered seeing one end of the pile beginning to smolder.

"Captain Fuller," he called out. "There's a bunch of new carpet in that house, and it must be on fire by now."

Fuller turned to him and nodded his head. "That's it!" he said. "Make sure that anybody else who goes into the house knows that."

Ben Fuller regularly hammered his crew about the dangers of cyanide—and that people don't usually die from being burned but from the toxic fumes and chemicals produced by a fire. Cyanide is a simple compound produced by the burning of numerous natural and synthetic materials, among which carpet is a frequent offender. When cyanide is released into the air and breathed in, it blocks the body's ability to use oxygen. The result is rapid asphyxiation and then death. If it doesn't kill you outright, you can expect headaches, dizziness, nausea, and vomiting. And you should count yourself lucky.

"Granny," the three-year-old suddenly whimpered, barely audible above the din of the crowd and the nearby engines.

"What is it, honey?" Fran asked her daughter. "What about Granny?" The three firemen looked down at the little girl.

"She's in the bathtub," she sobbed.

Sandy Russell was on his feet and running toward the front door, struggling to get his mask back on. He suddenly realized the grandmother must have climbed into the tub to try to hide from the spreading fire. That was the one place he hadn't looked.

"Sandy!" Fuller yelled after him. The fireman didn't hear him and disappeared into the flaming doorway.

"Doggone it!" Fuller muttered. Then he turned to Evans and said, "He didn't take an extra air mask with him."

Mac ran over to Engine #3 and opened one of the supply lockers, looking for a mask. It only took him a moment to find it, but he knew he didn't have much time. Cyanide was a quick killer. If they could smell it out in the yard, it must be pretty concentrated in the house.

He strapped his own mask back on and cinched it extra tight, knowing what he would be walking in to. He could feel the first twinges of fear as they began to tug at his mind, as they began to question what he was trying to do. But he didn't hesitate. He grabbed the extra mask and bolted toward the house.

Smoke was thick in the living room, and if he hadn't known the general layout of the house from his first entry he would never have found the hallway that led to the back. There were three bedrooms back there. And he would have to check each one, unless he got lucky and saw or heard Sandy. He passed the burning pile of carpet and grabbed his mask, making sure it was secure on his face. He tried to detect the telltale burnt-almond smell, but thankfully could smell nothing—his mask wasn't leaking.

The roar of the flames in the house was deafening. And then there was the occasional crash of a wall collapsing or a part of the ceiling caving in.

"Sandy!" he yelled as loud as he could, his voice stifled by the mask.

Mac listened intently but didn't hear anything other than the all-consuming fire. He didn't have much time.

Crouching in the hallway, he could just make out the outlines of the three bedroom doorways. Which one should he choose first?

Later, Mac would remember that moment and the choice he'd had to make. If he chose wrong, Sandy might not make it. Nor would the grandmother his partner was trying to save. All of that had flashed through his mind, but somehow, something else did as well. If he and his wife had their grandmother living with them, which bedroom would they give to her? There would be no question. They would want her in the room farthest from the noise and commotion of the den and living area.

Mac quickly turned to his right and crawled down the hallway to the last doorway. As he reached it, he called out once again.

"Sandy! Can you hear me?"

Nothing, except the sound of a window exploding somewhere behind him.

He inched into the room, peering through the dense smoke, desperately trying to find his partner.

There was another doorway in the back of the room that might lead to a bathroom, and maybe to the tub the little girl had mentioned. Mac decided to take a chance and spend what little time he had left searching there. He passed the bed, its mattress now in flames, and was almost at the door when he saw the foot.

It was a fireman's boot, lying at an awkward angle, and not moving.

"Sandy!" he screamed once again, moving as quickly as he could to the bathroom.

Sandy was lying facedown on the tile floor with his legs and arms sprawled in different directions. His helmet had been knocked off and was lying under the lavatory.

And his mask was gone!

Mac reached out and started shaking him, yelling out his name and then screaming for help. How could anybody hear him?

Through the smoke Mac could see his partner's blue and dusky face, but he couldn't tell if he was breathing. Then he glanced to his left, over by the tub, and saw a frail elderly woman. She was slumped against the side of the tub, her eyes closed. A fireman's mask was strapped to her face and she was taking shallow, feeble breaths. But she was breathing!

Mac grabbed her shoulder and shook it, trying to rouse her. Her eyelids fluttered but didn't open.

Then he looked back at Sandy's mottled face. He had only seconds to decide, but he already knew what he had to do. He knew it from months of training and from the constant instruction of Ben Fuller and Gardy Webster. But that had been lectures and sitting around the firehouse. Now he was faced with it—faced with this terrible decision.

He wasn't going to get them both out, and he sensed that the house was ready to collapse at any moment.

Mac leaned close to Sandy's ear and whispered hoarsely, "I'll be back." Then he turned to the woman, scooped up her tiny frame, and turned to the doorway. Her eyelids fluttered again but that was all—that and her feeble breathing.

He had just made it out of the bathroom, when he heard the voices.

"Mac! Where are you!"

It was Gardy Webster!

"Over here!" he called out, stopping in the doorway to the bathroom. He wasn't going to move until Gardy found Sandy.

Through the smoky haze he made out the shape of Webster moving quickly toward him. And then he saw someone else behind him. It was Captain Fuller.

"Here, give me that woman," Gardy said to Mac, stepping close and holding out his arms.

"No, it's okay," Mac said. "I've got her." Then he tilted his head toward the bathroom and said, "Sandy's in there, and he needs help."

Gardy bolted past him, and Ben Fuller stepped up close. "You okay?" he asked him.

Mac nodded, and then Fuller said, "You'd better get her out of here, and fast!"

The captain moved quickly around him, following Gardy into the bathroom. Mac raced for the front door.

When he got to the entrance, the living room was nothing but flames, and part of the roof had collapsed, partially blocking the entrance. Mac stooped as low as he could. And he managed to scramble onto the stoop. He almost collapsed going down the steps, and stumbled into the waiting arms of two firemen from one of the other engines. They took Granny from him and gently laid her on the grass. Two other firemen, both paramedics, came rushing up with their equipment and quickly began to assess her. In only a matter of minutes they had her airway secured and an IV going. As her family gathered around her, she began to gag and move her arms and legs. And then she began to fight the endotracheal tube placed in her windpipe.

She looked around confusedly. But when she saw Johnny standing over her, she nodded her head. She was going to make it.

Mac had been watching this from only a few feet away. He had ripped off his mask and fallen to his hands and knees, gasping for breath. For the first time, he realized he had a splitting headache. And then he started to retch. One of the paramedics knelt beside him and placed an oxygen mask on his face.

"Here, buddy—you're going to need this," he told Mac, helping him lie back on the grass. "And I want you to stay still and take it easy," he added.

Mac was still nauseated and had to lie on his side. In spite of his tight-fitting mask, he must have been exposed to the cyanide. What was that Captain Fuller had told them? "If you're still awake after a cyanide exposure, you're probably going to make it." Mac sucked hard on the oxygen.

There was a commotion in another part of the yard, and he looked over in that direction.

A group of firemen, their jackets partially open and their helmets thrown on the lawn, were huddled around a figure on the ground. One of them was kneeling, and as he shifted his weight to one side, Mac saw the body of Sandy Russell lying on his back in the grass. Someone was holding his head and bagging him, forcing air into his lungs. Another fireman had his palms on Sandy's sternum. His elbows were fully extended and he was feverishly administering chest compressions.

It was Gardy Webster, and he was sweating profusely. Something made him look over at Mac, and their eyes met. His face didn't change its expression, but Mac saw the hopelessness in his eyes. Then Gardy looked down again at Sandy Russell.

Mac fell back on the grass and stared up through the trees into the clear blue sky. His mind was a blur. Nothing seemed to be making any sense anymore. How could that be Sandy lying over there, fighting for his very life? Just an hour or so ago he was—

"Excuse me," the voice said, interrupting his tortured and confused thoughts.

Mac looked over into the faces of Johnny and his wife, Fran. They were both kneeling beside him, with their arms around each other.

"We just want to thank you for saving our little girl's life," Johnny spoke again.

"And for saving Granny," Fran added.

Mac didn't say anything, but just kept looking up into their eyes, searching for something else. But they didn't know. They had no idea of the sacrifice Sandy Russell had made for them, and that he was lying dead in another part of their yard.

Fran leaned over and patted him on the shoulder. "Thank you," she said. Then they stood up and walked away.

Mac closed his eyes for a moment, his world still reeling. Then he propped himself on his elbow and looked across the yard to the group of firemen.

They were motionless now. Gardy Webster was still at Sandy's side, but was sitting back in the grass, his arms locked around his knees. He was slowly rocking from side to side. Captain Fuller stood behind him, rubbing his eyes and staring at the lifeless body of his crewmate.

The other firemen slowly stood up and silently drifted away, leaving the two men with their partner.

Mac lay back again in the grass, and gazed up into the empty sky.

14

Bound Together

No cord or cable can draw so forcibly,
or bind so fast,
as love can do with a single thread.

ROBERT BURTON (1577–1640)

E MS 3, respond code 1 to 1400 East Bridge Street. Reference chest
pain."

The dispatcher's voice startled Archie Joiner and Sam Weathers.
They had returned to the EMS station not long ago, from a call on the
interstate. It had been a minor accident, with a couple of people needing transportation to the ER. Nothing serious, but it had taken up
most of the morning.

Now they had been trying to fix some lunch. In the kitchen, Sam
was studying his wife's "can't fail" recipe for lasagna, which he was
about to put in the oven after adding the last ingredients. He grabbed
his radio from the kitchen tabletop and pressed the send button. "Dispatch, this is EMS 3. We're on our way."

"10-4," was the response. "I'll get you some more info when we get it."

Sam looked wistfully at the lasagna, carefully put it in the refrigerator, and turned off the oven.

"How do they always know when we're getting ready to eat?" he
asked, grabbing his equipment bag and following his partner out the
door.

"I don't know," Archie answered. "It's just a universal thing, isn't it?"

They climbed into the front seat of the ambulance and belted
themselves in. Archie drove them out into the parking lot. When they

reached the highway, Sam flipped the switches for the lights and siren and they were on their way.

Archie glanced over at his partner and asked, "What's the problem? Indigestion?"

He had noticed him rubbing the upper part of his stomach. He hadn't seen him do that before, and he was curious.

Sam looked down at his hand, unaware he had been massaging his belly. He stopped, and quickly began to fiddle with some of the radio dials on the dash.

"Yeah," he answered. "That sauce for the lasagna was pretty spicy, and I guess I tested it too much on an empty stomach. I'm fine."

Archie Joiner and Sam Weathers had been partners for more than eighteen years. That was unusual for the EMS. Usually, a partnership would last a few years, four or five maybe, and then something would happen and the two paramedics would split and switch up. Which was okay. The team needed to work well together, to trust each other, and to complement each other's skills.

Archie and Sam did that. They had had their moments, but at the end of the day, they were close friends, and they enjoyed what they did.

That was a little unusual too. Both were in their late forties and had been paramedics for more than twenty years. The professional life expectancy of a paramedic is twelve to fifteen years. That's just a little longer than that of an ER doctor, which is around ten. About that time, the shift work, strain, and pressure wears you out, and it's time to find something else to do for a living.

A job change hadn't been a topic of conversation between the two, not until a week or so ago. They had responded to a call for a possible fractured hip. It was a woman in her late eighties who lived in one of the nicer but older sections of town. She had tripped over a loose carpet and fallen, breaking her right hip but fortunately nothing else. She had been able to crawl over to her phone and dial 9-1-1.

Sam and Archie had responded quickly, and made their way onto the front porch with their stretcher.

Archie knocked on the door and then tried the handle. It wasn't locked, and swung open easily.

As he stepped into the house, he heard a faint voice from a nearby room say, "I hope you're with the ambulance. I usually lock that door, but today I was in a hurry. I guess that's why I'm where I am." They heard her chuckle softly. "I would greet you properly," she added. "But I'm not getting around too well right now."

The voice was coming from the living room off to their right, and as they started in that direction, Sam said, "Yes, ma'am, we're with the ambulance. And we're here to help you."

The woman was lying in the middle of the room, actually looking pretty comfortable. She had managed to pull down one of the couch pillows and had propped it under her head. And she had put another one under her right knee, taking some of the pressure off her injured hip. Archie could see immediately that the right leg was shortened, an obvious indication of a fracture.

It was Sam, behind him, who spoke.

"Mrs. Rhinehart, is that you?" he asked in sudden recognition.

The woman on the floor squinted in his direction, studying his face.

"Sam? Sam Weathers?" she answered hesitantly. "Well, I'll be! And you!" she said, pointing at his partner. "You're Archie Joiner!"

Archie had been opening his emergency kit. He stopped and looked down, examining the face of this woman who seemed to know the two of them.

Suddenly he recognized her. Lying on the living-room floor at his feet was their first-grade teacher, Sarah Rhinehart.

"Mrs. Rhinehart…" he stammered in disbelief. The two men hadn't seen this woman in more than forty years, but there was no doubt who she was. She wore her hair in the same style, only now it was completely white. And her eyes were the same. And that voice! They should have recognized it immediately. How many times had she called them down? How many times had she singled them out as the misbehaving culprits in the back of the classroom?

"My, my!" she said wistfully. "How long has it been?"

They had gently splinted her injured leg, loaded her onto their stretcher, and taken her to the hospital. She was operated on that afternoon, and would do well. Her life was going to change, though. She would be in rehab for a while, and her out-of-town children weren't going to let her live by herself anymore.

Later that night, during a quiet stretch of the evening, Archie and Sam had had a chance to talk about Sarah Rhinehart.

"You know, Sam," Archie had said. "You're getting to be pretty old."

"Me?" Sam answered incredulously. He glanced over at Archie. For the first time, he noticed the crow's feet beginning to announce themselves at the edges of his partner's eyes. And where had those gray areas around his temples come from?

He knew what was on Archie's mind. Sam thought for a moment, and then said, "That was really something, seeing Mrs. Rhinehart after all these years. She hasn't changed all that much, just…"

He paused, and Archie said, "She's old, Sam. We were in the first grade."

Sam nodded, and neither of them spoke for a moment.

"Where have the years gone?" Archie said quietly. "How did she get to be so old? She used to chase us around the playground, remember?"

"Yes, I remember," Sam answered. "And she usually caught us!"

They both laughed at this, and then were silent again. This was something new for them, something uncomfortable and gnawing.

They hadn't talked about Sarah Rhinehart again. Someday soon they would need to—they both knew that. But now they were on the way to a chest pain on East Bridge Street.

The cars ahead of them were pulling over to the curb, allowing the ambulance to speed down Cherry Road. They made good time and were at the dispatched address in under five minutes.

As they pulled into the driveway, the front door of the house opened. Out walked a short, plump lady of about sixty years. She had on a blue gingham apron, and her hair was tousled. With her hands placed squarely on her hips, she called out, "You boys need to get a move on! We don't have all day!"

Sam looked over at Archie and smiled.

"Better not cross her," he warned his partner.

Fay Leinfelt was the name of the woman on the porch. Her husband, Freddy, was sitting in a recliner in the living room as the paramedics entered the house.

They immediately walked over to him, and Sam knelt down, checking his pulse and starting to ask some questions.

"Tell me about this pain—" he began, but was interrupted by a voice just behind his right ear. It was Fay, and she quickly provided the pertinent history.

"Freddy smokes too much," she began, shaking her finger at her seventy-year-old husband. "And he barely gets out of that chair. I told him that one day soon he was going to have a heart attack, and it looks like I was right."

She had her hands on her hips again, her feet wide apart. She was an imposing figure, and Sam wisely let her continue.

"Well, he started having some chest pain a little while ago," she explained. "Burping, and all that."

"Now just a minute, Fay," her husband feebly tried to interject.

"You just be quiet!" Fay scolded him. "Let these men do their work, and I'll tell them what's going on here. And yes, you were *burping*."

She proceeded to describe the events of the early afternoon and her decision to call 9-1-1 for an ambulance.

During this colorful recital, Archie opened the emergency kit, attached Freddy Leinfelt to a cardiac monitor, and started an IV. He carefully placed the oxygen pegs and tubing around Freddy's head and into his nose, and then printed off a rhythm strip from the monitor.

Fay became quiet and stepped over to where the paramedic was standing. She could barely see over his arm, and up on her tiptoes she asked, "What do you see, young man? What does that tell you?"

Archie held it so that Sam could see the two-foot strip of paper the monitor had spit out. Freddy's heart rate was normal, a little over 80, and his blood pressure was good. But the shape of his electrical complexes was bothersome, and was suggestive of an acute heart attack. You couldn't be sure from the rhythm strip, but the story fit, and they weren't going to take any chances.

"Your husband is stable right now," Archie told her. Then he looked down at Freddy and said, "You might be having a heart attack, Mr. Leinfelt," he began to explain.

"I told you so!" his wife exclaimed from behind Archie.

"Hush!" Freddy told her emphatically. And for the first time she seemed to shrink back a bit. Her mouth was starting to work a little, but she remained quiet.

Archie went on to explain what was happening and what they needed to do.

"We're going to get you to the hospital as fast as we can," he reassured him.

Fay went quietly to the back of the house to pack some things for her husband. She would be following them to the ER.

The two paramedics took their patient out to the waiting ambulance and carefully loaded him into the back. They secured the stretcher to the floor of the unit. Sam climbed in with Mr. Leinfelt.

"I'll be riding back here with you," he told his patient. "How do you feel right now?"

Freddy folded his hands over his sizable abdomen and said, "I'm okay right now, I think. The pain is better. Maybe the oxygen is helping."

"Could be," Sam responded, making sure the monitor's electrodes were securely attached to Freddy's bare chest, and that his IV was running smoothly. Everything looked fine. They should be at the hospital in seven or eight minutes.

Archie walked around to the driver's side of the ambulance. He was about to climb in, when he saw Mrs. Leinfelt hurrying out the front door of the house. She was carrying an old and battered suitcase.

"You take care of my husband!" she called out, waving at Archie and then pointing at him. "I'll be right behind you!"

From inside the ambulance, Freddy heard his wife. He smiled and settled back on the stretcher.

"He'll be fine," Archie called to her, swinging into the seat and buckling himself in. He closed the door and reflexively reached up to adjust the rearview mirror. It allowed him to see what was happening in the back.

He could see the top of Mr. Leinfelt's head, and beyond that, his protuberant belly. On Freddy's left side, he could see his partner quietly working, checking on all the equipment and lines.

And then, there it was again. Sam was kneeling beside the partially lowered stretcher, and he straightened up, grimacing just a little. He was rubbing the top of his stomach just below the breastbone.

Archie backed the ambulance out of the Leinfelts' driveway and had just flipped on the lights and sirens. He checked to make sure everything was clear, then carefully pulled out into the street.

He glanced back in the mirror again. This time, Sam was gripping the stretcher rail with one hand, and his head was bowed. There was that same grimace on his face. Something was wrong.

"Sam, you okay?" Archie called back to him.

His partner looked up at him and said, "I don't feel so good. This indigestion is getting worse, and now it's..." He started rubbing his neck, indicating a new location of his pain.

Archie stared at Sam in the mirror, unwilling to think the worst.

The angry blast of a car horn got his attention, and he looked out of the driver's window. He was out in the street, lights flashing and siren wailing. And he was traveling five miles an hour. A car had pulled up beside him and its driver was gesturing angrily. He was rolling his hand in the air, as if to say, "Get moving!"

Archie raised his palm in response and nodded to the driver. He began to accelerate. But then he suddenly pulled to the side of the street and came to a complete stop. He switched off the lights and siren and twisted around in his seat, looking at his partner and studying him carefully.

Sam Weathers was sweating profusely, though the ambulance was comfortably air-conditioned. And his face had a pasty, ashen color. He looked up at his friend and partner, and there was fear in his eyes.

Archie Joiner had seen this too many times. His brain switched into a different gear, and he unbuckled his seat belt and started toward the back of the ambulance. Then he stopped, reached toward the dash, and grabbed his radio.

"Dispatch!" he called calmly yet firmly. But he heard in his own voice a growing sense of apprehension. "This is EMS 3! I need a backup unit at 1400 East Bridge Street. And I need it now!"

There was an awkward pause before the dispatcher responded.

"You need what?" she questioned, wanting to be sure she had heard his request correctly.

Archie shook his head and repeated, "I need backup and I need it now! I've got a heart attack in the ambulance, and I think Sam is having…I think Sam is having one too!"

He tossed the radio onto the front seat, not waiting for a response.

Sam had heard this last comment and just stared at his partner. He knew what was happening, and he had just needed to hear the words.

"I…I'd better put on some electrodes," he mumbled, clumsily beginning to unbutton his shirt.

There was something strangely comical about this, and at the same time touching. Archie couldn't help smiling. But only for an instant. His partner was in trouble, and he needed help.

In his decades as a paramedic, Archie Joiner had been through countless training sessions. He was certified in everything certifiable. And he had taught young EMTs and paramedics for a lot of years. But nothing in his training had prepared him for this scenario. He had dealt with multiple injuries from auto accidents, multiple gunshot victims, even a triple suicide attempt. This time he would be flying by the seat of his pants.

Quickly he was at Sam's side. He put his fingers to his partner's neck, checking his pulse. Nice and regular…wait! He kept his fingers in place, and there it was again—an extra heartbeat, and then another.

"Sam, I want you to lie down on the floor here," he told him. Then he grabbed a blanket from the shelf behind him and spread it out, wanting to provide at least a little comfort for his partner.

Sam did as instructed, sitting down and lying flat on his back. He continued to fumble with the buttons of his shirt.

"Here, let me do that," Archie told him, moving his partner's hands out of the way. With one forceful jerk he ripped his shirt open, exposing his chest.

"That'll cost you," Sam said, barely above a whisper. He wasn't smiling.

Archie looked around the ambulance and realized there was only one monitor. And it was connected to Freddy Leinfelt. He glanced at the screen, watched to make sure the rhythm was nice and regular, then he printed out a recording on a foot-long strip of paper.

"Mr. Leinfelt," he said to him. "How are you feeling?"

Freddy looked up at him and answered, "I'm okay, son, no pain now. But I don't think your partner here is looking so good." He nodded in Sam's direction and shook his head.

"No, he's not," Archie agreed. Then he reached out and disconnected Freddy's electrodes from the monitor, leaving the adhesive patches attached to his chest.

"I'm going to borrow this monitor for a minute," he told him.

"You go right ahead," Freddy said. "Do what you need to do. I'm okay."

Archie quickly placed a new set of electrodes on Sam's chest and connected them to the monitor. The small screen came to life again, showing him what he feared—what he already knew.

His partner's electrical complexes were more abnormal and distorted than Freddy's. And every few beats, there was an irregular and premature complex—the telltale sign of cardiac irritability and potential sudden disaster.

"What ya see?" Sam asked weakly, not venturing a look behind him at the monitor.

"It looks okay," Archie lied. "But I'm going to start an IV just to be safe. And I need to check your blood pressure."

He listened twice, making sure his ears were not betraying him. 82 over 60—dangerously low. He felt sweat trickling down his neck and upper back. Yet he remained calm and efficient and in control.

"Mr. Leinfelt, you okay?" he asked without looking up.

"Yep, fine," he answered. "You got any music in here?" he asked lightly.

Archie glanced up at this, looking at the man and appreciating his attitude. He had two partners now.

From somewhere outside, he heard the faint sound of an approaching ambulance—his backup. He felt himself relax a little, sensing just the tiniest bit of relief.

Suddenly Sam grabbed his arm and it all went bad.

Archie looked down into his friend's face and saw a desperate plea for help in his eyes. Then he looked up at the monitor, and his breath caught in his throat. Sam was in v-tach—ventricular tachycardia—an unstable electrical rhythm that could quickly deteriorate into something worse. It had to be stopped.

His blood pressure was even lower now, due to the ineffective pumping of his heart. It was beating too fast and this rhythm didn't allow it to fill properly.

This time, Sam twisted his head around and stared at the monitor. Then he looked again into Archie's eyes. There was still a plea for help there, but the fear seemed to be gone now. He understood.

"Do what you need to do," he whispered to his partner.

The ambulance siren was much closer now, maybe just outside. And it sounded to Archie like there might be two of them. But he had no time to wait.

He reached for the paddles on the defibrillator, just as he and Sam had done hundreds of times before. Then he set them down on the ambulance floor, slapped two jellied pads on Sam's chest for solid contact, and pushed the charging button on the defibrillator.

The machine made a whining sound as its batteries charged to the designated voltage level. At the all-too-familiar noise, Sam looked up once more at his partner. He nodded his head, settled back down, and closed his eyes.

Archie looked again at the monitor. Still the tachycardia, but the complexes were beginning to widen. That wasn't a good sign. It meant that Sam's heart was wearing out from the demand placed on it, and it would soon stop altogether. There wasn't any more time.

"All clear!" he called out, then wondered at his own absurdity. There was no one else in the ambulance who needed to stand clear. It was just Sam and him—and Freddy, who was in no condition to move anywhere. *Just habit,* he realized.

The doors of the back of the ambulance burst open and two paramedics stood staring in surprise at the scene before them. Archie didn't turn around. He looked at his partner once more and said, "Hold on, buddy." Then he pressed the buttons on the paddles and waited the few milliseconds for the sensor to detect the right instant to fire.

There was a dreadful thumping sound as the paddles fired their electricity through Sam's chest. He arched upward a little, not much. He grimaced, but his eyes didn't open.

Archie looked over at the monitor, hoping to see a nice, regular electrical pattern.

A voice from behind him said, "He's still in v-tach."

It was Mike Brothers, one of the paramedics on EMS 2.

Mike was right. The jolt of electricity had not converted Sam's heart back to a normal rhythm. Archie reached over to the defibrillator and adjusted one of the knobs, ramping up the voltage that would be delivered with the next shock.

"Here," Mike said, leaning down and reaching for the paddles. "Let me do that, Archie."

Without saying a word, Archie used his left elbow to move his would-be helper back out of the way. Then he again pressed the paddles onto the pads on Sam's chest. He pushed down firmly, making sure he had good contact.

"One more time," he said quietly. His partner didn't respond. His color was worsening, and there was a terrible slackness to his face.

Thump! The paddles delivered a stronger shock this time, and Sam's body arched up off the floor. Archie leaned back on his heels and looked over at the monitor, praying silently.

The line on the screen was completely flat—no electrical activity. The shock had worked and wiped out the v-tach. The two paramedics waited, unaware they were both holding their breath, their eyes glued to the monitor.

And then, there it was. First one blip, then another, and then Sam was back in a regular rhythm. Almost immediately his color improved, and then his eyes opened.

Archie reached down to check the pulse in his neck—good and strong. He wasn't out of the woods yet, not by a long shot. But he had survived this episode—one that easily could have taken his life.

Mike put his hand on Archie's shoulder and gently said, "Here, let us take over now. You've done your part."

Archie looked up at him, now grateful for the help.

He sat back and leaned against the side of the ambulance, giving the other paramedics room to do their work. It was a crowded space, with Sam on the floor and Freddy Leinfelt still on his stretcher.

Archie Joiner's shoulders slumped, and his chin fell to his chest. He was sobbing. He covered his face with his hands, not wanting to upset Sam. He was exhausted and drained, more than he could ever remember being.

There was a flurry of activity as the two EMS crews worked to stabilize Sam and reattach Mr. Leinfelt to a monitor. They were going to move the stricken paramedic to another stretcher and get both men to the hospital as quickly as possible. The ER had been notified, and the cath lab alerted. Sam was resting quietly, his eyes closed.

Something made Archie look up. He glanced down at his partner, and then up to Freddy Leinfelt. The older man had rolled onto his side and was looking quietly down at Archie Joiner. Their eyes met, and for a moment they were silent.

Then Freddy nodded his head and said, "You love him a lot, don't you?"

The tears began to flow down Archie's cheeks again, but this time he didn't cover his face.

He looked into the eyes of this stranger, this man who somehow understood him.

"He's my brother."

> *Treasure each other in the recognition*
> *that we do not know*
> *how long we will have each other.*

JOSHUA LIEBMAN (1907–1948)

15

Just When You Think You've Seen It All

You k'n hide de fier,
but what you guine do
wid de smoke?

FROM THE "PLANTATION PROVERBS" OF UNCLE REMUS
JOEL CHANDLER HARRIS (1845–1908)

Sharon Brothers was standing at the back of her ambulance in the emergency parking area of Rock Hill General. Her radio suddenly crackled to life.

"EMS 1, respond to Dave Lyle Boulevard, right at the overpass of Charlotte Avenue. Bicyclist struck by auto."

She slammed the back closed and hurried around to the driver's door. Flinging it open, she called out, "Joel, did you hear that?"

Joel Carver was sitting in the passenger seat of EMS 1, making notes on a large clipboard.

"Yeah, I did," he answered, looking over at his partner. "We'd better get going."

The engine roared to life as Sharon snapped her seat belt securely in place and switched on their lights and siren.

"That's pretty close," she told the young paramedic beside her. "Should only take four or five minutes to get there."

Joel had been riding with Sharon Brothers for a little over two months, the same amount of time he had been working with the hospital's EMS. He was twenty-one years old and had just finished his paramedic training. Randy Green, the head of EMS, knew from the start that Joel would someday be a good paramedic. But right now he needed some experience, and Green had paired him with Sharon, one of their most seasoned staff members.

They made a good team, and Sharon knew her role. She had broken in quite a few rookies in her twenty-plus years with EMS.

"You can never tell about these things," she said knowingly as they sped down Ebenezer Road. "Sometimes a bicyclist just gets bumped a little and crashes in somebody's yard—nothing bad. But then again, if a car is going pretty fast and really catches the bicycle…well, we've seen some bad ones."

Joel looked over at her, nodding his head in understanding.

"Traffic moves pretty fast on Dave Lyle," he said. "Especially coming around that turn. There are some blind spots there, too, even though it's a four-lane road."

Brothers quietly nodded her head, and carefully made her way through the intersection of Cherry Road and Oakland Avenue.

"Could be anything," she said quietly, wondering what they were about to find.

As EMS 1 turned onto Dave Lyle, Sharon and Joel had to come to a sudden stop. Several cars were pulled over on the grassy shoulder, and the right lane of traffic was completely jammed.

"Look! Over there!" Joel called out, pointing to a group of about a dozen people huddled together near a large maple tree. They were ten yards off the highway and were standing around, looking down at something or someone.

A teenage boy in the group looked up, saw the ambulance, and frantically began to wave to them. Others looked up and started to wave as well.

Sharon pulled the ambulance as close as she could, then turned off her siren.

"Let's go," she calmly instructed her partner.

"Over there," Joel said again, this time pointing to the other side of the road. A crumpled blue bicycle was lying on its side in the median, its front wheel irreparably bent but somehow still spinning. The bike had seen better days, even before its unexpected meeting with an automobile. It seemed to be held together mainly with duct tape and rust. Sharon noticed the twisted metal basket attached to the handlebars and the scattered aluminum cans on the ground around the front of the bike.

"Must have been doing some collecting and wasn't paying attention," she observed.

Joel was halfway out the door and heading to the back to get their stretcher and emergency kit. Sharon reached for the radio at her side and called dispatch, letting them know they were at the scene.

Together they hurried over to the knot of people standing under the tree. As they approached, the group began to move to both sides, making way for them. *Like Moses parting the Red Sea,* Sharon thought.

"Oh my Lord!" Joel cried out in shock and disbelief. He stopped dead in his footsteps, staring at a figure propped against the maple tree.

The suddenness of his outburst got Sharon's attention, and she quickly glanced over at him. Then she followed his gaze to the source of alarm.

Sitting on the ground with his back against the trunk of the tree was a man who looked to be in his thirties. His head hung down, cocked to one side, with his chin on his chest. He was skinny and wore a tattered white dress shirt that was four or five sizes too big for him. His blue jeans were spattered with paint and grease, and—

"Look!" Joel exclaimed. He was completely stunned, and his jaw hung slack, his mouth wide open. He was pointing to something over in the grass about ten feet away from this man.

It was his leg!

Sharon's head jerked around and she stared again at the man by the tree. This time she noticed his right leg was missing and his pants leg lay empty, crumpled in the grass.

Joel rushed over to him in a panic, beginning to open his emergency kit. Before he could set it down, some of its contents spilled haphazardly onto the ground, causing him to move even more frantically.

"Petey," a voice behind him pronounced. It was Sharon, and Joel thought she was much too calm for this situation. She should be—

"Petey," she repeated. "What in the world have you done to yourself today?"

She casually walked over to the man on the ground and put her hand on his shoulder. Sluggishly he responded, trying mightily to raise his head and look at the person calling his name. His headed rolled from side to side, and his eyes opened, though only to small slits.

When he was able to focus, he mumbled, "Miss Sharon, I'm okay." Then his head slumped back onto his chest.

As he spoke these words, the scent of cheap alcohol filled the air around him. Joel stepped back from the unexpected assault on his nostrils.

Sharon just shook her head, patted the victim on the shoulder again, and asked, "Are you hurt anywhere?"

Petey managed to shake his head from side to side, but never looked up.

"But what about his leg?" Joel asked anxiously, looking over into the grass again.

Before Sharon could answer, a middle-aged man in a business suit stepped up behind her and tapped her on the shoulder. Surprised, she turned around to face him.

"Ma'am, I...let me explain," he humbly began.

"I was driving down Dave Lyle, when this fellow here veered off the sidewalk and right into the middle of the road. I swerved to miss him and slammed on the brakes." He paused and pointed over to the median. "That's my car over there."

"Are you okay?" Sharon asked him.

"I'm fine," the man responded. "But I'm worried about him," he said, pointing at Petey. "I don't think I hit him, but he swerved again and ran up on the curb and then into that tree. He's been talking and everything, and I think he's pretty drunk, but I want to be sure he's okay."

"We'll check him out," Sharon told the worried driver. "And you're right, it looks like he's been drinking again."

"But what about his leg?" Joel asked with persistent concern.

"Oh, that," Sharon answered, nodding toward the grassy area. "Better go get it, Joel. He'll be wanting it later."

"He'll *what?*" her partner stammered in amazement.

"Yeah, he'll probably be asking for it pretty soon," she added, turning again to Petey.

"Asking for it?" he repeated, incredulous at her seeming lack of urgency. There might still be time to re-attach it, or something. "What if the surgeon needs it? Shouldn't we…"

"The surgeon?" Sharon asked, surprised. She turned to her partner, trying desperately to suppress a smile. "Joel, that's Petey's *wooden* leg."

His shoulders slumped forward and his mouth hung open.

"His…wooden…" Joel stammered.

Sharon and Joel had loaded Petey onto their stretcher and into the back of the ambulance, and they were on their way to the ER. He had only a few scratches and some tenderness around his left shoulder. Otherwise he seemed to be fine. He would need to be checked out and sobered up a little before being released.

Then Sharon began to explain the legend of Petey Brewster.

Petey had been an auto mechanic at one of the large dealerships in town, and a good one at that, according to people who remembered those days. Then, sadly, he had fallen in love with the bottle and grown accustomed to cheap whiskey—Rockin' Rye being his favorite libation. One Saturday night, having emptied a rather large bottle, he fell asleep near the railroad track that runs through the middle of town, and lost his right leg to the 2 a.m. Southern. He was lucky to have lived, and that was thanks in large part to the engineer who made an emergency stop and called for an ambulance. That was the end of his mechanic days. But it wasn't the end of his acquaintance with Rockin' Rye. For a variety of reasons he was never able to get a driver's license and resorted to an old bicycle as his mode of transportation. He had become quite proficient with his artificial limb. Every once in a while, he would have a bump-up and land in the ER. Fortunately, most of these episodes were minor, and he had never been seriously hurt.

Sharon turned to Joel and said, "One night in the ER, Lori Davidson said there's a special angel that looks over Petey. And she must be right. But one day, even *that* angel is goin' to get tired of lookin' out for him."

Joel glanced back at their sleeping patient and at the wooden leg lying against the side of the ambulance.

They wheeled him into the department, and Abby James, one of the nurses on duty, directed them to the ortho room. It was empty at the moment, and would be a good place for Petey to sleep it off.

"One of the doctors will be back in a few minutes to check on him," Abby told Sharon as the stretcher passed by the nurses' station.

The paramedics carefully picked up Petey and transferred him to the ortho stretcher. He didn't weigh much to start with, and without his leg he seemed light as a feather.

"Be sure to pull that rail up," Sharon directed her partner, pointing to the side of the stretcher. "We don't want him falling out and bustin' somethin'."

Joel nodded, pulled up the rail until it snapped into position, and then looked down at the snoozing Petey Brewster.

"He gave me quite a scare," he admitted to Sharon. "Seeing that leg over in the grass and all."

"Usually does," she chuckled. "The first time you meet him. But now you know."

They pulled the sheet off their stretcher and tossed it into the linen hamper near the door. Then they pushed the gurney out into the hallway. Halfway to the nurses' station they passed Michael Lewis, the ER doctor on duty. He had the clipboard for ortho in his hand, and was on his way to examine the patient.

"Petey?" he asked Sharon, stopping by their stretcher.

"Yep," she answered. "It's Petey. Seems okay, though—just a few scratches and bumps."

"Well, we'll be sure," Lewis said. "He's got nine lives, it seems, but I don't know where the count is."

Sharon laughed and was about to say something, when—

"Code blue—cardiac!"

It was the overhead intercom. Michael Lewis spun around and headed for the cardiac room and the patient who had just stopped breathing.

"Let's get out of their way," Sharon said, quickly pushing their stretcher up the hallway and toward the ambulance entrance. "Looks like it's going to get busy."

Things *did* get busy. The respiratory arrest in cardiac was only the first of the dilemmas facing Michael Lewis and his staff. Two EMS units called in, on the way with several severely injured auto-accident victims, and one of the local nursing homes was sending in an elderly woman in with fever and confusion. The waiting room was overflowing with people who wanted to be seen, and within an hour, almost every bed the department was occupied.

Meanwhile, Petey Brewster slept quietly back in the ortho room.

Abby checked on Petey periodically, making sure he was alright. His vital signs remained stable, and he was beginning to wake up a little. He wasn't complaining of any pain, but was requesting something to eat.

That's a good sign, Abby thought, walking back to the nurses' station. When she got there, she asked Amy Connors, the unit secretary on duty, to order a dinner tray from the kitchen. It would be awhile before Dr. Lewis would be able to get back to Petey.

The ER never slowed down that evening, with a dozen or so other ambulance cases, and a constant flow of patients from the standing-room-only waiting area. Abby checked on Petey Brewster when she could, and he seemed to be doing fine. He had inhaled his tray of food and asked for another.

"That'll have to do," Abby told him. "Anyway, it shouldn't be much longer until Dr. Lewis gets back here to see you, and then you should be able to go home."

He just sat there, scratching his chin. Then suddenly he asked, "Who's got my leg?"

Abby was walking out of the room. She turned around upon hearing this question, a little startled.

"Your leg?" she repeated, just to be sure she had heard him correctly.

"Yeah—you know, my leg," he answered, patting the stump of what remained of his right leg.

"Oh, your *leg*," Abby said, now understanding his question. She had forgotten about his being an amputee. She didn't know Petey Brewster that well, but when he came in this evening she had heard someone mention he was missing a leg.

"Last time I saw it, it was flyin' through the air and landed over in a ditch," he mused, now rubbing the top of his head. "Need that thing, for sure," he added.

"I'll check with EMS," Abby responded, smiling a little, and then turning again to the doorway. "I'm sure they know where it is."

"Umm," he muttered as she walked up the hall.

He's going to be fine, Abby thought. He was fairly alert now, and seemed to be in good spirits after having had something to eat. And he wasn't complaining of any pain anywhere. She just hoped Dr. Lewis could get back there to check him out and get him on his way. They would need that bed before the night was over.

Forty-five minutes later she was standing at the nurses' station, when Sharon Brothers and Joel Carver pushed their stretcher through the ambulance doors.

"What ya got?" Amy Connors called out from behind the counter.

Abby walked over to the stretcher and looked down at the young man lying there. He was tightly gripping the sides of the bed, obviously in severe pain.

"Twenty-two-year-old, looks like he has a fractured ankle," Sharon answered. "Fell off a bronco over at the rodeo. And we need to get him something for pain. It looks pretty bad."

Abby noticed the cowboy chaps the young man was wearing and the awkward angle of his right foot. Sharon and Joel had placed him in a splint, but the ankle was obviously fractured and probably dislocated.

"One of the beds is open in ortho," Abby told the two paramedics.

"Why don't you take him back there and get him settled. I'll grab Dr. Lewis and we'll be right back."

"Ortho it is," Sharon responded, then headed down the hallway to the back of the ER.

As they entered the ortho room, Sharon noticed that the bed on the right had its curtain drawn around it. Someone was occupying it, and…Wait—wasn't that where they had taken Petey Brewster a couple of hours ago? Surely he was gone by now, and this was a new patient.

Then she heard it. The man behind the curtain had started to sing, and she immediately recognized Petey's voice. Actually, he was pretty good, and the first refrains of Percy Sledge's "When a Man Loves a Woman" didn't sound too bad. Then he began to slur some of his words, and the melody began to waver. When Sharon heard, "When she be bad, he don't shee it," she pulled the curtain aside and stepped over to his bed.

"Petey?" she exclaimed, her nose suddenly assaulted once more by the odor of bad booze. "What in the…"

Petey Brewster was lounging back on his bed, with his eyes closed and his head lolling from side to side. His arms were waving around in the air, as if he was directing a singing ensemble.

"She can't do no wrong…" he mumbled, obviously intoxicated. His eyes opened a little at the sound of his name being called.

His head flopped to one side, allowing him to briefly focus on Sharon's face.

"Officer…I didn't do nuthin'…" he mumbled. Then his eyes closed again and his head flopped down on his chest.

"Mm-mm," Sharon muttered, her head shaking from side to side. "Still drunk as a skunk."

She stepped back through the curtain, pulled it closed behind her, and helped Joel get the injured young man onto the ortho bed.

"Someone will be right back with you," Sharon told him as they wheeled the EMS stretcher out into the hallway. "And we'll make sure you get something for the pain."

"Thanks, ma'am," the cowboy replied politely, still grimacing.

At the nurses' station, Sharon dropped her clipboard onto the countertop and looked over at Amy Connors.

"Now don't that beat all," she sighed.

"What?" Amy asked, looking up from behind the counter. "What are you talkin' about?"

"Petey Brewster," Sharon answered, starting to write on the chart of Petey's young roommate back in ortho.

"We left him here a couple of hours ago, pretty much drunk," she continued. "And doggone if he isn't *still* drunk…maybe even more so."

"He's what?" Abby James asked, walking up behind Sharon. She had heard this last part and was confused. "I was back there just a little while ago, and he was sitting up eating and even asking for more food. He was sober—"

"Well he's drunk *now*," Sharon interrupted. "I take it back. He's plastered."

Amy Connors chuckled at this and remarked, "That's Petey Brewster alright."

"That can't be, Sharon," Abby persisted. "He was awake and—"

"Go see for yourself," Sharon told her. "And if he's not drunk, I'll… take myself back there and give him a great big kiss right on his lips."

Amy Connors shuddered at this thought and muttered, "Ooo, I don't know about that."

Abby spun around and headed toward ortho. With a determined look, she glanced back over her shoulder and said, "I'm going to find out for myself."

When she walked into ortho, she immediately smelled alcohol. Glancing quickly over at the young man that had just been brought in, she could tell he was completely sober. Smiling briefly at him, she stepped over to where Petey was lying behind the closed curtains. Pulling them aside, she stepped over to his bed.

"What the…!"

Abby James couldn't believe what she was seeing. Petey Brewster was lying on the stretcher with his sheet pulled down to his knees—or where his knees should have been. His right leg was of course missing, but…his left leg was gone as well! In his lap was another wooden leg, his left one. And from the hollowed-out upper part of it, where his thigh should have been, he was withdrawing a half-empty fifth of Rockin' Rye.

His eyes were closed, and he was starting to lick his lips when Abby reached over and snatched the bottle of whiskey out of his hands. And then, without thinking, she grabbed his wooden leg.

"Petey Brewster!" she exclaimed. No more words came to her, and she turned, pulled the curtain closed behind her, and marched up the hall to the nurses' station.

Sharon and Joel were still standing there, and they looked over as she huffed her way to the counter beside them. She slammed the artificial leg down and then unceremoniously placed the bottle of Rockin' Rye in front of Sharon.

"What in the world?" Sharon said, looking from the bottle to the leg, then back again.

"Let me see that," Amy Connors said, standing and picking up the prosthesis. Then she picked up the bottle, and after a few maneuvers said, "Well, will you look at this!"

She inserted the whiskey bottle into the cavity that Petey had created, then held the leg upright. It fit perfectly, snugly enough not to rattle around and break.

"Now that's pretty ingenious," she declared.

"Well, I never," Sharon said, awestruck. "How did he—"

"I never knew he had *two* wooden legs," Amy remarked. "I wonder when *that* happened."

"I don't know either, but he must have been partyin' hearty back there in ortho," Sharon opined, laughing.

"I told you he was sobering up awhile ago." Abby shook her head as she began to realize what had been happening behind those curtains.

"Well, he might have been, but he's not now," Sharon reluctantly allowed. "But I sure ain't gonna kiss him."

Amy chuckled, and was about to say something when—

"I want my legs!"

They all looked toward the end of the hallway.

Then suddenly, there it was again—but louder.

"I want my legs! Who's got 'em?"

As the group at the nurses' station watched, several heads started peeping out from behind closed curtains. Wide-eyed with curiosity as to the source of this pitiful and persistent request, they began to sheepishly look up and down the hallway.

Then it happened. Petey came out of the ortho room and into full view, accompanied by scattered gasps from the growing audience.

Sharon looked over at Abby in amazement, and then stared back down the hall.

"I want my legs back!" he bellowed again. "And I want 'em RIGHT NOW!"

His voice was getting louder, and more agitated…and closer!

Petey Brewster was coming up the hallway and coming fast! He was planting his hands in front of him, swinging his trunk forward, landing on the stumps of his thighs, and then repeating this awkward but effective maneuver.

"Good Lord!" Amy Connors exclaimed. "He looks just like R2-D2!"

One of the staff from the kitchen came out of room 5, carrying a dinner tray. As she turned the corner, there was Petey.

He looked up at her and hollered, "Give me back my legs!"

The tray went up in the air, uneaten food flying toward the ceiling. As the utensils, plate, and tray crashed loudly to the floor, Petey never flinched. Sharon thought he might have smiled a little when the woman screamed, waved her hands over her head, and ran toward the back of the department.

Then Petey resumed his relentless march toward the nurses' station.

Sharon, Abby, and Amy watched in disbelief—speechless, and not knowing what to do.

Suddenly, like the Archangel Michael swooping down onto the field of battle, Jeff Ryan stepped out of triage, where he had been assigned to work this evening. Quickly assessing the situation, this gentle mountain of a man strode toward Petey Brewster and effortlessly scooped him up. Holding him under one huge arm, he walked back down the hallway.

"GIVE ME BACK MY LEGS!" Petey persisted, his arms and thighs flailing in protest as he disappeared into ortho.

And then there was silence. Sharon and Abby looked at each other, and Amy Connors just shook her head.

The elderly wife of the patient in cardiac had been leaning out into the hallway and silently watching all that had just transpired.

"Stars and garters," she quietly declared. Then she stepped back into the room and pulled the curtain closed behind her.

*Apparently there is nothing
that cannot happen.*

MARK TWAIN (1835–1910)

16

Deliverance

The first question which the priest and Levite asked was:
"If I stop to help this man, what will happen to me?"
But…the Good Samaritan reversed the question:
"If I do not stop to help this man,
what will happen to him?"

MARTIN LUTHER KING JR. (1929–1968)

Tuesday, 9:48 p.m. Richard Blanton was standing at the nurses' station when patrolman Pete Jeter shuffled clumsily through the triage entrance to the ER. Richard was the overnight doc and was finishing up the chart of his patient in room 5, a three-year-old with an ear infection.

He looked up when he heard the unit secretary suddenly exclaim, "Good Lord, Pete! What happened to you?"

Amy Connors was staring wide-eyed over Richard's shoulder, and Dr. Blanton turned, following her gaze. When he saw Pete Jeter, he immediately understood Amy's reaction.

Lori Davidson, the triage nurse, was helping Pete into the department, steadying him with one hand on his left elbow and her other on his shoulder. He was a bloody mess.

The two stopped in front of Richard, and Pete looked up at him, trying to smile. As he did so, the ragged gash of his upper lip rose a little, revealing several fractured teeth. Blood was streaming down his forehead and into his eyes, apparently coming from an open wound in his scalp. He was holding a blood-soaked towel on the top of his head wound in an unsuccessful attempt to stop the bleeding.

Pete's highway-patrolman uniform was torn in several places, and the knees of his trousers were abraded and grass-stained. He was trying to say something to Richard but his mouth wasn't working. He winced and grabbed his jaw with his right hand. There was an unnatural movement of his jawbone, and the doctor thought he heard a faint crunching sound. It was obviously broken. He reached over to the man, putting his hand on his shoulder.

"Don't try to talk, Pete," he told him. Then looking over at Lori he said, "Let's get him back to minor trauma. I'll be there in just a minute."

Pete Jeter nodded his head thankfully and let Lori lead him down the hallway. Richard glanced down and took note of the trail of blood spatters that followed them.

He turned to the counter again, picked up the chart of room 5, and put it in the discharge basket.

"Boy, Pete's a mess!" Amy said, shaking her head. "He must have been in a bad accident or somethin'. He's really busted up. Did you see his mouth?"

Richard nodded without saying anything. Then he asked, "Did EMS call anything in? Anything about an auto accident involving Pete?"

Amy thought for a moment. "No, there haven't been any runs called in for at least an hour or so. That's odd, isn't it?"

It *was* unusual. Pete obviously had a radio in his car and could have called for help. Something didn't add up.

"Dr. Blanton." It was Jeff Ryan, the nurse assigned to minor trauma. The big man was standing in the hallway, beckoning Richard with his hand. Then he disappeared into the room.

Whatever had happened to Pete remained a mystery, but it must be serious judging from the way Jeff was acting. "I don't know, Amy," Blanton said over the counter to her. "I guess we'll find out."

He walked down the hallway and into the four-bed treatment room. Pete Jeter was the only patient in minor, and he was lying on the first stretcher on the left, bed A. Jeff was standing at the head of the stretcher, pressing a stack of gauze to the top of Pete's head.

The patrolman looked up at the doctor as he approached, and once again tried to smile. His jaw must have been really starting to hurt. He grimaced at the effort and then gave up and looked down at his chest.

Jeff waited for Richard to get to the head of the bed, and then he removed the gauze from Pete's scalp. A pencil-lead-sized stream of blood immediately shot straight toward the ceiling, at least a foot and a half into the air. Jeff replaced the gauze, again applying pressure to the wound. Then he looked up at Richard, waiting on his instructions.

Richard had seen the bleeder and the laceration. It was almost eight inches long, with jagged and ugly edges. At the base of it he had seen exposed bone.

He glanced over at the nurse with questioning eyes. What could have caused this? What had he hit his head on in the car that would have caused this bad a gash? Jeff met his eyes, shook his head, and shrugged.

Richard explained to their patient what needed to happen next. He told him about the laceration and about the bleeding blood vessel. That was the first order of business—to get the bleeding controlled and then to close the wound in his scalp. Then they would start on his mouth and jaw. This was going to take awhile.

As Pete nodded his understanding, Lori Davidson walked into the room, leading a middle-aged man dressed in mechanic's overalls. He was gingerly holding his right hand, cradling it against his left shoulder.

Lori led him over to bed B, the stretcher beside Pete Jeter. Jeff leaned over and grabbed the curtain that separated the two beds. He was starting to pull it closed when the patrolman became agitated. He shook his head at the big nurse, then reached up and grabbed Richard's arm, pulling him close to his face.

Pete grabbed his injured jaw and muttered something to Richard. He was having trouble forming any coherent words, and when he tried to talk, blood splattered from the wound of his lip. The doctor couldn't understand anything he was trying to say.

"Slow down, Pete," Richard said, leaning toward him and placing his ear close to his mouth. "Take your time and try whispering."

When Jeff noticed Pete's agitation, he had stopped pulling the curtain. He was still holding it, and when their patient seemed to calm down, he started to pull it closed again. Pete looked up at him and started shaking his head again. Richard looked back at Jeff and then at the man lying on the next stretcher. Something was going on here—something that was obviously bothering Pete Jeter.

"Just leave the curtain open for now," Richard told Jeff. "And go ahead and set up a surgical tray." He looked down again at the top of the patrolman's head. "And you'd better get a lot of suture material," he added.

Jeff let go of the curtain and walked over to the supply cabinet, glancing back at Pete and then over at the new patient in bed B.

The doctor leaned down to Pete once more and said, "Okay, what are you trying to tell me, Pete? Go slow, and just whisper."

Pete nodded his head and jabbed his finger in the direction of the man in bed B. Then he murmured something that Richard still couldn't understand.

"Take your time," the doctor repeated. "And just whisper. I'll hear you."

Pete took a deep breath and squinted his eyes, frustrated with his inability to communicate. Then he looked up at Richard and whispered, "That man…" he paused, pointing again to bed B. "That man… saved…my…life."

It took awhile for Richard to piece together what had happened to Pete Jeter earlier that evening, but he had some time. It would take awhile to piece together Pete.

It was a little after 8 p.m., and Patrolman Jeter had been heading south on I-77, something he routinely did during this part of his shift. Traffic was moving smoothly, and he hadn't noticed anyone speeding or driving erratically—at least not until he saw the white Impala fly down the ramp from Gold Hill Road.

The car was moving fast, at least 75 miles an hour, but the driver must have seen the patrol car as he merged onto the interstate. He immediately slowed down and veered to the right, the tires on that side of his car almost running off the shoulder. He quickly corrected himself, and Pete could see him glance back at him in his mirror.

Pete pulled close to the car and just followed. He wasn't going to pull him over for nothing more than coming down the ramp too fast. But he was going to follow him for a while, just to be sure he didn't veer off the road again or display some other evidence of being impaired.

This was routine procedure—and nothing out of the ordinary. However, the patrol car following behind him did seem to be making the driver of the Impala nervous. He glanced back in his mirror again and seemed to hunch over the steering wheel. The next time he glanced back, he started to slow down. The speed limit in that section of the interstate was 65, and the Impala was soon doing 60. Then 55. Pete was having to adjust his speed to the slowing vehicle and was about to pull around him and head down the highway, but he didn't. The driver glanced in his rear-view mirror again and slowed down even more, this time to 45 miles an hour.

Something was wrong here. The Impala hadn't veered to one side or the other or erratically changed its speed. It had just been gradually slowing down, obviously bothered by the presence of the highway patrol officer behind it.

That's when Pete Jeter made the decision to hit his lights. The circling blue flashes signaled the man in the car ahead to pull over, and Pete radioed that he was making a stop. He gave the mile marker and the license-tag number. That's when he noticed that the tag was from Georgia.

At first, the Impala sped up a little, maybe to 60. But then, as if the driver had had a change of mind, it slowed and drifted off the road and onto the shoulder. Pete pulled in behind it, grabbing his flashlight after patting his holster to make sure his revolver was snapped in place.

As he got out of his patrol car, he swept his flashlight beam over the rear window of the Impala, confirming that there was only one person inside. Pete approached the car carefully, from the driver's side. As the door ahead of him began to open, he called out, "Stay in your vehicle!"

The door stopped moving, and Pete continued to walk toward the car. Then the door began to slowly swing open again.

"I said stay in your vehicle!" the patrolman called out again, stopping where he stood and putting his hand on the butt of his pistol.

He had to steady his hat as the rush of wind from a passing car almost knocked it off.

"It's okay, officer," a man's voice spoke from the darkness within the Impala. "Look, here're my hands."

Two large hands protruded from the car, and then a heavyset man awkwardly stepped out. He was at least six-foot-four and a lot bigger than Pete Jeter.

"Get back in the car!" Pete insisted, now drawing his revolver and pointing it at the man. Both of his hands were occupied, and he used his right elbow to locate his radio. It should have been attached to his belt, but it wasn't there. He had left it in the car.

The driver started walking toward him, slowly, while keeping his eyes fixed on the barrel of the weapon.

"Get your hands on your head and get back in the car!" the patrolman ordered him, raising his gun to eye level.

This seemed to get the man's attention. He stopped his advance and halfheartedly raised his hands to shoulder height.

Pete Jeter had been trained for this, and he was prepared to take this man down if it came to that. But he had never had to shoot anyone, and he didn't want to now. He tried once again to convince the man to cooperate.

"Get back in the…"

It was a faint noise, barely heard between the whooshes of the passing cars, but Pete had heard it. He was standing near the back of the Impala, and the sound seemed to have come from inside the trunk.

There it was again. A thump, and then another. And then a muffled sort of…scream.

The driver of the car had heard the noise too, and when Pete took his eyes off him and glanced down at the trunk, he sprang forward.

He moved with an agility unusual for his size, and unanticipated. He was on top of the patrolman in a split second and easily knocked him to the ground, the pistol flying into the ditch. Then the man reached behind him and snatched the small crowbar he had tucked into his belt.

The fall had stunned Pete, and he lay on his back, trying to clear his head. Still holding his flashlight, he tried to ward off the man now straddling him. The driver easily pinned his arm to the ground and then struck a crushing blow to the top of his head. Pete almost lost consciousness and tried to free himself by rolling from side to side. It didn't work, and the man struck him in the face with the crowbar, splitting his lip and shattering his jaw.

Pete knew he was going to die, but all he wanted was for the searing pain in his face to stop. He tried to struggle against this unknown assailant, but he could no longer raise his arms. He thought of his wife, and of his little boy, and of—

Then suddenly, from some distant and cloudy place, he thought he heard a yell, or a scream. And just as suddenly, the crushing weight of his assailant was somehow gone and he was able to breathe. He looked up at the night sky and saw a half-moon and millions of stars, and he felt the chill of the evening air on his face, and though he tried desperately, he couldn't move.

Somewhere behind him, he heard the sound of men's voices, angry and threatening. And somehow he knew it was the sound of a determined and deadly struggle.

Jasper Willingham had been driving his eighteen-wheeler down the interstate, when he had seen Pete's patrol-car lights flashing up ahead. He had slowed, trying to give the patrolman some space as he passed by. He had seen the white Impala, and in the instant he passed the two cars, he thought he had seen two men on the ground, violently thrashing about.

The trucker didn't hesitate. He hit the switch of his emergency flashers and pulled off the highway as quickly as he could. Looking around his cab, he tried to locate anything that could be used as a weapon. He grabbed his flashlight, jumped out, and began running back toward the Impala and the flashing blue lights. As he ran, he struck the handle of the flashlight against his left palm. It was heavy and solid and it would work. It was all he had.

Jasper was fifty-two years old and hadn't done any running in quite awhile, but he covered the hundred or so yards like a much younger man. As he ran down the side of the interstate, the headlights of passing vehicles nearly blinded him. A few blasted their horns at this strange vision, but no one stopped.

He reached the front of the Impala and slowed to a walk. Behind the car, he could hear someone moaning and then an awful, crunching sound as metal struck flesh and bone. He raised the flashlight in his right hand and hurried around the vehicle. The lights of the patrol car lit the scene as if it were a play. He could see the patrolman lying on the ground, on his back, his face bloodied. There was a giant of a man sitting on his chest, raising an arm into the air. And then he saw the crowbar, dripping blood and poised to deliver another deadly blow.

Jasper took a couple of strides toward the attacker, and with all of his strength, he struck him on the back of his head. It was a sickening sensation, and the trucker expected the man to fall over unconscious, if not dead. He didn't. He lowered the crowbar and turned to him, staring with a fiery anger into Jasper's eyes. He seemed totally unaffected by the blow. Then he started to shift his weight, readying himself to come after this uninvited intruder.

Jasper didn't wait. He raised the flashlight again, and this time he swung with all of his might and all of his weight. His feet came off the ground as he struck the left side of the man's face, just below the ear. He heard a crunching sound and heard the man grunt loudly. Something snapped in his right hand. Jasper heard it more than felt it. He raised his arm again and was ready to strike another blow, when the driver slumped and then fell over onto his side, freeing the patrolman beneath him.

The trucker stood over the man, ready to hit him again if he so much as moved. But he just lay there. He was breathing, but it was an awful, gurgling sound.

Then Jasper stepped over to the officer and bent down. "Are you okay?"

The patrolman had been staring straight up into the sky, and when

Jasper spoke to him, Pete's eyes slowly moved until they found his. He tried to smile, and then shook his head. He wasn't.

Richard Blanton had been sitting on his rolling stool, transfixed as he listened to Jasper tell the story. Then he looked down again at Pete and put the final stitches in his lip.

Jeff Ryan walked into the room, followed by two of Pete's fellow highway patrolmen. They took their hats off as they approached his stretcher.

"Pete," one of them spoke. "Are you going to be alright?"

The other officer looked over at Dr. Blanton. Richard nodded his head and said, "Pete's a pretty tough guy. He's going to need to have his jaw wired, and he'll have a headache for a few days. But he's going to be okay."

They seemed to relax when they heard this, and then one glanced over to where Jasper was lying.

"I guess you heard what this man did," one of the officers said to Richard.

"I was just getting all the details," he responded. "Pretty amazing."

"Well, you haven't heard all of it," the officer said, patting the injured patrolman on his knee.

Pete looked up at him, waiting.

Richard shifted around, getting a good look at the man who had just spoken. The officer took a deep breath and then continued relating the events out on the interstate.

Not long after Jasper had subdued the driver of the Impala, a county deputy had seen the cars on the side of the road and pulled over. After cuffing the patrolman's assailant, he immediately called for backup and helped the trucker get Pete into his patrol car. When another deputy arrived, he found the assailant, still unconscious, lying in the grass on the side of the road. EMS was on the way and should arrive shortly.

Pete and Jasper were sitting exhausted in the back of the patrol car, when suddenly the injured patrolman motioned to the back of the Impala, mumbling incoherently and shaking his head.

Jasper understood, and he got out of the car, gesturing to the deputy. He walked over to the back of the white car, followed by the other man, and looked down at the trunk. He listened, but didn't hear anything. Then he tapped lightly on the trunk and waited.

He and the deputy both heard the sound. There was a thumping from within the trunk, insistent and growing in intensity. They both looked at each other. The deputy glanced down and grabbed the bloody pry bar that still lay on the ground.

In less than a minute the trunk was open and the deputy was shining his light into the well. There, bound and gagged, was a teenage girl. Her forehead was bruised from where she had desperately been banging the roof of the trunk, signaling for help.

At first her eyes had searched their faces in desperate and hopeless fear. But when she had seen the deputy's uniform, she had closed her eyes and begun sobbing.

"She was kidnapped just outside of Atlanta," the officer explained. "This guy grabbed her in the parking lot of a big mall earlier today. Who knows where he was headed? But Pete, you saved that girl's life."

Then he turned to Jasper and said, "And you saved both of them."

Pete just looked straight ahead, and slowly nodded his head.

"What about the guy who did this?" the trucker asked. "Did I kill him?"

There was no anxiety in his voice, just a quiet resignation.

"No, but you busted him up pretty good," the officer told him. "When the EMS got on the scene, they took him straight to the trauma center in Charlotte. One of my friends up there said he got pretty crazy when he came in. Started waking up some, and caused quite a ruckus. Had to be put down again, this time with some heavy-duty drugs. That must have been one big dude."

Both injured men nodded their heads, not saying a word.

After Jasper's broken hand was taken care of, he walked over to Pete's stretcher and put his hand on his shoulder.

"I'm going to look you up next time I'm in the area," he said quietly.

"Thanks," was all Pete could manage to say. It was all he needed to say.

And then Richard Blanton was alone in the room with Pete Jeter. They were waiting for the OR crew to come and take him to get his jaw repaired.

The doctor sat down again and leaned back on the stool, grabbing his left knee with both hands.

He was bothered by something, and finally decided to ask the question.

"Pete, do you think anybody else out on the road tonight saw what was going on?"

They both knew the answer, and it really troubled Richard that Jasper Willingham was the only person who had stopped out on the interstate.

Pete looked over at him and did his best to smile.

"Doesn't matter. Jasper did."

But a Samaritan, as he journeyed,
came to where he was;
and when he saw him,
he had compassion.

Luke 10:33 RSV

17

His Hands and Feet

When God's finger points,
God's hand will open the door.
CLARENCE W. JONES (1900–1986)

June 1976. Lieutenant Cole Anderson pressed the doorbell button and waited. He and his partner, officer Charlie Kimmons, could hear the faint ringing inside the house. And then they heard footsteps approaching.

The 9-1-1 call had been dispatched to any available unit. "Unknown disturbance" was the information they were given. Every other patrol car was out on another call, and Anderson and Kimmons were the only ones available to respond. They had come all the way across town to this house, curious as to the nature of this "disturbance."

The door opened and Anderson stepped back a little, his hand resting cautiously on the butt of his holstered revolver.

Standing in the doorway was a middle-aged man. He was barefoot and dressed in khakis and a T-shirt.

"Hello, officers," he spoke, hesitantly. "I…thank you…there's been a mistake."

"Is it the police, honey?" a woman called from somewhere in the house.

"Yes, Sarah," he called back to her, his eyes still on the officers.

"What seems to be the problem here?" Anderson asked him.

At this, the man looked down and began to shuffle his bare feet.

"Well, sir, like I said, there's been a mistake," he began. "My wife heard some noises in the attic and got scared. She said someone was trying to break in, and before I knew it, she had called 9-1-1. I had my suspicions, so I pulled down the attic stairs and took a look for myself."

He paused and looked up at Cole Anderson, hoping for some sign of understanding. Both officers remained stone-faced.

"It was squirrels, just like I thought," he stated flatly. "That was what was making the noise—squirrels. No one was trying to break into the house."

He stood silent now. And from the back of the house his wife called out, "What'd they say?"

The man cleared his throat and said, "So you see, it was all a mistake. I was going to call 9-1-1 again and explain, but one of those squirrels jumped down into the house, and we were chasing it, and…"

Lieutenant Anderson pulled a small writing pad from his back pocket and began making some notes.

"Okay, okay," he said. "Now, I'll need your name and phone number."

Anderson was trained to be dubious, but this man seemed to be telling the truth. And it did make sense. Still, he and Kimmons would need to check the house, just to be sure.

"My name is Arthur Dugans," the man answered. "And our telephone number is—"

A loud crashing noise ripped through the quiet summer morning. It was thunderous, and they could almost feel the reverberation as it echoed off the nearby houses. It had come from somewhere behind them, somewhere through the pine trees, and close by.

It was the sound of metal on metal. The two officers quickly looked at each other, immediately recognizing the awful sound of a vehicular collision. It had come from Highway 5, just through the woods.

Anderson jammed the notepad in his pocket, and he and Kimmons bolted for the patrol car.

As they sped out of the drive, Kimmons saw Arthur Dugans standing dumbfounded in his doorway, his curler-headed wife now peeking out over his shoulder.

Anderson flipped the switch for the patrol car's flashing lights and siren, and tore through the neighborhood.

"That was big," Kimmons said. "Didn't sound like a little fender bender."

Anderson nodded silently, trying not to imagine what they might find on the highway.

He came to the entrance of the Dugans's neighborhood, wondering which way he should turn. Immediately, he swerved to the right, toward the plume of black smoke that was drifting up from the middle of the four-lane road, about a hundred yards away.

"Good Lord..." Kimmons muttered, his eyes widening.

In the center of the highway was a smaller-size dump truck turned on its side. Its front end was crumpled and distorted, with smoke spewing from under the destroyed hood.

Seemingly attached to the front end of the truck were the remains of a light-blue two-door Chevette. Its front end was gone, accordioned into the passenger compartment.

"Must have been head-on," Kimmons said, as the patrol car screeched to a stop beside the tangled mess of steel and glass.

"Look," Anderson cautioned his partner, nodding to an expanding pool of gas and oil. "We're going to have a big problem in a minute."

They jumped out of the car and headed around to the other side of the truck. They hadn't seen anyone yet, and if anyone had survived this wreck, they needed to be found and moved safely away before the whole thing blew up.

"Dispatch, this is Officer Kimmons," Charlie spoke excitedly into his radio. "We're on Highway 5, just beyond the school, and we need backup. We need EMS, and we need the rescue squad. And we need them fast!"

He shoved his radio into the holder on his belt and ran to catch up with Cole Anderson.

His partner had come to a sudden stop just on the other side of the smoldering dump truck. Leaning against the top of the cab was the driver, a middle-aged man dressed in T-shirt, overalls, and work boots.

Blood was dripping from a large gash on the top of his head, and he was gingerly holding his left shoulder.

He dazedly looked up as the officers came around his truck. Raising one hand, he pointed to the Chevette and said, "You'd better go check on that guy."

The effort caused him to lose his balance, and he quickly grabbed the top of the cab to keep from falling to the ground. That was when Kimmons noticed his mangled left knee. His pants were torn there, and soaked with blood. And his left foot was planted on the ground at an unnatural angle. The policeman winced as he hurried over to the man and put his arm around his shoulder.

"Let's get you away from this rig and over onto the grass," he said, leading him away from the smoldering wreckage.

"You'd better check on that guy," the driver repeated, dazed and confused.

The policeman helped him down to the ground, trying to support his injured leg as best he could. Grateful, the man sat down on the grass. He reached up to the top of his head, felt the gash there, and then looked vacantly at his bloody hand.

Charlie Kimmons hurried over to his partner, who was now on the driver's side of the Chevette.

"What ya got?" he called out to Anderson.

"You'd better come over here," Cole answered, an unfamiliar foreboding in his voice.

Kimmons and Anderson had worked a lot of wrecks together and had seen a lot of bad stuff—things they didn't talk about. Charlie knew it took a lot to get to Cole, but something was bothering him now as he looked into the Chevette.

Kimmons got to his partner's side and looked down. He froze.

The dash of the car had been pushed back into the cab, almost up against the front seat. The car's driver, a middle-aged man with blond hair and glasses, was sitting straight up, his head lying back in the seat, almost comfortably. His eyes were closed. Kimmons noticed the unnatural appearance of his glasses. They rested on his nose unevenly, the right lens shattered and the earpiece on that side bent outward at 90 degrees. His face was a pasty color, and his breaths came in short, grunting gasps.

It was the steering wheel that caused them to stare in disbelief and horror. It had been driven back into the man's chest, impaling him and crushing him against the seat. All they could see of it was the steering column.

The driver took another gurgling breath and weakly raised his left hand. His eyes remained closed.

The two officers looked at each other, knowing they needed to do something, but not sure what.

Cole Anderson reached for the door handle of the Chevette, thinking how ludicrous this action must appear to be. The car was crushed, barely recognizable, and he was nonchalantly going to open the door and get the driver out.

To his surprised and amazed relief, the handle clicked and the door swung open. Then it came loose from its hinges and fell to the ground.

Kimmons quickly stepped in beside his partner and reached down for the steering column, trying to pull it one way or the other.

At the same moment, Anderson was trying to manipulate the seat adjustment in the hope of sliding it back, if only just a little.

Something clicked, and the driver's seat shifted. Then there was a terrible crunching sound as the steering wheel was pulled out of the man's chest.

There was just enough room for the two of them to get hold of the driver and slowly edge him out of the car and onto the ground. His head flopped uncontrolled to one side, and he somehow managed to take another shallow gasp.

"What was that?" Kimmons asked, baffled by the sound he had just heard.

Cole had heard it too, and he knew what it was. He had his hand over the man's carotid artery, searching for a pulse that wasn't there. He immediately reached down to the man's shirt and ripped it open, pulling it away as much as possible.

There it was again—a bubbling, sucking noise. There was a hole on the right side of the driver's chest, and each time he took a breath, air was making its way into and out of his chest wall.

Cole grabbed the tattered shirt and ripped a piece loose. Then he folded it twice and pressed it firmly against the sucking chest wound.

"Charlie," he said, looking up at his partner, "we need to start CPR. This guy doesn't have a pulse."

Kimmons was quickly down on his knees, placing his hands over the man's sternum, and starting chest compressions. He could feel a sickening crunching with each effort.

"We're going to need some help," Cole stated calmly.

Just then, coming from back toward town, they could hear the sirens of approaching emergency vehicles. Charlie looked over at his partner and nodded. Sweat was starting to drip from his face and onto the man's chest.

"Did you see anybody else in the car?" Cole asked him. "I took a quick look, but didn't see anybody in the front or in the back."

"I didn't either," Charlie responded, taking rapid breaths now, and timing them to his compressions. "All of the doors were closed, so I don't think anyone was thrown out of the car."

The man's color was getting worse, but he continued to take feeble, shallow breaths. His eyes were half-closed now and had rolled back into his head.

Behind them, they heard car doors closing and the sound of running footsteps.

Kimmons looked up thankfully to see two paramedics coming up beside them.

"Here," one of them said. "Let us take over now."

Anderson kept his hand pressed tight against the man's chest.

"It looks like he has a pneumothorax here," he explained to them. "This is a sucking wound, so we need to keep it covered."

One of the paramedics nodded and reached down, replacing the policeman's hand with his own.

Two other paramedics rushed up, each carrying an emergency kit.

"The driver of the truck is going to need some attention," Kimmons told one of them, pointing to the other side of the Chevette. "He's over there in the grass." He stood up painfully, stretched his back and legs, and then wiped the sweat from his face.

"Let's check the car out," Cole told his partner, moving slowly around the battered vehicle.

None of the other doors would open. But almost all of the glass in the car was shattered, and they had no trouble seeing inside.

There was nobody else in the vehicle, and nobody lying anywhere around it.

"Looks clear to me," Kimmons said as they walked over to where the truck driver was now getting help.

"You've got a really messed-up leg here," they heard one of the paramedics trying to explain to him.

The driver just nodded his head absently and stared over at the Chevette.

"I don't know what happened," he mumbled. "I must have hit somethin' in the road, and the next thing I knew, he was right in front of me. I tried to swerve, but it was too late...and then the truck flipped over and..."

He paused and stared off over the trees. Then focusing once again, he asked Lieutenant Anderson, "Is he okay? I can still see the look in his eyes...we must have only been ten feet apart when..."

"Don't worry about him right now," Cole told him calmly. "We need to get you taken care of first."

Then he turned to his partner and said, "See what information you can get, Charlie. But go easy."

Anderson turned and walked back over to the group of men huddled around the driver of the Chevette. Some curious onlookers had started to congregate around the scene, edging closer for a better look. Another police unit had arrived, and those officers were beginning to move the growing crowd out of the way.

"We'd better get this guy away from the car as soon as we can," he told the paramedics, pointing to the pool of gas and oil spreading down the asphalt. He had seen too many cars suddenly explode, injuring a lot of people, and he was starting to get nervous about the situation.

One of them looked up and nodded his head. He called over to his partner and told him to bring their stretcher over. Then he looked up at Cole again and said, "Rock Hill Rescue should have some foam they can spray on this. They ought to be here in just a few minutes."

Anderson stepped closer to the group and looked down. The driver of the Chevette had been intubated, and one of the paramedics was ventilating the man's damaged lungs while another continued chest compressions.

"Any change?" Cole asked the group.

A paramedic looked up and shook his head slowly. There was little if any hope for this man. He wasn't going to make it.

Anderson stepped back from the crowd and leaned against the side of the Chevette. He was beginning to form a picture of what had happened here, a painful realization of how terrifying the last seconds of this man's life must have been.

It never got any easier, no matter how many times you witnessed things like this.

His breath caught in his throat and he froze.

There was a sound he had recognized, but he couldn't yet place its origin. He listened intently, trying to block out all the noise around him. He had heard something, and it sounded like it was coming from somewhere in the car.

Charlie Kimmons walked up just then and began to report, "That guy's too shook up to tell me very much. We'll just—"

"Shh!" Anderson said, holding up his hand but not looking up. He was staring intently at the ground, concentrating all his abilities on hearing.

"What's the—" Kimmons started, confused by his partner's actions.

"Shh! Listen!" Cole told him again.

This time Charlie stepped closer to Anderson, not saying a word. He cocked his head toward the car and waited.

Nothing. There was not a sound, other than the excited voices of the men gathered around the driver of the car. They had managed to get him onto the stretcher and away from the wrecked vehicles, all the while continuing their desperate efforts to save him.

A unit from Rock Hill Rescue had arrived with their emergency equipment, and they had started to spray foam over the entire area. It was none too soon, what with the black smoke from the truck seeming to fill the sky above them.

The hissing of the sprayer made it even harder to hear, but Cole was convinced he had heard something—something important, yet…

Then the sprayer stopped, and it was suddenly quiet.

A whimper. Just barely a whimper. And it was coming from somewhere in the car.

"There!" Cole cried out. "Did you…"

"I heard it!" Charlie answered, immediately jamming his upper body through the back window of the Chevette. "It's a kid!"

He was pawing through the jumble inside the wrecked car, trying to lift the backseat, looking under anything and everything that might conceal a small child.

At the same time, he was listening for another sound, something that would help him find the child that seemed to be hidden somewhere in the interior.

Anderson dashed around to the passenger side of the car and glanced quickly through the window. The dash was pressed against the front seat, leaving no space for anything or anyone. He turned his attention to the backseat, helping Charlie move what they could.

Nothing. They had searched the entire back area of the car and had even managed to open the trunk. No sign of a child.

"Maybe we heard a hydraulic line leaking, or something like that," Kimmons ventured, frustrated by their failure.

"No, I heard a kid and they seemed to be hurt," Anderson resolutely answered, staring into the car. "There's a child in here somewhere."

He put his hands on his hips and listened.

Still nothing. Then he called out softly, "Honey, can you hear me?"

They waited.

After a bit, he looked down and shook his head. Maybe he hadn't heard a child after all.

"Help me."

It was the voice of a little girl, and it was coming from somewhere in the front seat. But how could that be? There was no space there. The engine and dash were collapsed against it.

The two men scrambled desperately, trying to pull the seat back and free the child from this metal prison. They ripped the seat out and peered into what used to be the foot space of the passenger side.

A tiny hand reached out for them, and they grabbed it.

Kimmons yelled over to the members of the rescue squad and they came running. When they saw what was going on, two of them ran back to their truck for some special equipment. Within minutes, the little girl was free, and standing beside the car. Her name was Betsy, she said, and she was five years old. From what they could see at first, she only had a small scratch on her forehead—a miracle, considering what she had just been through.

Cole Anderson stooped down and gently patted her head.

"Are you okay?"

"Emmy," she answered.

"What did you say?" he asked her.

"Where's Emmy?" the little girl quietly repeated.

Cole glanced up at Charlie, then looked at Betsy intently and asked, "Is Emmy your doll?"

"Emmy's my sister," she answered, staring up at him with large, brown eyes.

Charlie Kimmons was back in the car in a flash, reaching into the recesses of the tiny space where they had found Betsy. He couldn't see anything, but he frantically swept his hand back and forth.

Then he felt a small hand grab his, and he yelled out, "I've got her!"

Carefully, he managed to get Betsy's two-year-old sister out of the car and onto the ground. She immediately grabbed her sister and began sobbing. But she looked okay, except for some ugly swelling about her left wrist.

"Anybody else in there?" Cole asked Betsy. At this point he wasn't going to be surprised by anything.

She just stood there, holding her sister tight and shaking her head.

Cole Anderson grabbed the two girls in his big arms and walked over to the patrol car. His partner opened the back door, and Anderson set them down on the backseat.

"You girls stay right here, and then we'll go for a ride, okay?" He and Kimmons would take them to the ER to be examined.

The little girls nodded their understanding and sat back quietly, Emmy sucking her thumb.

The two officers walked back over to where the paramedics were still working on the driver of the Chevette.

"Anything new here?" Cole asked the lead paramedic.

The other man stood up and stretched, shaking his head. "He's not responding to anything. Flail chest, pneumothorax, probably a contused heart. That must have been one bad collision."

The policeman nodded his agreement. Then he felt a tugging at his right pants leg, and he looked down into Betsy's bright brown eyes.

"Where's my daddy?" she asked innocently.

The paramedic looked at the little girl and then up at Cole Anderson. He turned and walked away.

Cole leaned over and scooped Betsy into his arms again, making sure she was shielded from any sight of the battered man lying on the stretcher. Her father.

"Let's go back to the car, honey," he whispered to her. "We'll go on that ride now."

"Where's my daddy?" she asked once more.

The ER was ready for them when they arrived. The staff had been informed of the wreck and of the condition of the girls' father. He had arrived a few minutes earlier and was in the trauma room.

Lori Davidson was in triage, and she quickly guided the two officers down the hallway. Charlie was carrying Emmy, and Cole had Betsy.

After a couple of hours, the ER doctor came over to where the officers were sitting and explained what he had found.

"The little one," he began, "Emmy, I think. She has a broken wrist, but nothing else that we can find. She's mighty lucky."

Relieved by this news, Cole asked, "What about Betsy? How is she?"

The doctor rubbed his chin and shook his head.

"That's the darnedest thing," he said, and then paused. "That little girl has a broken neck and a fractured vertebra in her low back. It doesn't seem possible, but she has no neurologic damage, none at all."

"A broken neck?" Charlie repeated, dumbfounded.

"Yes, a C-3 fracture. Middle of the neck, and stable. But she's going to be in the hospital for quite a while. Several weeks, at least."

"What about Emmy?" Cole asked the doctor. "Will she need to be in the hospital too?"

"Her mother's with her now. We're going to keep her overnight at least, considering the magnitude of that wreck. They're lucky to be alive."

Cole nodded his head. "It was awful, Doc."

"And you know their father didn't make it," the doctor added.

They hadn't heard this yet, but weren't surprised by the news.

The officers were left sitting alone in the hallway. Charlie turned to his partner and said, "Let's go find Emmy and her mother. I'd like to meet her."

"Good idea," Cole said, wearily standing and heading back into the ER.

Emmy went home two days later. Her fracture healed without any complication, and she never remembered anything about that summer morning.

Betsy was in the hospital for three months. Cole Anderson made it a point to visit her at least twice a week, sometimes more. They became friends, and he was a little disappointed when she finally walked through the automatic doors and climbed into her mother's car. He was going to miss seeing her. She waved to him and then buckled herself in.

Her mother walked around to where he stood and said, "Lieutenant

Anderson, I expect to see you and your partner at the house a lot. Here's our address." She put a slip of paper into his hand. "I want the two of you to stay in my daughters' lives."

She glanced over at her car and then back to Anderson.

"This little girl thinks the world of you," she told him. "And someday, she'll understand that you and your partner saved her life. And Emmy's too."

There were tears in her eyes, and Cole had to look away.

He slipped the piece of paper into his pocket and said, "Take care of them, and be sure you drive safely."

"Don't worry about that," she said, walking back around to the driver's side and getting into the car.

She drove away, with Betsy waving to him from the backseat. He just stood there until they disappeared from view.

Every month or so, Cole Anderson and Charlie Kimmons would make sure their rounds took them through Betsy and Emmy's neighborhood. They would stop and check on the girls, keeping up with their activities. Later, at their mother's encouragement, they would pass judgment on any potential boyfriends that happened to come calling. A police officer can be pretty intimidating to a teenage boy, if need be.

For years, Betsy never mentioned the wreck, and Cole wondered if she had somehow forgotten about it. Or maybe she had just repressed the terrible memory, locking it away in some dark and dangerous box.

Then one day in early June, when Betsy was twelve years old, Cole and Charlie had stopped by to visit the girls and their mother. The officers were leaving, and Betsy was standing on the front porch.

"Lieutenant Anderson," she called out, stepping down and walking toward him.

He turned and walked back to her.

"Yes, Betsy, what is it?" he asked her. He looked down into those same large, brown eyes he had first seen that tragic morning, and it was almost as if he were once again standing in that highway beside the crushed Chevette.

"I just want to say thank you," she quietly said, looking intently into his eyes. "I know what you two did for us, and I…I just want to say thanks."

He had no words, but somehow managed to gently pat the top of her head, just as he had that morning so many years ago.

They never talked about it again. They didn't need to.

⌘

May 1989. Anderson and Kimmons got into their patrol car and sat quietly for a few moments, just staring out at the crowd swirling through the high-school parking lot. Moments before, Betsy Marshall had graduated with honors. The two officers had been sitting near the stage and had watched proudly as she walked toward the podium and received her diploma. There was no limp in her walk, no sign of the terrible injuries from that long-ago day out on Highway 5.

Afterward, they had talked with Betsy and her sister, Emmy. Their mother had been there as well, along with several aunts and uncles.

It was Charlie Kimmons who spoke first.

"Cole, I know you're thinkin' about it, that summer day, and the wreck, and all…"

Cole Anderson just nodded his head, and mumbled, "Uh-huh."

They were quiet again, and then Charlie asked, "Does it ever make you wonder—why we were out on that side of town? I mean, that wasn't our patrol area. And nobody else was available to respond to that goofy call. And if we hadn't been there right at that very minute…who knows what might have happened? If that truck had blown, those little girls…" His voice trailed off into a choked silence.

Cole took a deep breath and slowly let it out.

He turned and put his hand on his partner's shoulder.

"Charlie, I've thought about that a lot of times. And seeing Betsy up on that stage just now…It was no coincidence we were there that morning. We were *meant* to be there. I *know* that. We were instruments that day, and just knowing that…overwhelms me."

Charlie nodded his head and looked down at the floor.
The dash radio crackled, breaking into their thoughts.
"All units, respond code 3. Unknown disturbance."

Christ has no body now on earth but yours,
no hands but yours,
no feet but yours,
Yours are the eyes through which
Christ's compassion is to look out to the earth.
Yours are the feet with which he is to go about doing good;
Yours are the hands with which he is to bless men now.

TERESA OF AVILA (1515–1582)

18

A Dark and Stormy Night

From ghoulies and ghosties
And long-leggedy beasties
And things that go bump in the night
Good Lord, deliver us.

TRADITIONAL SCOTTISH PRAYER

A re you sure this is okay?" Danny asked Denton Roberts. Roberts had just turned off Highway 21 onto a narrow dirt road. It was a little after nine in the evening, and pitch-black. Low-hanging clouds smothered whatever sliver of a moon might be above them.

"Of course it's okay," Roberts answered, glancing over at the young paramedic sitting next to him in the pickup truck.

Danny Godoski had finished his training a few weeks ago and had immediately joined the hospital's EMS. He was a good-looking kid— quick, bright—and everyone seemed to like him. But tonight he was a little nervous.

"Should be just a little farther," Denton added, switching on his high beams. "You're not getting cold feet, are you?" he chided.

"No, sir, it's just that…well, we're pretty far out in the country," the young man answered hesitantly.

"I told you she lived a little ways out of town, Danny," Denton responded. "We should be getting pretty close."

The car lights reflected off two red eyes just up ahead. Roberts blew the truck horn, and the deer turned, then quickly disappeared into the brush off to their right.

"Gotta keep your eyes open around here," he told Danny.

The two men were partners on EMS Unit 5 and were off duty tonight. It was Halloween, and Denton explained that after twenty years with the EMS, he was always glad to be off this particular holiday.

"Strange things happen around here on Halloween," the older paramedic warned.

Godoski squirmed a little in his seat, but didn't say anything. He was beginning to wonder just why in the world he had agreed to come out here with Denton Roberts.

"You're young and single," his partner had said to him a few days earlier. "And you're a good-lookin' kid. There's a girl that lives just out of town, Darlene Higgins, and she's always wanting to meet young paramedics. Likes a man in uniform," he had added, winking.

He'd assured Danny that Darlene was something special—a really beautiful girl. She and Denton were related somehow, and he was willing to introduce Danny to her. It had sounded fine at the time, but now…he was starting to have second thoughts.

The road was getting narrower, and rougher. Roberts ran over a big rock in the road, and they both bounced up off the seat.

"Yahoo!" he hollered, slapping the wheel. "Now *this* is fun!"

Then he started to slow down, and reaching toward the dash, he turned the high beams off.

"Better be careful," he whispered. "We're close now. It's just around the next turn."

For some reason, Danny caught himself slumping down in the seat.

"And remember," Denton added. "What did I tell you about her father, Eugene?"

Before Godoski could answer, Roberts went on.

"Eugene Higgins is a little touched, if you know what I mean. I don't think he'd hurt anybody, but he's very protective of his daughter. Always has been. Now, Darlene knows we're coming," glancing down at his wristwatch as he said this. "She might be out in the yard right now. But if not, and if Eugene comes out—well, we'll just say howdy and turn right around. Understand?"

This seemed a little strange to the young man, but he was in no position to question Denton Roberts.

"I'll just follow your lead," he answered.

"Good," Roberts whispered. "There's the house up ahead."

He turned off the truck lights, slowly coasted to a stop, then switched off the motor.

"Now, like I said," he whispered to Danny, "any sign of Mr. Higgins and we're outta here."

They got out of the truck and started up the graveled drive. Just then, the clouds overhead parted, and the quarter moon shone brightly down on them and the opening in the woods just ahead. For the moment, they didn't have any trouble seeing.

Danny suddenly felt goose bumps on his forearms, and the hairs on the back of his neck stood straight up. He wondered if it was the chill of the October night, or something else.

He looked ahead and could see the outline of what seemed to be some sort of ramshackle structure. It might have been a house at one time, but now it seemed to be slowly falling in on itself. Through one of the front windows, he could see the flickering light of a solitary candle.

"Denton, are you sure about this?" he whispered nervously.

"Shh!" his partner responded, turning around to Danny and holding up his hand, motioning for silence.

It seemed to the young paramedic that their footsteps were making way too much noise on the gravel, with the loud crunching obviously signaling their approach.

He was ready to call this thing off. He reached out to tap Denton on the shoulder, when suddenly the front door flew open.

Danny was almost blinded by the sudden appearance of the beam of a flashlight, and both men froze where they stood.

"Who's out there?" an angry and raspy voice called out. "I can see you guys! Who is it?"

"Don't go any farther," Denton said quietly, with an obvious tremor in his voice. This was going bad, and they both knew it. "Start backing up, real slow," he told Danny.

"I see you two!" the voice on the front porch called out again. "You're out here to see Darlene, ain't ya?"

"Daddy, now don't do anything crazy." The voice belonged to a young woman, and it came from somewhere just inside the house.

"I warned these boys about comin' out here! And I've had just about enough of this foolishness!"

Denton was slowly moving back toward the truck, guiding his partner as he went. They both had their eyes glued on the flashlight. It didn't seem to be moving, so Higgins must still be standing on the porch.

"Easy, Danny," Denton told him. "Just take it easy. We'll get in the truck and—"

He stopped in mid-sentence as the flashlight dropped to the wooden boards, clattering loudly. Its light now spread up to the clapboard façade, and for the first time they could see Eugene Higgins. He had something in his hands now, and seemed to be raising it up to his shoulders. Then they heard the unmistakable metallic click of a shotgun being cocked.

"Run!" Denton called out, turning clumsily in the gravel and heading for the truck. Danny turned around too, and was just a few steps behind Roberts and a little off to his left side.

The blast of the shotgun shattered the quiet of the moonlit night. A couple of large birds had been roosting in some nearby trees. Startled by the noise, they made an unearthly racket of their own, flew up out of the forest, and disappeared over the tall pines.

Danny heard more than saw his partner fall to the ground in a crumpled heap. There was a single moan and then an anguished gasp. Then silence.

Godoski stopped and knelt beside Denton, feverishly fumbling over the fallen paramedic, shaking him and calling his name.

"Denton! Denton!" he yelled. "Get up! We've got to get out of here!" There was no response.

"I told you boys to stay away from here!" It was Higgins again, and he was walking down the driveway toward them.

Danny shook his friend, trying desperately to rouse him.

"Denton! Denton!" he called out again.

The young man froze as he heard Higgins once more cock the shotgun. He closed his eyes and waited for the blast, wondering what it would feel like to be shot.

The man seemed to be fumbling with the gun, and then…*blam!* He must have been only thirty or forty yards away. But he missed!

Danny was torn, not knowing whether to stay with his fallen friend or run for help. The gun cocked again, making up his mind for him.

"I told you guys—!" Higgins called out.

"Daddy! Don't shoot those boys!" Darlene screamed from the front porch.

Godoski jumped to his feet and was about to head for the truck. Suddenly he remembered seeing Denton put the keys in his pants pocket. No time for that!

Trying to get his bearings, he made his decision. He raced into the thick woods off to the right of the road. He felt the briars viciously grabbing his face and arms, but nothing was going to stop him.

Danny heard one more blast from Higgins's shotgun as he thrashed his way through the underbrush and in the direction of what he hoped would be Rock Hill.

Strangely, there had been few 9-1-1 calls for EMS this evening. Strange because it was Halloween, and stranger still because it was a Friday night. The main EMS headquarters on Heckle Boulevard housed three units, and the three two-man teams were all sitting in the dayroom, enjoying this rare time together.

The door opened, and they were joined by two visitors.

"So, how'd it go?" Ben Carson, the lead paramedic on Unit 4, asked the first man through the door.

Denton Roberts was grinning from ear to ear as he walked into the room and flopped down in the nearest recliner.

"It was perfect!" he exclaimed. "I couldn't see Godoski's face, but from the sound of his voice, and the way he took off into the woods, he must have been scared to death."

262   **Angels** and **Heroes**

"And this guy," he added, pointing to the man behind him. "He was great! You should have heard him."

Eugene Higgins was standing in the doorway, dressed in a dirty T-shirt, grease-stained overalls, and well-worn boots. Actually, it was Frankie Peppers, another off-duty paramedic.

"Took off like a scalded dog!" Frankie proudly announced. "At the rate he's runnin', it probably won't take him long to get back to town. By the way, did you guys call down to the police station and give them a heads-up?" he asked the room.

Carson spoke first. "Yeah, we called dispatch and told them what was going on, and not to pay any attention if Godoski calls in a shooting out in the country. She's gonna go along with him, just like always."

This wasn't the first time a rookie had been introduced to the Higginses. And it wouldn't be the last.

"I just hope that boy's going to be okay," Ron Hartley said. He was the oldest of the group, and he felt a little guilty about being part of this prank. But only a little.

"He'll be fine," Roberts assured him. "And I bet you didn't worry too much about *me* the night you left me in those woods."

Hartley and the other paramedics chuckled. "That was different," he said. "Godoski is a *good* kid."

"What?" Denton asked, feigning insult.

Frankie Peppers plopped down on the sofa beside Hartley and said, "Being this is Halloween and all, Dr. Gee had an interesting case the other night in the ER. Something sort of spooky."

The room fell quiet as the other paramedics settled in their seats waiting for Frankie to continue. He could tell a story.

"Dr. Gee, we've got a problem in room 4."

It was Lori Davidson, the overnight nurse. EMS had just brought a sixty-two-year-old woman in with the complaint of "unresponsive." Lori had directed the paramedics to room 4, where they had transferred the patient to the ER stretcher and left her there with her son, Jackson Given.

Without looking up from the chart in front of him, Johnny Gee asked, "What's going on, Lori?" She didn't sound that worried, and if something needed his immediate attention, he knew she would have told him.

Lori had the chart of room 4 in her hand and was making some notes on it.

"I don't think we've ever seen this woman before," she began. "Her son called 9-1-1 tonight and told them his mother was lying on the floor, unconscious."

Dr. Gee looked up at this and said, "Unconscious?"

"Well, *he* said unconscious," Lori answered. "She seems more…catatonic. Her vital signs are fine, and she withdraws from pain. But she's just lying there, sort of rigid, not moving. It's peculiar."

Johnny put his ballpoint pen in his coat pocket, slid the chart he had been working on over to Amy, the unit secretary, and said, "Let's go check this out."

Sadie Given was lying on the stretcher in room 4, with a sheet pulled up to her neck. She was a large woman, and occupied almost all of the narrow gurney. Standing to one side of her was a forty-year-old man, dressed in jeans and a navy-blue parka. Jackson Given was gently stroking the woman's forehead, and he looked up as Lori and Dr. Gee entered the small room.

"Are you the doctor?" he asked Johnny.

"That's me," Johnny answered, smiling. "I'm Dr. Gee. And you are…?"

"I'm Jackson, Jackson Given," the man answered, looking down again at the woman. "And this is my mother, Sadie."

Johnny stepped over to the stretcher and pulled the sheet down. Then he reached for Sadie's wrist, checking her pulse as he questioned her son.

"Tell me what happened tonight. When did this start?"

Jackson stood quietly for a moment, and then started shaking his head.

"I should have listened to her this morning," he murmured. "She told me, but I didn't pay any attention."

Johnny could barely hear the man, and he moved closer, cocking his head.

"Listened to what?" he asked the visibly distraught son.

"She told me that May Beth Randle had put a root on her, but I just went on with my business. I left her this morning and went downtown. She was fine, but when I got home, she was...she was just like this. Won't talk. Won't move. Won't do nothin'."

"A root?" Lori asked, confused.

Johnny Gee looked over at her and nodded knowingly. Then he put his hand on Jackson's shoulder.

"When did this happen, this root business?" he asked him.

"Last week, I think," Jackson answered. "Sometime last week, maybe Thursday. Mama and May Beth got in some kind of argument, and mama came home all upset. May Beth has always been no-count, and she threatened to put a root on her."

He paused, and patted the top of his mother's head. "Looks like she did."

"Okay," Johnny responded. "We're going to need to check some things and see if we can't help Sadie get rid of this thing."

He glanced over at Lori and nodded toward the curtained opening of the room. She was staring down at Sadie Given, her brow furrowed in confusion. Then they left Jackson alone with his mother.

At the nurses' station, he pulled Lori aside and said, "We need to make sure there's nothing serious going on. We'll need blood work and an EKG. Probably a CT scan of her head before we're finished. I'll go take a good look at her, but I think everything will turn up negative."

"What do you think is going on?" the nurse asked, worried. "What's this about a *root*?"

"A root?" Amy Connors, the unit secretary, exclaimed from behind her desk. "Did someone put a root on that woman?"

"Shh!" Johnny silenced her, glancing over to the closed curtain of room 4. "That's what her son says."

"Well, I'll be!" Amy whispered, shaking her head.

"Would someone please tell me—" Lori began.

Johnny interrupted her with an index finger to his pursed lips. "Let's check things out, and then we'll talk."

Dr. Gee was right about Sadie Given's workup. He was unable to find any evidence of a neurological problem, and all of her studies were normal. Yet she still lay on the stretcher, her eyes closed, not talking, not moving. Lori was right—she appeared to be catatonic. And she didn't appear to be faking.

Johnny was standing at the nurses' station, studying the stack of Sadie's reports.

"What now, Dr. Gee?" Lori asked him. "What can we do for her? Has she had some kind of psychotic break?"

"No, I don't think so," he ruminated, stroking his chin. "I thought about that, but she has no history of any mental problems. I think it has to do with this 'root' business."

"That's where I'd put my money," Amy Connors chimed in. "Seen it happen before. Sometimes even worse than this."

"What exactly is this 'root' thing?" Lori asked, perplexed. She had never heard of such a thing.

"It's kind of like voodoo," Johnny began to explain. "Someone puts a curse on you—the 'root,' they call it. And it can cause some real problems. But only if the victim believes in its power."

"Looks like Sadie believes in that power," Amy said. "I don't think she's moved a muscle since she got here."

"That's true," Lori agreed. "But how does it work?"

"Nobody really knows," Johnny said thoughtfully. "But back in medical school, I remember a visiting lecturer speaking to our psychiatry class one afternoon. He was especially interested in the Charleston area, with its history of black magic and all. Anyway, Samuel Lightfoot was his name, I think. And he gave a really interesting talk. I don't think any of us believed much of it, maybe none. But it was interesting just the same. And I remember him talking about some of his patients having the root put on them. Some acted just like Sadie. And I think he even said he had a couple of them die."

"Die?" Lori exclaimed. "You mean people can die from this stuff?"

"Sure can," Amy said matter-of-factly. "I remember a woman from down in Great Falls—"

"Come to think of it," Johnny interrupted her. "He talked about what he did to try to get people to snap out of this. It was all pretty bizarre, but he claimed it would work. You just had to be convincing and committed."

"Sounds like you'd be committed, all right," Amy quipped.

Johnny Gee didn't pay her any attention, but turned to Lori and said, "We're going to need a couple of things. Actually, a bunch of things."

He proceeded to give her a list of the items necessary for his root exorcism.

Amy Connors just sat at her desk, listening quietly and shaking her head.

"Boy, am I glad I'm on duty tonight!" she commented under her breath.

Fifteen minutes later, Jackson Given looked up as Dr. Johnny Gee and Lori Davidson walked into room 4. His eyes widened and his jaw dropped.

"What in the world…" he stammered.

Lori looked odd enough. She had a hospital sheet wrapped around her, with only her eyes peeping out of a small opening.

But it was Johnny Gee who had gotten Jackson's attention. He had taken his lab coat off and attached over a hundred two-to-three-foot strips of surgical tape to his shirt and pants. They were hanging loose, giving him the appearance of a shagbark hickory tree, only he was moving. He had borrowed someone's bright-red scarf and tied it around his forehead. Within the lost-and-found drawer, Lori had discovered two dozen plastic loop bracelets, oversize and brightly colored. These were flopping around on his forearms. The same drawer had yielded some gaudy silver loop earrings, and these were dangling from his ears. The total effect was one of a gypsy soothsayer, all save the surgical cap jammed onto the top of his head. It had slipped a little to one side, giving him the appearance of a probable lack of sobriety. The kids' sticker on the cap that read, "I was brave when I got my shot!" didn't help much either.

"What the…!" Jackson muttered again, backing away a little from this approaching apparition.

Johnny just looked at him and slowly nodded his head. Then he looked over at Sadie and walked up beside her stretcher.

He raised his arms, and for the first time Jackson noticed the metal bedpan in one of the doctor's hands, and the butt end of a large flashlight in the other.

The silence of the room was suddenly shattered by a ghostlike wailing from Lori. Jackson looked over to see her swaying from side to side, her barely visible eyes closed, trancelike. He backed up against the far wall of the room, and began searching for somewhere to hide.

The clattering of the flashlight against the bedpan caused Given to snatch his head around once more. He was staring in disbelief at the spectacle in front of him, when Johnny began to chant. It sounded like a bad rendition of an Indian war dance from a B movie of the early 1960s. Maybe a C movie.

Then Johnny began to move slowly around the stretcher, banging and chanting his way to the head of Sadie's bed. Through all of this, she had not flinched. The doctor had been studying her face closely, looking for some sign of awareness. Nothing.

He knew he was going to have to pull out all the stops. Carefully, he put the bedpan down on the foot of the stretcher and pulled a kazoo from his shirt pocket. It was another donation from lost-and-found, and he wondered where in the world it had come from. But he'd thought it might come in handy.

He put the instrument in his mouth and began playing what sounded like a medley of "The Star-Spangled Banner" and "You Ain't Nothin' but a Hound Dog." It wasn't a bad effort, and Jackson caught himself starting to place his hand over his heart.

But something stopped him. It was his mother. Her eyelids had fluttered a little, and her left hand had flinched.

Johnny Gee had seen it too, and he took the kazoo out of his mouth and began chanting some garbled mantra, with the word "root" clearly discernible every few syllables. Then he picked up the bedpan again and started rhythmically beating it.

That seemed to do the trick. Sadie Given opened her eyes and started looking around the room. When her gaze landed on Johnny Gee, she let out a gasp and sat bolt upright on the stretcher.

"Mama!" Jackson exclaimed, stepping quickly over to her bed and putting his arms around the startled woman. "Mama! You're all right!"

By the time Johnny and Lori had gotten out of their therapeutic garb, Jackson and Sadie Given were making their way out of the department. They stopped at the nurses' station, and it was Jackson who spoke first.

"Thank you, Doctor, for helping my mother," he said earnestly. "And you too, Miss Nurse."

Johnny stepped over to Sadie and put a hand on her shoulder.

"Are you feeling okay now, Ms. Given?"

"Thanks to you I am, Doctor," she replied. "If you hadn't gotten that root off me, I just don't know what would have happened. I'm gonna have a word with May Beth when we get home."

"Now mama," Jackson said, taking her by the hand and leading her toward the ambulance entrance. "You're gonna leave that woman alone, you hear?"

He winked at Johnny and Lori, then turned and guided his mother out into the parking lot and their waiting car.

"Oh my gosh! Now that was somethin'!" Amy exclaimed. "I almost wet my pants when the two of you came out of room 4! I just wish I'd had my camera."

"Don't you breathe a word of this," Johnny warned her. "I'm not sure any of that was FDA-approved."

"Well, it worked, didn't it?" Amy responded, smiling.

"It sure did," Johnny Gee answered. "Thanks to Samuel Lightfoot— and whoever left us that kazoo."

⊂◎⊃

"You need to ask Dr. Gee about that the next time you see him," Frankie Peppers said, concluding his story. "We'll be talking about that one for quite a while."

Denton Roberts glanced down at his watch. It was getting late, and he was a little worried about Danny Godoski.

"How do you think the kid is doing?" he asked the group. "Shouldn't we have heard something by now?"

"Nah," Ben Carson said. "That's a little bit of a trek, especially at night. He won't be back for another hour or so, I'd guess."

"I'm sorta thinkin' about headin' home," Denton said. "I'm not sure I want to be here when he shows up."

The door suddenly burst open, startling everyone in the room. Danny Godoski stumbled in, slamming the door behind him.

He was a mess. His face and hands were covered with scratches, his shirt was torn, and his pants were covered in mud. One of his shoes was missing.

"Something terrible has happened to Denton Roberts," he stammered breathlessly. "And it's all my fault!"

"Here, sit down, boy," Ben Carson said, jumping up from his chair near the door.

Danny collapsed into the recliner and was about to speak again, when he heard snickering from somewhere in the room.

He looked up and glared at his fellow paramedics. "This isn't funny! Denton is—"

The words froze in his mouth as his eyes came to rest on Denton Roberts. He was sitting in a chair, hands folded in his lap...smiling, and very much alive.

Danny's eyes slowly began to scan the room. His jaw dropped when he saw the man sitting beside Roberts. It was Eugene Higgins in his T-shirt and overalls.

The paramedics watched in amusement as the look on Godoski's face changed from shock and confusion to a dawning understanding.

He jumped up from his chair.

"You mean…Denton, you were…and Higgins…but what about… all you guys knew…!"

Ron Hartley leaned over in his chair and took a Gatorade from the ice chest on the floor beside him. He stood up and walked over to Danny. Handing him the cold drink and putting an arm around his shoulders, he said, "Welcome to the family."

19

Going Home

This world is not our abiding place.
Our continuance here
is but very short.

JONATHAN EDWARDS (1703–1758)

The stretch of Highway 5 from Blacksburg to York was always lonely and somehow forbidding. A lot of people thought its twisting turns too dangerous, causing them to choose an alternate route for their travel. But not Jordan McClendon. The twenty-one-year-old was on his way home from Clemson for the Thanksgiving holiday, and his spirits couldn't be higher. He had received word yesterday that he been accepted into the highly competitive architecture program there. After his final exam this afternoon, he had packed his Honda Accord and headed toward Rock Hill.

He reached down to the dash and turned up the CD player, singing along with it as he passed the Highway 55 cutoff. The music reminded him of his sister, and he smiled.

It was eight o'clock, and the countryside was pitch-black. He hadn't seen another car since he'd left Blacksburg.

And then up ahead, around one of the sharp turns in the road, he saw the headlights of an approaching car playing through the leafless trees. He glanced down at his speedometer—50 miles an hour. His father would be proud of him. He began to brake a little as he headed into the turn.

Something was wrong. The headlights of the car coming at him were swerving from one side of the road to the other. Jordan gripped his steering wheel as tight as he could and slammed on his brakes, trying to guess where the car in front of him was going to go.

First it swerved to Jordan's left, away from him, and toward some trees. Then suddenly the driver jerked the car back into the middle of the road and then directly toward Jordan. He had nothing else to do but turn his car as hard as he could to the right, into the trees looming just off the road. He braced for the impact he knew was coming.

"EMS 2, what's your 10-20?"

A truck driver had called 9-1-1 about a wreck on Highway 5, and the county dispatcher was trying to learn the location of Denton Roberts and his partner, Bill Jenkins. They were responding to the incident and were just now pulling up to the site.

"Dispatch, this is EMS 2," Denton spoke into his radio. "We just got to the scene, and it looks like we're going to need backup."

"10-4. We'll get some more units on the way."

The radio crackled once more, and then there was silence as Roberts and his partner pulled to a stop on the side of the road, their ambulance lights shining on a horrifying sight. In the middle of the road, completely overturned, was an older-model Ford pickup truck. The left front wheel was still slowly spinning in the night air, and smoke was wafting upward from beneath the smashed front hood.

"Looks like he hit those trees over there and then spun back into the road," Jenkins said, indicating the splintered remains of several small cedars.

"Check out the truck, Bill, and I'll head over there," Denton pointed to the silver Honda that was pinned between two giant oak trees just off to their left.

"Should we put up some flares first, in case someone comes flying down the road?" Bill asked, worried about the truck in the middle of the highway.

His partner paused and glanced back at the ambulance, its multiple lights flashing blues and whites and reds.

"No, we should be okay," he said. "We need to see what we've got here first."

Jenkins reached the overturned truck and shot the beam of his flashlight through the smashed driver's side window. The cab was empty. Puzzled, he painted a wide arc with the light, searching the road and nearby woods for any sign of the driver or passengers. Then he stepped toward the front of the truck and looked. Still nothing.

When he got to the passenger side, he stopped in his tracks, his flashlight shining down ahead of his feet. There, halfway under the truck and sprawled on the asphalt, was the bloodied body of a middle-aged man. His right arm was obviously broken through the humerus, and his neck was twisted in an unnatural and sickening angle. The man wasn't breathing, and Jenkins reached down to check for a pulse. From the size of the pool of blood spread across the road, the paramedic didn't expect to find one, and he didn't. This guy was gone. As he hovered over the body, making sure there was no sign of life, the smell of alcohol struck him full force.

"Bill, come over here!" Denton Roberts called from the other side of the road.

Jenkins stood and hurried over to his partner. Denton had opened the driver's door of the Honda and was leaning in, working feverishly with the young man behind the wheel and still strapped in his seat belt.

As Bill stepped up behind Denton, he glanced over at the windshield. It was still intact, but there was an area of cracked and shattered glass just where the driver's head would have struck it. Looking down, he could see the bruised and bleeding forehead of the young man.

"What ya got?" he asked.

"He's got a good pulse and he's breathing fine," Denton answered, reaching over and releasing the seat belt. "But he's not responding to anything. Not to pain, or yelling in his ear. Nothing. We need to get his neck stabilized and then get him on a stretcher. How about the pickup?"

"Just the driver," Bill answered. "I didn't see anyone else. He must not have been wearing his seat belt, 'cause he was thrown out of the truck and pinned under it. Looks like head and neck and chest injuries. Nothing we can do for him."

"Well, we can do something for this kid," Denton said. "Grab the emergency kit and give dispatch a call. Find out where our backup is."

The Honda's CD player was still on, and Denton Roberts had been absently listening to the familiar tune. He reached over the young man's body and turned it off.

Melissa was setting the table in the dining room. Tomorrow would be the big meal, but tonight Jordan was coming home, and they were preparing his favorite dinner.

"Mom," she called. "When do you think Jordan will be home?"

Melissa was a senior at Northwestern High School and idolized her older brother. It had been a few weeks since he had been home, and she was excited she would soon see him.

Laura McClendon was in the kitchen, putting the finishing touches on the pork tenderloin. She put it back in the oven just as her husband, David, walked through the garage door.

Laura looked up and smiled at her husband, then answered her daughter. "Anytime now. He left school about—"

She stopped, stood straight up, and stared out the kitchen window to the front yard beyond. She couldn't move. Something was wrong. She knew it with the sureness that only a mother can know.

David had seen his wife suddenly stiffen. "What's the matter, honey?" he asked.

She turned to him, her face pale and worried. "Something's wrong, David. I just feel it. Something's terribly wrong. Jordan..."

David stepped over to his wife and took her in his arms. "Everything's fine," he reassured her. "Stop worrying. He'll be home in just a few minutes."

When Laura had these premonitions, he always got a nervous feeling in the pit of his stomach. And he had one tonight. But he knew it was only her worrying about her boy. That was all.

"He's fine, Laura. Don't worry. And dinner smells great," he added, stepping away now to arm's length and smiling, trying to calm his troubled wife.

Melissa came bouncing into the kitchen.

"Hey, Daddy!" she said. "I didn't hear you come in." She headed around the island to hug her father.

Laura was looking into her husband's eyes. "No, David—something's wrong..."

The phone rang.

Laura McClendon dropped her basting brush to the floor.

Lori Davidson walked back into the trauma room.

"Dr. Daniel," she said, closing the door behind her. "Dr. Evans is on call for neurosurgery, and he'll be down in a few minutes. He's finishing up a case in the OR."

Les Daniel looked up at Lori and nodded his head. He had once again checked the pupils of this young patient for any reaction to light, any sign that something was going on in his brain.

EMS had brought him in thirty minutes earlier, after picking him up on Highway 5. Denton Roberts had given Les his report about the scene of the accident, and about what he had observed with the young driver.

"I couldn't find any obvious injury," Denton had told him. "Just the bruises on his forehead. But the windshield was pretty busted up, so he must have hit it mighty hard."

Dr. Daniel hadn't been able to find any other significant injury either. The young man's chest X-ray, neck films, and abdominal CT scan were all normal, as were his blood work and urinalysis. The only study pending was the CT of his head, and they should be getting that report soon.

"Do we have a name yet?" Les asked Lori.

She glanced down at the clipboard in her hand and said, "Yes, his name is Jordan McClendon. Twenty-one years old. And Amy told me his family is on the way in."

The beeping of the oxygen saturation monitor got Daniel's attention and he glanced over to the head of the stretcher. The alarm indicated a fall in his O2. His breathing had become a little more irregular, and it was worrying the doctor.

Since his arrival in the ER, Jordan had maintained a good blood pressure and adequate respiratory efforts. But he had not responded to any of the usual stimulations—loud noises in his ear, a brisk sternal rub, and most bothersome, a bright light in his eyes.

"Oh," Lori added, flipping up a lab slip on the clipboard. "His blood alcohol is 0."

Les nodded, not expecting this test to turn up anything. Denton Roberts hadn't noticed any alcohol in the Honda, and the doctor hadn't smelled any on the young man.

The O2 monitor continued to beep, and Daniel listened again to Jordan's lungs. Still moving air, but his respirations seemed to be getting slower.

He turned to Lori and was about to ask for an airway tray to be set up. She had already pulled an instrument stand up behind him and was tearing open the paper wrapping of the sterile tray.

"I'll ask Amy to get one of the respiratory therapists to come down," the nurse said, organizing the various endotracheal tubes and laryngoscope blades. She knew Jordan McClendon was going to need airway support if he was going to have any chance of survival.

The door suddenly opened, and Dr. Richard Evans walked into trauma. He was still in his surgical scrubs and cap. Lori glanced down at his blood-spattered shoe covers and at the sweat that almost completely soaked his shirt. She knew he worked hard, and dealt with a lot of tragic and hopeless things. Yet he always seemed to be in a good mood. And what she appreciated most was that he was always kind to his patients and their families.

"Les," he said in greeting, pushing the door closed and walking over beside the ER doctor. He looked down intently at Jordan McClendon and then, with his right thumb, gently raised one of the young man's eyelids. No pupillary response.

This didn't seem to surprise the neurosurgeon, and he looked up at his colleague and said, "I stopped by radiology on the way over and looked at this fella's head CT. It's not good. The frontal lobes are significantly contused. And as you'd expect, there are occipital changes as well."

Daniel had anticipated this. The mechanism of injury would have bruised the front of the brain, and as it bounced back and forth in the skull, the back would also have been injured.

"The main problem is his brain stem," Evans continued. "It's been almost completely severed." He glanced down again at Jordan and watched his chest slowly rise and fall. "I don't know how he's still breathing. Or how he's still alive at all. But I'm afraid he's not going to last very long."

It was what Les Daniel was afraid of. It was the right explanation for what he was seeing, but it was a death sentence for this young man.

"I'm afraid there's nothing I can do for him," Evans said, shaking his head and laying a tired hand on Jordan's shoulder. If I can help with the family, or anything…just give me a call, Les. I'll be up in the surgical ICU for a while."

"Thanks, Richard," Les Daniel murmured. "We'll see how things go."

Evans left the room, and Lori stepped over beside the stretcher.

"Do we need to ask respiratory to bring down a ventilator?" she asked quietly.

Daniel glanced over at the oxygen monitor, its numbers slowly drifting south.

"Yes," he answered. "We need to secure his airway, at least until we get a chance to talk with the family."

The door opened again, and this time it was Amy Connors, the unit secretary. In one hand she held some loose papers, part of Jordan's medical record, and she put these down on the counter.

In her other hand, she held his driver's license. In this kind of situation, it was her job to keep track of certain administrative details about the patient.

She stepped over to the stretcher and said, "The family is in the waiting room. I don't think they know anything yet."

Lori glanced up at Dr. Daniel. He just kept staring down at the strangely peaceful face of this doomed young man.

"Amy, would you take them back to the family room?" the nurse asked without looking over at her.

"Sure," she answered. Then, handing her Jordan's driver's license— "We need to put this on his chart."

Lori took the plastic card and looked down at it as Amy left the room. Her drawn-out sigh caused Les Daniel to look up. He followed her eyes to the license in her hand.

There was Jordan McClendon, alive and smiling. And there were his height, weight, and date of birth. And just to the left side of his picture was a red circle, with a heart in its center.

Jordan McClendon was an organ donor.

"When can we see our son?" Laura McClendon asked Lori. She was trying desperately to maintain her composure, but was coming close to losing her struggle.

The family room was crowded. Laura and her husband, David, were sitting on the sofa, and their daughter, Melissa, was standing at her mother's side. Lori was standing by the door when it opened and Les Daniel walked in.

He closed the door behind him and introduced himself. Then he began to explain Jordan's condition, and what they should expect to see when they went into the trauma room.

Daniel didn't tell them of the hopelessness of the situation. He wanted the chance to talk with them a little before he explained it. There was never an easy way to do this, but if he could just ease into—

"Is he going to be alright?" Laura asked him. "Is my son going to be alright?"

There was a rising urgency in her voice, and David McClendon gently put his hand on his wife's arm.

"Let's go to the trauma room, and we can talk more there," Daniel said, opening the door and stepping out into the hallway, not giving her a chance to ask him again. Not just yet.

Les explained there would be a tube in the young man's mouth and into his airway, and that a ventilator would be breathing for him. In spite of his attempt to prepare them for this, Melissa and Laura gasped as they walked into trauma and saw Jordan lying on the stretcher, the ventilator hissing with each artificial breath.

They all stepped to his side, and Lori watched as each of them reached out and put a hand somewhere on the young man's body. David put his hand on his son's shoulder, while Melissa reached out and grasped Jordan's hand in her own.

Laura laid her hand over her boy's heart, and sobbed quietly.

Daniel let them stand there for a few moments while they tried to come to terms with what was happening to Jordan and to all of them.

Laura McClendon looked up at the doctor, her eyes helpless, pleading. He knew what she wanted to ask, and he knew she could no longer find the words.

There was a heavy silence in the room, broken only by the rhythmic hissing of the ventilator. Then Les Daniel said, "I'm sorry, Mrs. McClendon. He's not going to wake up."

An hour later, Lori Davidson was with the McClendons back in the family room. It had been an awful time in trauma, but as best they could, they had begun to come to terms with Jordan's condition. Lori had been surprised by their responses. David McClendon now sat quietly, staring at the floor, while Laura seemed to be composing herself—still sobbing, but trying to comfort her husband.

It was Melissa who calmly took charge. She had called several family members and told them what had happened, and she was asking Lori about the things that needed to happen next. The nurse wasn't sure how long her calmness would last, but she was impressed with this remarkable young woman, and admired her courage.

Les Daniel stood outside the family room door and gathered his own courage. This was one of the most difficult things he had to do in the ER. It was hard enough to tell people their loved ones were dying or dead. But to tell them that and then raise the issue of organ donation was somehow…it somehow seemed heartless. But he knew it had to be done. If you didn't ask the family about it, it would never happen. But he wished there was another way to do this, or better yet, somebody else to do it.

He took a deep breath, tapped on the door, and once again stepped into the room.

As Les began to tell them about what needed to happen, he closely studied Laura McClendon's face. He was most concerned about her and her reaction. Her response was initially one of shock, maybe even horror. She couldn't imagine her son's organs being shipped out to all parts of the country. How would they get them? She squeezed her eyes shut and sank deeper into the sofa, sobbing, with her face in her hands. This was her son, her baby boy. She turned white, swayed a bit, and swallowed hard.

"Organ donor," she whispered. "I had no idea he had done that."

David moved over beside her on the small couch.

"Let's just think about this for a minute," he said to her.

"Dad, Mom, this is something that Jordan and I talked about a couple of months ago." It was Melissa, and she stepped over and put her hand on her mother's shoulder.

"We never thought it would ever really happen," she continued. "Not like this. But it was something we both wanted to do."

"But how would they…" Laura began, but was unable to finish the lingering question.

Melissa looked over at Lori and Dr. Daniel and said, "Can you give us a few minutes? Just let us talk a little."

"Sure," Lori said.

She and Les Daniel stepped out of the room and walked toward the nurses' station.

"Good," Amy Connors said, looking up as the two reached her counter. "I was gonna have to come get you. Here, this is for you," she added, handing a fax to Daniel. "It's from the organ donation center."

Les studied the piece of paper, then nodded his head. "Hmm."

A few minutes later, the door to the family room opened and Melissa stepped out, motioning for Lori to rejoin them. She called for Dr. Daniel, and they retraced their steps back to the McClendons.

Lori wasn't sure how Melissa had done it, but David and Laura seemed more at peace now, more comfortable with the idea of Jordan being a donor.

"I do have a question," David McClendon said. "Is there any way to know who is going to receive any of Jordan's...organs?"

It was customary for the recipients to be completely unidentifiable. A lot of things could go wrong, just adding more suffering for everyone involved.

Les Daniel paused for a moment, then reached into his lab-coat pocket and took out the folded fax Amy had just handed him.

"This is all supposed to be anonymous, and I certainly can't give you any names," he began to explain. "But I will tell you there's a fourteen-year-old girl in Chattanooga who had a viral infection of her heart a few months ago. She's dying, and Jordan is going to save her life."

Melissa's breath caught in her throat. She sat down heavily and stared at the floor.

It was Laura this time who spoke up. "Thank you for sharing this with us, Dr. Daniel."

Two hours later, after Richard Evans had pronounced Jordan brain-dead, with no chance of recovery, the surgical team wheeled him around to the OR. His heart would be taken by helicopter to the local airport, and then by jet to Tennessee.

The McClendons were standing outside, talking with some friends and family members who had come to the hospital. It was still dark, now three or four in the morning, and soon David, Laura, and Melissa found themselves alone, standing under the ambulance entrance portico.

It was a beautiful night, with an occasional cool, almost chill breeze. The stars were exceptionally radiant in a black and cloudless sky. It was almost as if they were alone in the universe, and on any other night, in any other place...

Exhausted, they just stood and looked at each other. They needed to get home and get some rest, but none of them wanted to leave the hospital. Jordan was still here…somehow. And yet, they all knew he wasn't.

The ambulance doors opened behind them, and Denton Roberts walked out, pushing an empty stretcher in front of him. He had just brought another patient to the ER and was headed back out to his ambulance.

Recognizing the McClendons, he stopped and said, "I'm awfully sorry about what happened to your son tonight. I just wish we could have done something for him."

"You did all you could," David told him. "Thanks for that."

Denton quietly muttered something to himself and then said aloud, "Oh, I almost forgot." Reaching into his jacket pocket, he took out a CD, enclosed in its plastic jacket.

Melissa was standing closest to him, and he handed it to her.

"This was in the CD player in Jordan's car, and I wanted to make sure you got it. It was playing when we got to the accident."

He grabbed the end of his stretcher and started off once more toward his ambulance.

"Good night," he called back to the huddled family.

Melissa looked down at the CD, trying to find enough light under the portico to see what it was.

Suddenly a loud noise caused all of them to look overhead. They heard the thumping of the helicopter's blades before they could see its lights. And then there it was, seemingly right above them.

Without anyone speaking a word, they all knew. The helicopter was carrying a most precious cargo—Jordan's heart.

They watched in silence as it crossed the parking area and then disappeared over the tall oaks in the distance. They stood completely still until they could no longer hear its engine, each with their own thoughts, but each of them thinking about Jordan.

Then Melissa broke the painful silence.

"Look at this!" she said excitedly.

She had recognized her own writing on the jacket of the CD, and immediately knew what it contained.

"I made this for him last summer! It's B.J. Thomas's version of one of Jordan's favorite songs, and he must have been listening to it when he...as he was coming home."

David and Laura leaned closer and read the title of the CD. The words of the familiar song ran through their minds and into their hearts.

They say that heaven's pretty,
and living here is too.
But if they said that I
would have to choose between the two,
I'd go home,
going home,
where I belong.

While I'm here I'll serve him gladly,
and sing him all my songs.
I'm here,
but not for long. *

Suddenly, out of the deep darkness of the night, the hint of a softer, warmer breeze, almost a breath, blew over the McClendon family. It surrounded them, comforting and drawing them closer.

Jordan had made it home.

---

* From "Home Where I Belong" by Pat Terry. Used by permission.

"Teacher, which is the greatest commandment in the Law?"
Jesus replied:
"Love the Lord your God
with all your soul
and with all your mind.
This is the first and greatest commandment.
And the second is like it:
Love your neighbor as yourself."

MATTHEW 22:36-39

Also by Robert Lesslie, MD

ANGELS IN THE ER
Inspiring True Stories from an Emergency Room Doctor

If you don't believe in angels... you should spend some time in the ER. You'll learn that angels do exist. Some are nurses, a few are doctors, and many are everyday people.

...such as well-starched head nurse Virginia Granger, whose heart of compassion hides behind a steely gaze.

...or William Purvis—a.k.a. "Max Bruiser"—a beefy pro wrestler who has a tussle with an unexpected opponent.

...Or Macey Love, whose determination to love her two granddaughters—and everyone else she meets—is expressed in just the radiance of her smile.

In this bestselling book of true stories—some thoughtful, some delightful, some heart-pumping—you'll see close-up the joys and struggles of people like you.

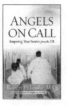

ANGELS ON CALL
Inspiring True Stories from the ER

Dr. Robert Lesslie shares experiences—some heartwarming, some edge-of-your-seat—that reveal answers to those often unspoken pleas of "Who can I turn to?" "Who's on call for me?"

...Sally Carlton and Wanda Bennett are both in desperate situations. But sometimes the passion for life burns where least expected.

...Wesley Wood is rushed through the doors on a stretcher, undergoing CPR from a 300-pound nursing attendant sitting on his chest. He clearly needs some help—but how?

Throughout these remarkable accounts, you'll also catch glimpses of those who are now asking, "Who am I on call *for*?" It is these people who have found the kind of healing we all need.

MAKING LIFE RICH WITHOUT ANY MONEY
Phil Callaway

Phil Callaway shares six fascinating characteristics of rich people—characteristics that have nothing to do with money and everything to do with wealth. You'll nod your head and laugh as you read about...

- the perils and joys of a SITCOM family (Single Income Three Children Oppressive Mortgage)
- a lasting male friendship forged over the murder of a lawn mower
- Phil's new appreciation for his wife after a memorable "Mr. Mom" experience

The best things in life are not really *things*, says Phil...and surprisingly, they just may be in your own backyard.

THE STORY OF YOUR LIFE
Inspiring Stories of God at Work in People Just like You

Matthew West and Angela Thomas

When Grammy-nominated recording artist Matthew West invited people to share their stories, he received nearly 10,000 responses. As he read every one, entering into other people's joy, pain, and hope in God, his heart was transformed.

In *The Story of Your Life*, Matthew and fellow author Angela Thomas respond to 52 of those stories, considering what God is doing in each situation. You'll read about...

- Wendy, the unmarried girl who gives birth to her daughter in jail, and how God turns her life around
- Kristen, the foster girl who is about to turn 18 and has nowhere to go, and how she discovers that God is her true Father
- Greg, the pastor whose congregation lines the streets with banners and cheers when he and his wife bring home Lily, the little girl they adopt from Guatemala

In these inspiring glimpses into people's lives, you'll see how God is at work in everyone's story—including yours.

HORSE TALES FROM HEAVEN
Reflections Along the Trail with God
Rebecca Ondov

Drawing on 15 years of living "in the saddle" while guiding pack trips and working as a wilderness ranger, writer and avid horsewoman Rebecca Ondov shows how the outdoors can open up people's hearts and minds in true stories about…

- a frisky cayuse and an early morning chase
- the special friendship between a night-blind horse and a mule
- snoring at base camp—and a startling cure for it

Horse Tales from Heaven captures authentic Western life and reveals how God gets involved when you hit the trail with Him.

THE WHISPERS OF ANGELS
Stories to Touch Your Heart
Annette Smith

This bestselling collection of true stories will help you find a heavenly perspective in the midst of everyday experiences… as you meet people like Hope, a ten-year-old blind girl who found her place in a brand-new school. Or Sam and Lily, childhood sweethearts whose love never stopped growing. Or Mr. Simmons, a heart-attack patient who taught his nurse about proper healing. Take a few moments to stop and listen, and perhaps you too will hear the sounds of heaven—*The Whispers of Angels.*

FOUR PAWS FROM HEAVEN
Devotions for Dog Lovers
M.R. Wells, Kris Young, and Connie Fleishauer

Friend, family member, guardian, comforter—a dog can add so much to our lives. These furry, four-footed creatures truly are wonderful gifts from a loving Creator to bring joy, laughter, and warmth to our hearts and homes. These delightful devotions will make you smile and perhaps grow a little misty as you enjoy true stories of how God watches over and provides for us even as we care for our canine companions.